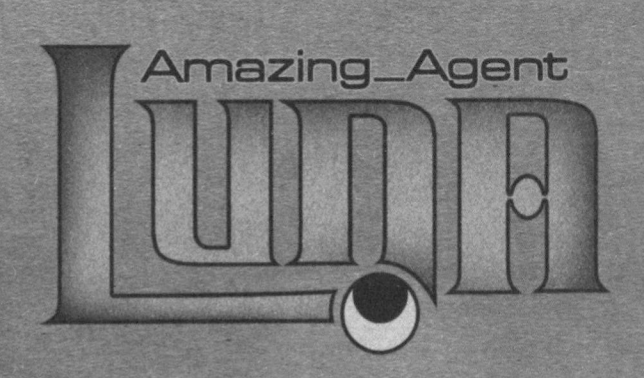

Amazing_Agent
LUNA

art by Shiei

story by Nunzio DeFilippis
and Christina Weir

[CONFIDENTIAL]

VOLUME 009

Amazing Agent LUNA

VOLUME 9

art by **Shiei**

story by **Nunzio DeFilippis & Christina Weir**

STAFF CREDITS

lettering	**Nicky Lim**
toning	**Ludwig Sacramento**
layout	**Alexis Roberts**
design	**Nicky Lim**
proofing	**Shanti Whitesides**
managing editor	**Adam Arnold**
publisher	**Jason DeAngelis** **Seven Seas Entertainment**

AMAZING AGENT LUNA VOL. 9
Copyright © 2013 Seven Seas Entertainment, LLC and Nunzio DeFilippis and Christina Weir

No portion of this book may be reproduced or transmitted in any form without written permission from the copyright holders.

This is a work of fiction. Names, characters, places, and incidents are the products of the author's imagination or are used fictitiously. Any resemblance to actual events, locals, or persons, living or dead, is entirely coincidental.

Seven Seas and the Seven Seas logo are trademarks of Seven Seas Entertainment, LLC. All rights reserved.

SBN: 978-1-937867-29-4

Printed in Canada

First Printing: June 2013

10 9 8 7 6 5 4 3 2 1

FOLLOW US ONLINE: www.gomanga.com

READING DIRECTIONS

This book reads from **right to left**, Japanese style. If this is your first time reading manga, you start reading from the top right panel on each page and take it from there. If you get lost, just follow the numbered diagram here. It may seem backwards at first, but you'll get the hang of it! Have fun!!

FROM THE JOURNALS OF KNIGHTFALL DIRECTOR, MASTER CONTROL:

Our efforts to destabilize the Agency by targeting Project Luna have met with mixed results.

Project Luna is a highly classified project run by my former protégée, **Jennifer Kajiwara** (Agency Codename: Control, see attached photo), which has created a genetically superior super-agent, code-named **Agent Luna** (see attached photo). Project Luna is the culmination of work that got Kajiwara recruited into the Agency, work that was once intercepted by the leaders of the rogue nation of Bruckenstein.

When **Count Heinrich Von Brucken** (see attached photo), ruler of that nation, targeted Nobel High School in New York, Agent Luna was sent into the school as a sophomore. She was given a handler, **Dr. Andrew Collins** (see attached photo) to pose as her father, with Kajiwara posing as her mother, an ironic cover as Kajiwara is actually Luna's biological mother, a fact she cannot reveal due to pressures from the Agency.

Project Luna has been coming apart ever since. Romantic complications between Kajiwara and Collins led to the end of their fake marriage, and Agent Luna has been troubled by this turn of events. She has also been troubled by the recruitment of Count Von Brucken by the Agency to assist as Project Luna turned its attention to **Countess Elyse Von Brucken** (see attached photo), the former Agency operative who turned against her nation years ago. Project Luna arrested the Countess, but we have since liberated and recruited her.

In addition, one of our agents had briefly been placed at Nobel High and reports that Agent Luna's problems worsened there. **Anders Haugen** (see attached photo) infiltrated the school as a student, and began dating Luna, now a junior. He found her to be troubled by problems with her two best friends, **Oliver Riggs** and **Francesca Aldana** (see attached photos), troubles caused by her double life.

With Project Luna in disarray, and the Agency tasking another control agent, code-named **The Controller** (see attached photo) to create a replacement for Luna, Knightfall decided to recruit both Luna and Kajiwara to join our efforts, which target countries and their intelligence agencies, and disrupt them all.

Kajiwara's recruitment did not go as planned. Due to her history with me, she was wary. And she showed surprising concern when I fatally wounded Heinrich Von Brucken. She refused to join and threatened to kill me.

However, Anders reports that he has had different results. As he and Agent Luna clashed over the MacGregor Device, which would allow us to mimic voices and faces of anyone communicating electronically, he told her of the Agency's plans to replace her and terminate Project Luna.

And thus, we have successfully brought Agent Luna over to our side.

File 45
GONE

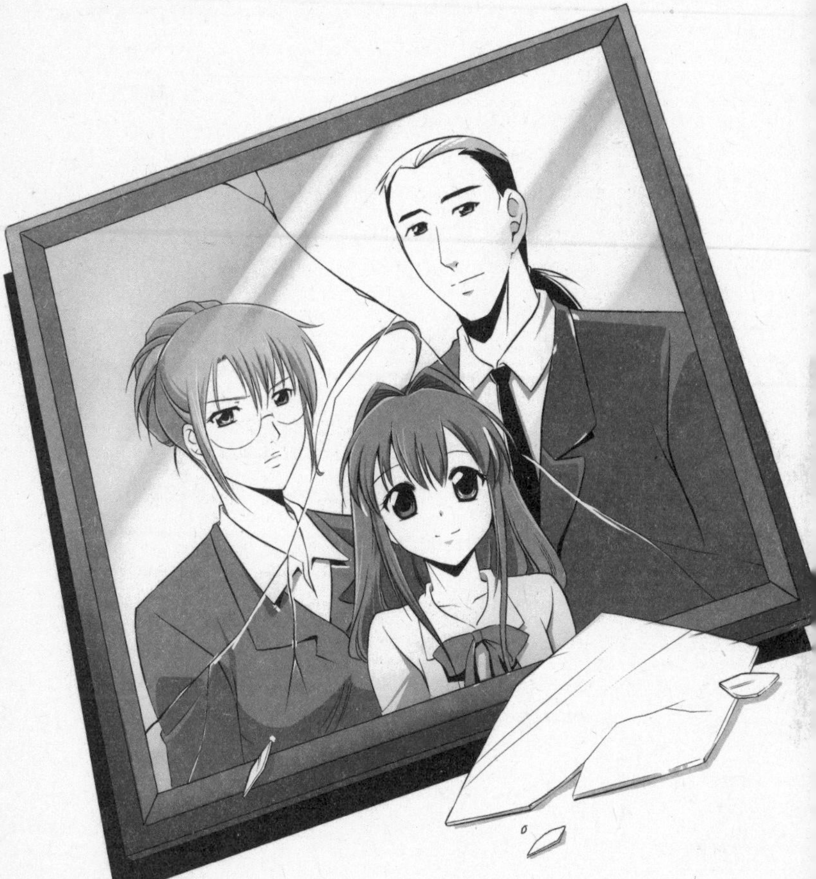

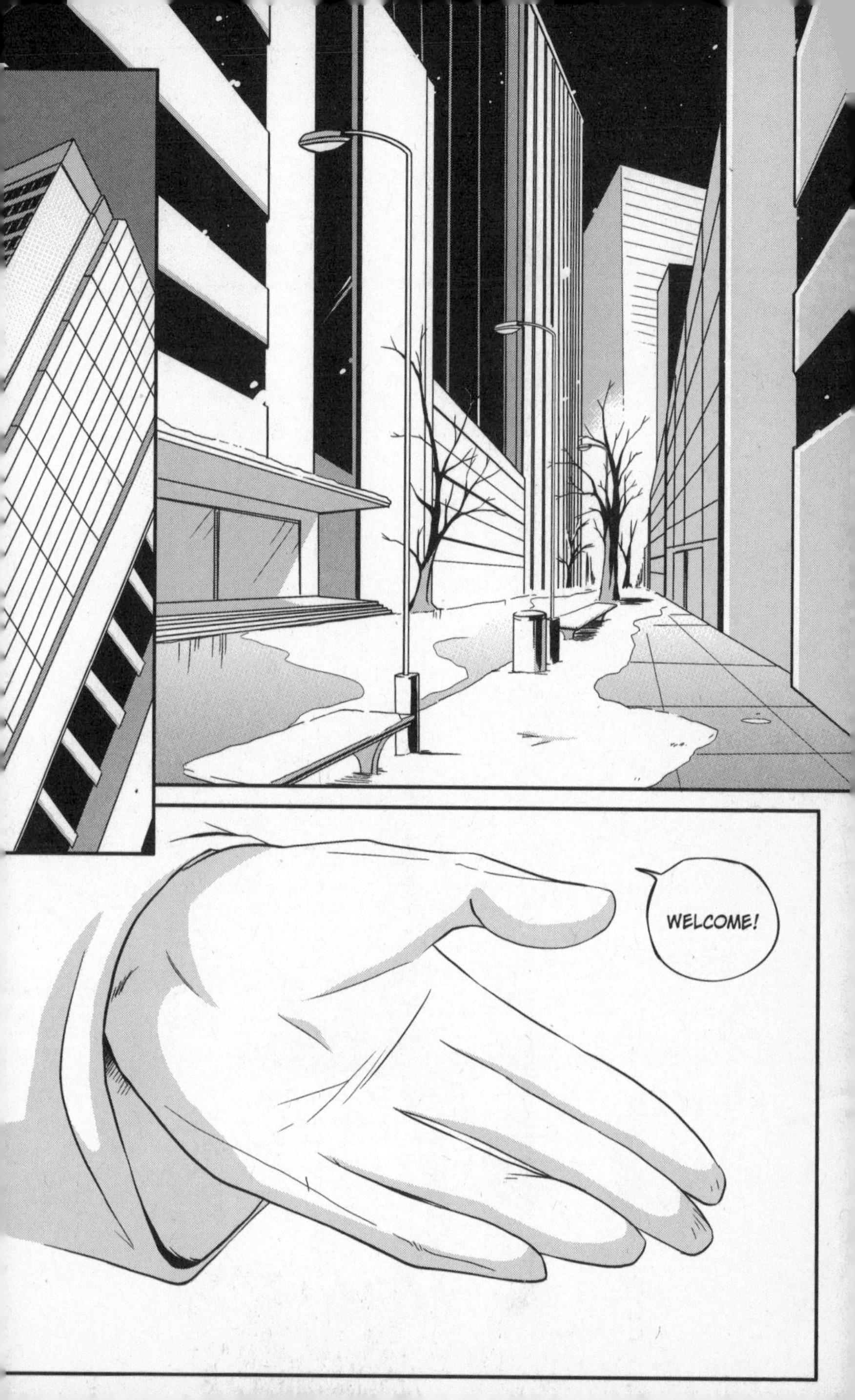
WELCOME!

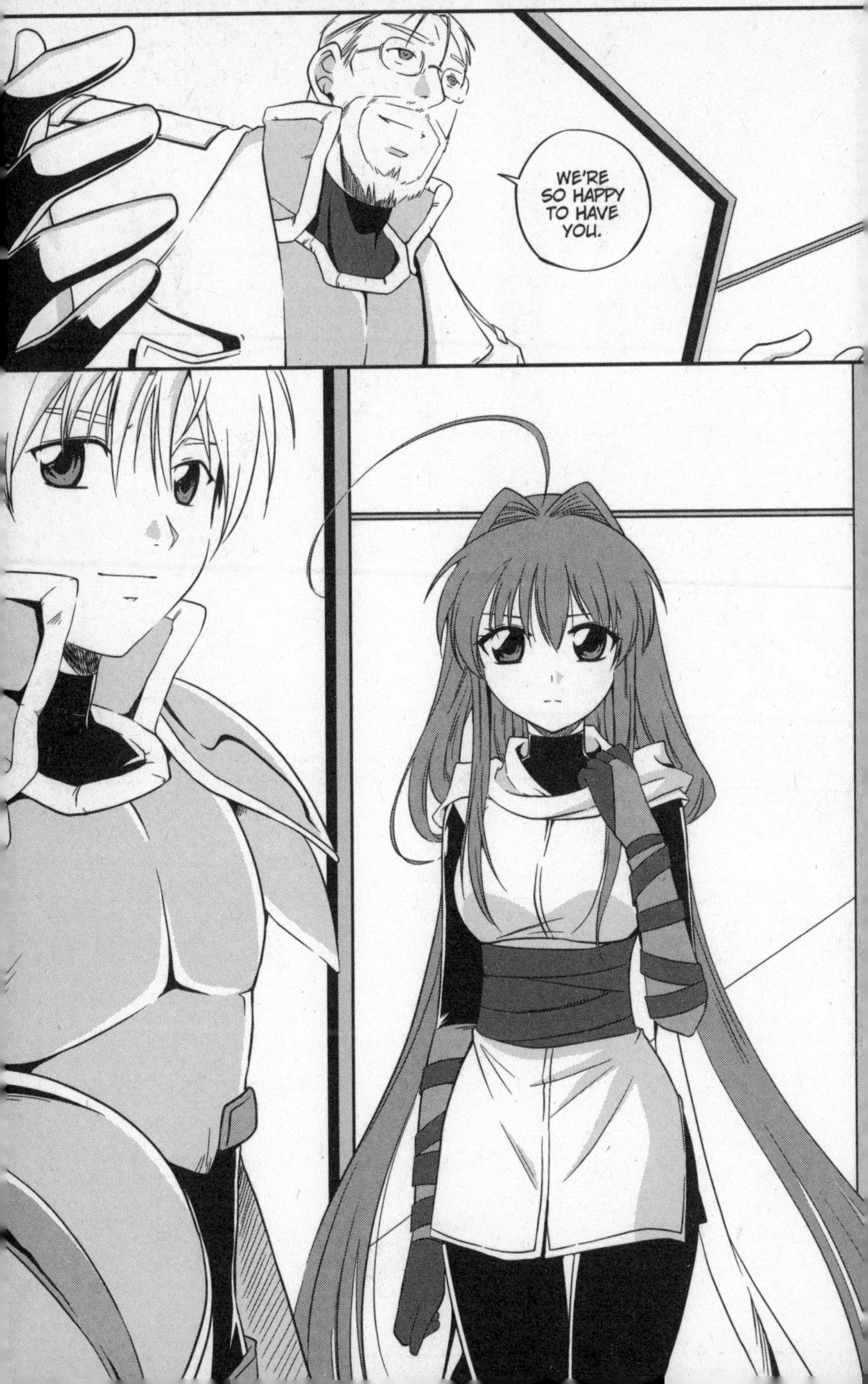
WE'RE SO HAPPY TO HAVE YOU.

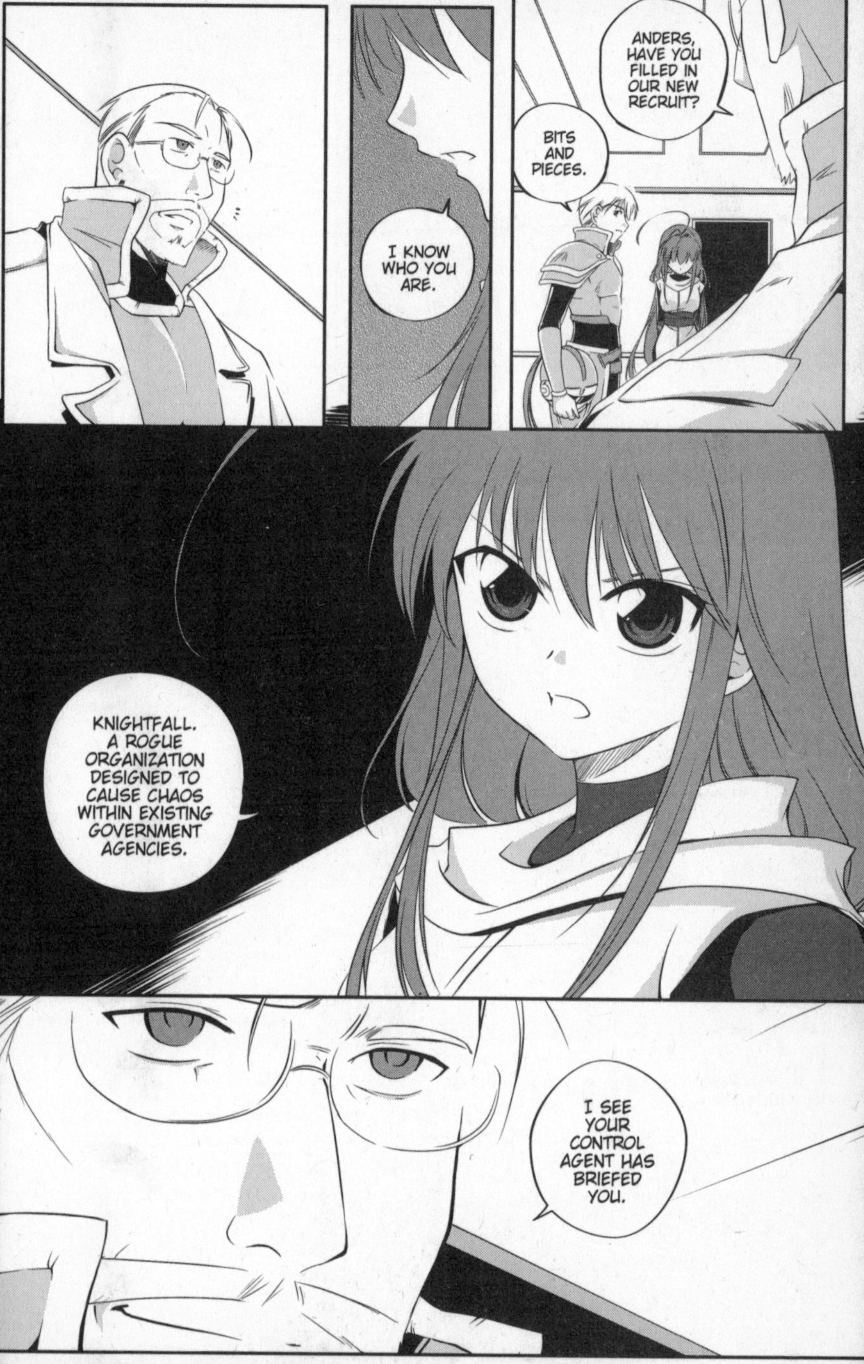
ANDERS, HAVE YOU FILLED IN OUR NEW RECRUIT?
BITS AND PIECES.
I KNOW WHO YOU ARE.
KNIGHTFALL. A ROGUE ORGANIZATION DESIGNED TO CAUSE CHAOS WITHIN EXISTING GOVERNMENT AGENCIES.
I SEE YOUR CONTROL AGENT HAS BRIEFED YOU.

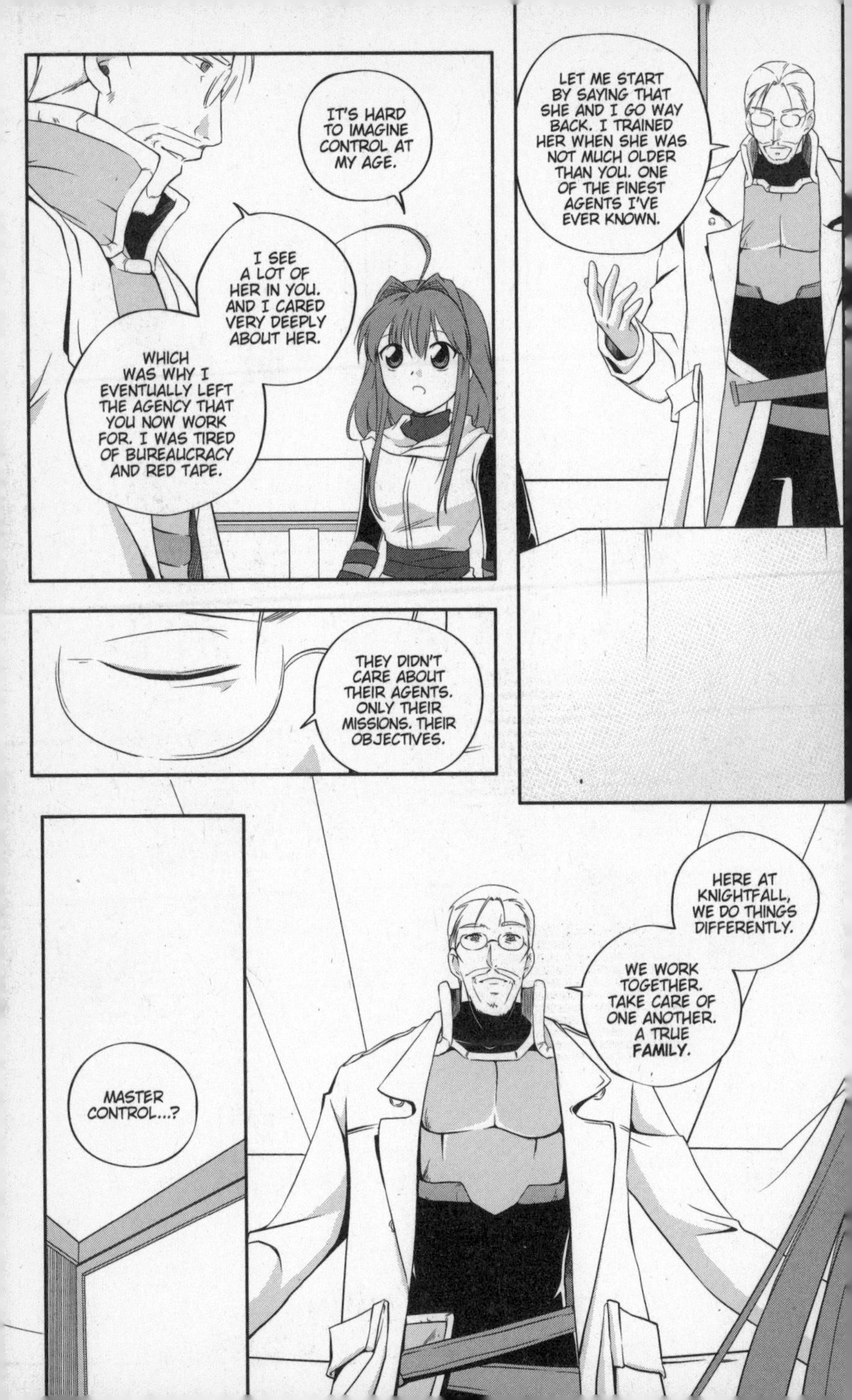
LET ME START BY SAYING THAT SHE AND I GO WAY BACK. I TRAINED HER WHEN SHE WAS NOT MUCH OLDER THAN YOU. ONE OF THE FINEST AGENTS I'VE EVER KNOWN.
IT'S HARD TO IMAGINE CONTROL AT MY AGE.
I SEE A LOT OF HER IN YOU. AND I CARED VERY DEEPLY ABOUT HER.
WHICH WAS WHY I EVENTUALLY LEFT THE AGENCY THAT YOU NOW WORK FOR. I WAS TIRED OF BUREAUCRACY AND RED TAPE.
THEY DIDN'T CARE ABOUT THEIR AGENTS. ONLY THEIR MISSIONS. THEIR OBJECTIVES.
HERE AT KNIGHTFALL, WE DO THINGS DIFFERENTLY.
WE WORK TOGETHER. TAKE CARE OF ONE ANOTHER. A TRUE FAMILY.
MASTER CONTROL...?

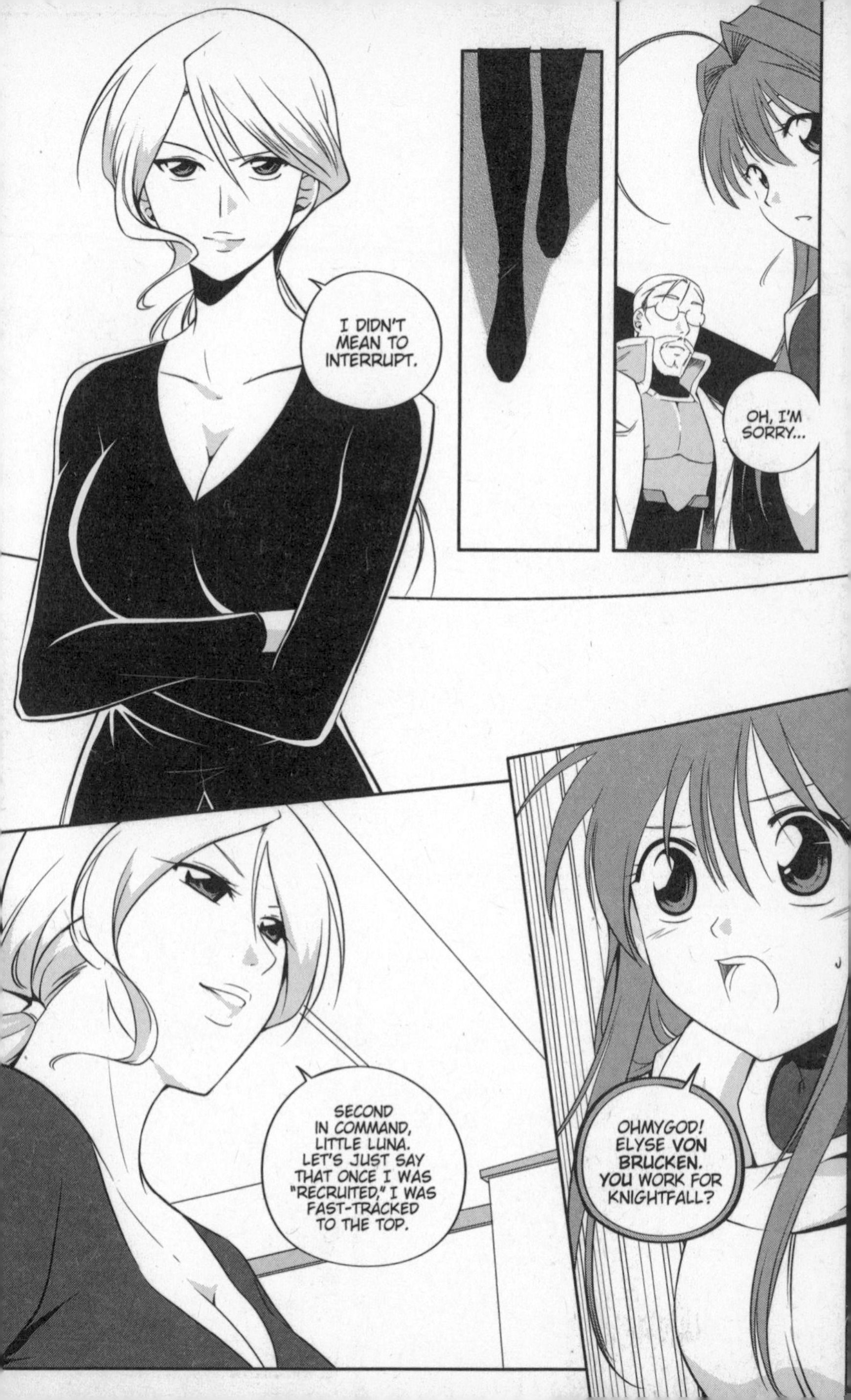
OH, I'M SORRY...
I DIDN'T MEAN TO INTERRUPT.
OHMYGOD! ELYSE VON BRUCKEN. YOU WORK FOR KNIGHTFALL?
SECOND IN COMMAND, LITTLE LUNA. LET'S JUST SAY THAT ONCE I WAS "RECRUITED," I WAS FAST-TRACKED TO THE TOP.

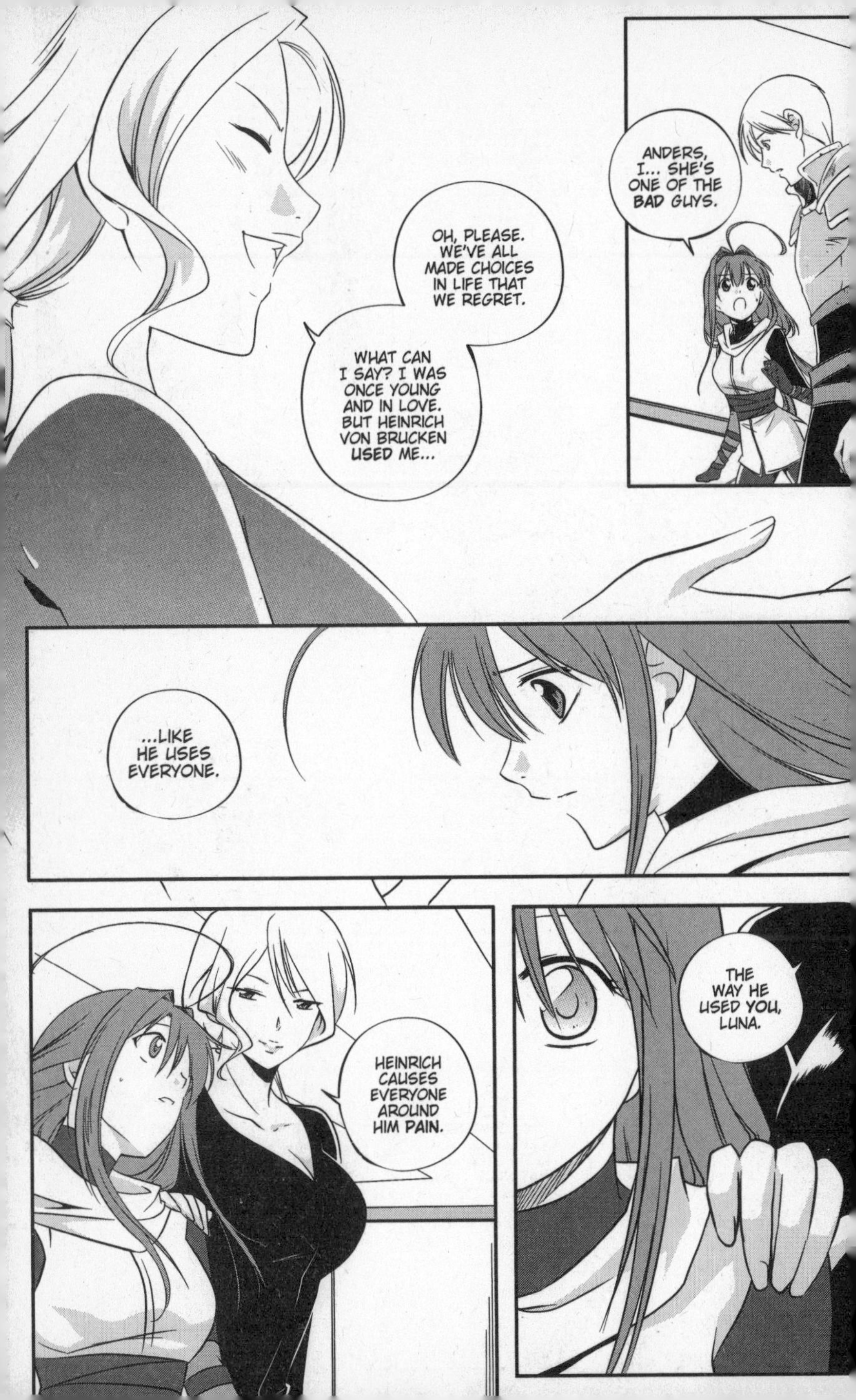
ANDERS, I... SHE'S ONE OF THE BAD GUYS.
OH, PLEASE. WE'VE ALL MADE CHOICES IN LIFE THAT WE REGRET.
WHAT CAN I SAY? I WAS ONCE YOUNG AND IN LOVE. BUT HEINRICH VON BRUCKEN USED ME...
...LIKE HE USES EVERYONE.
THE WAY HE USED YOU, LUNA.
HEINRICH CAUSES EVERYONE AROUND HIM PAIN.

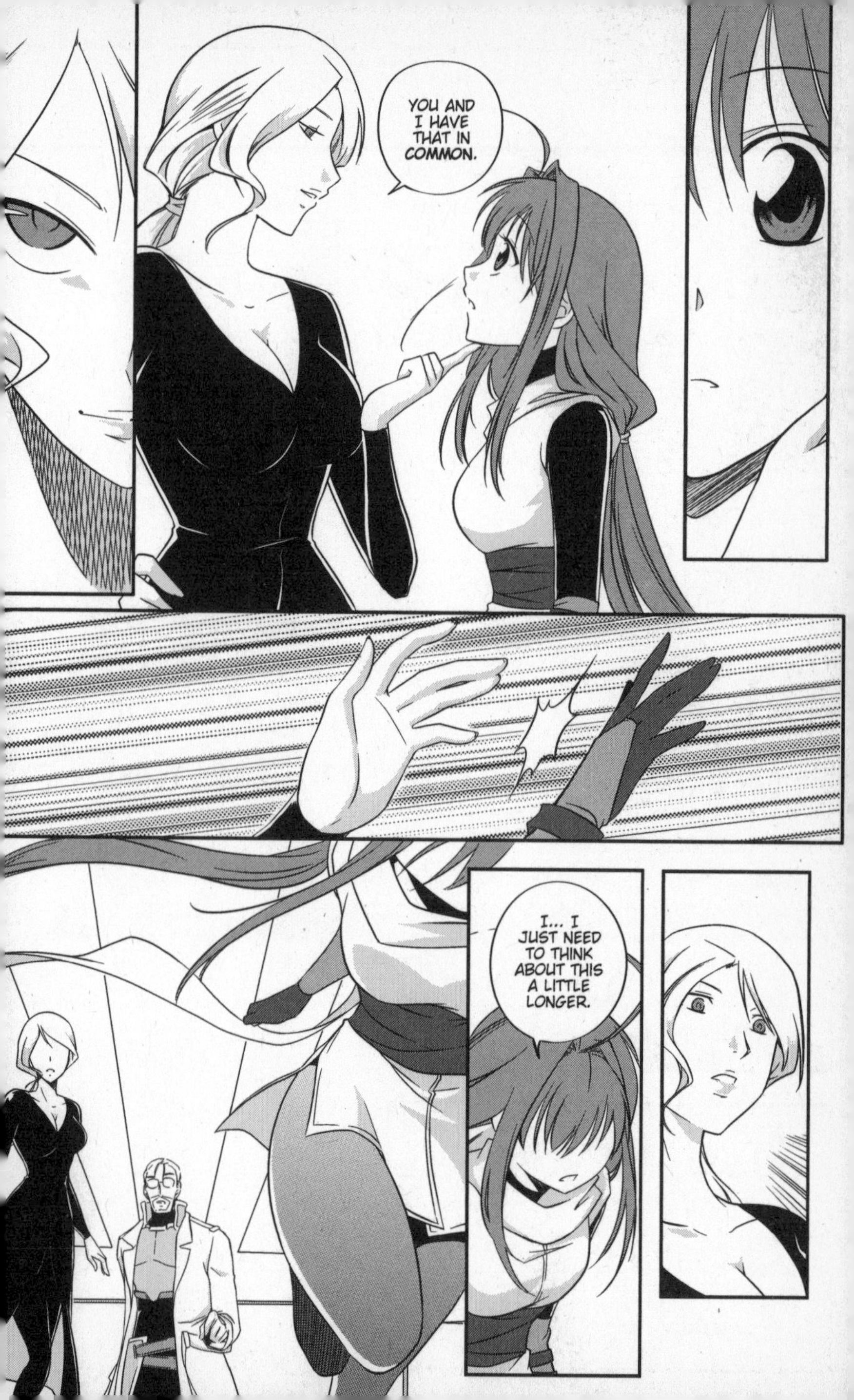
YOU AND I HAVE THAT IN COMMON.
I... I JUST NEED TO THINK ABOUT THIS A LITTLE LONGER.

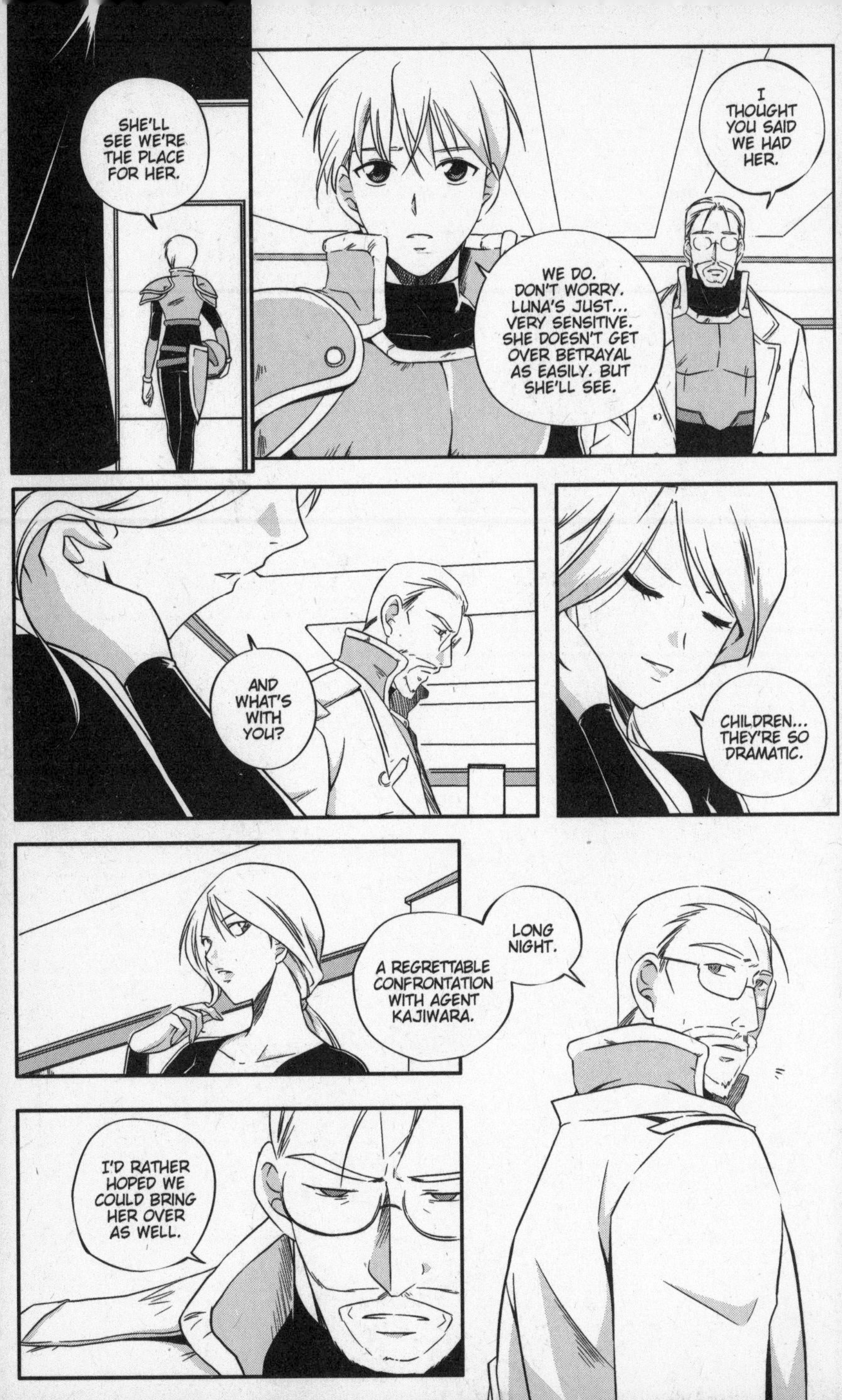
I THOUGHT YOU SAID WE HAD HER.
WE DO. DON'T WORRY. LUNA'S JUST... VERY SENSITIVE. SHE DOESN'T GET OVER BETRAYAL AS EASILY. BUT SHE'LL SEE.
SHE'LL SEE WE'RE THE PLACE FOR HER.
CHILDREN... THEY'RE SO DRAMATIC.
AND WHAT'S WITH YOU?
LONG NIGHT.
A REGRETTABLE CONFRONTATION WITH AGENT KAJIWARA.
I'D RATHER HOPED WE COULD BRING HER OVER AS WELL.

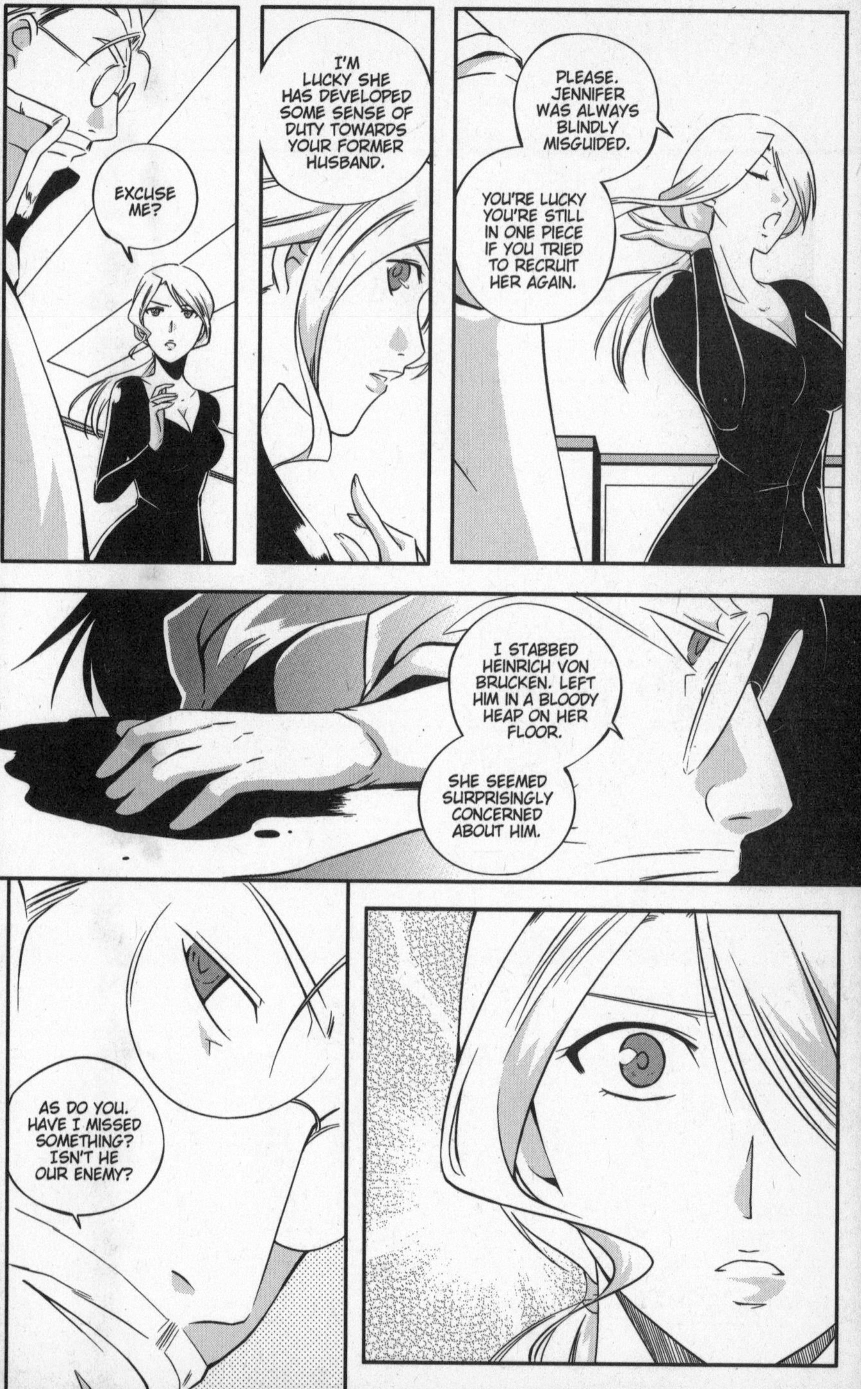
PLEASE. JENNIFER WAS ALWAYS BLINDLY MISGUIDED.
YOU'RE LUCKY YOU'RE STILL IN ONE PIECE IF YOU TRIED TO RECRUIT HER AGAIN.
I'M LUCKY SHE HAS DEVELOPED SOME SENSE OF DUTY TOWARDS YOUR FORMER HUSBAND.
EXCUSE ME?
I STABBED HEINRICH VON BRUCKEN. LEFT HIM IN A BLOODY HEAP ON HER FLOOR.
SHE SEEMED SURPRISINGLY CONCERNED ABOUT HIM.
AS DO YOU. HAVE I MISSED SOMETHING? ISN'T HE OUR ENEMY?

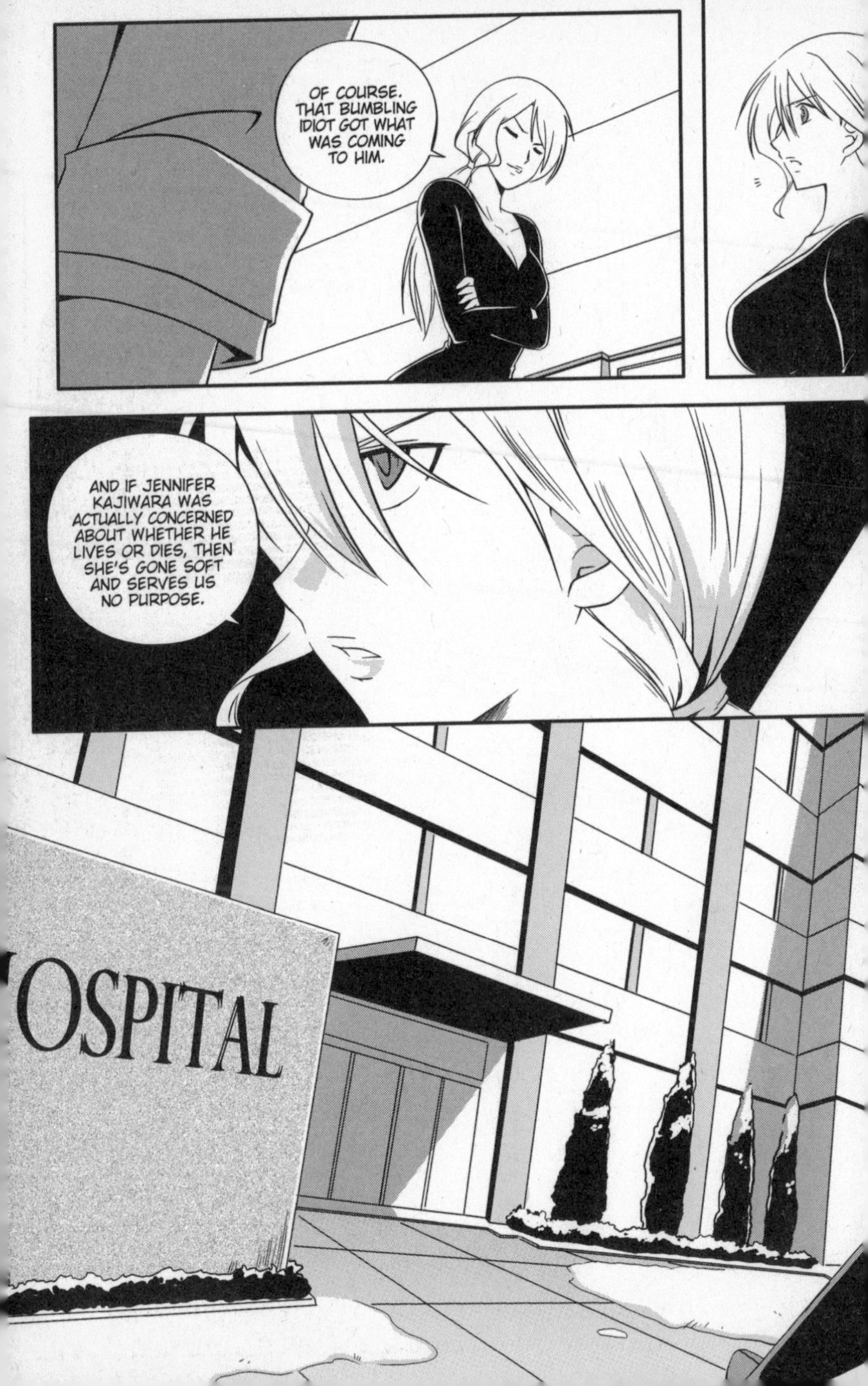
OF COURSE. THAT BUMBLING IDIOT GOT WHAT WAS COMING TO HIM.
AND IF JENNIFER KAJIWARA WAS ACTUALLY CONCERNED ABOUT WHETHER HE LIVES OR DIES, THEN SHE'S GONE SOFT AND SERVES US NO PURPOSE.
OSPITAL

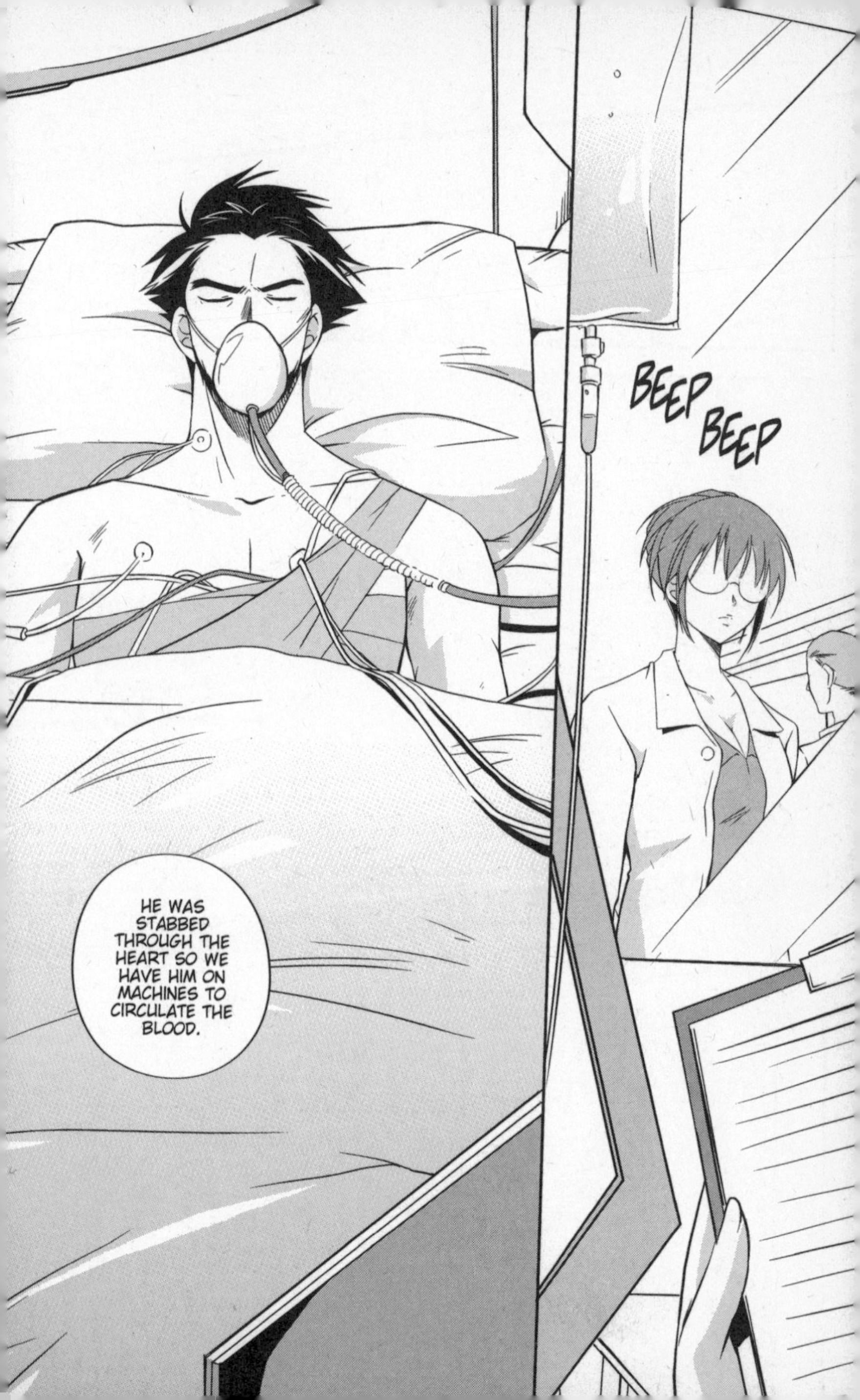
BEEP BEEP
HE WAS STABBED THROUGH THE HEART SO WE HAVE HIM ON MACHINES TO CIRCULATE THE BLOOD.

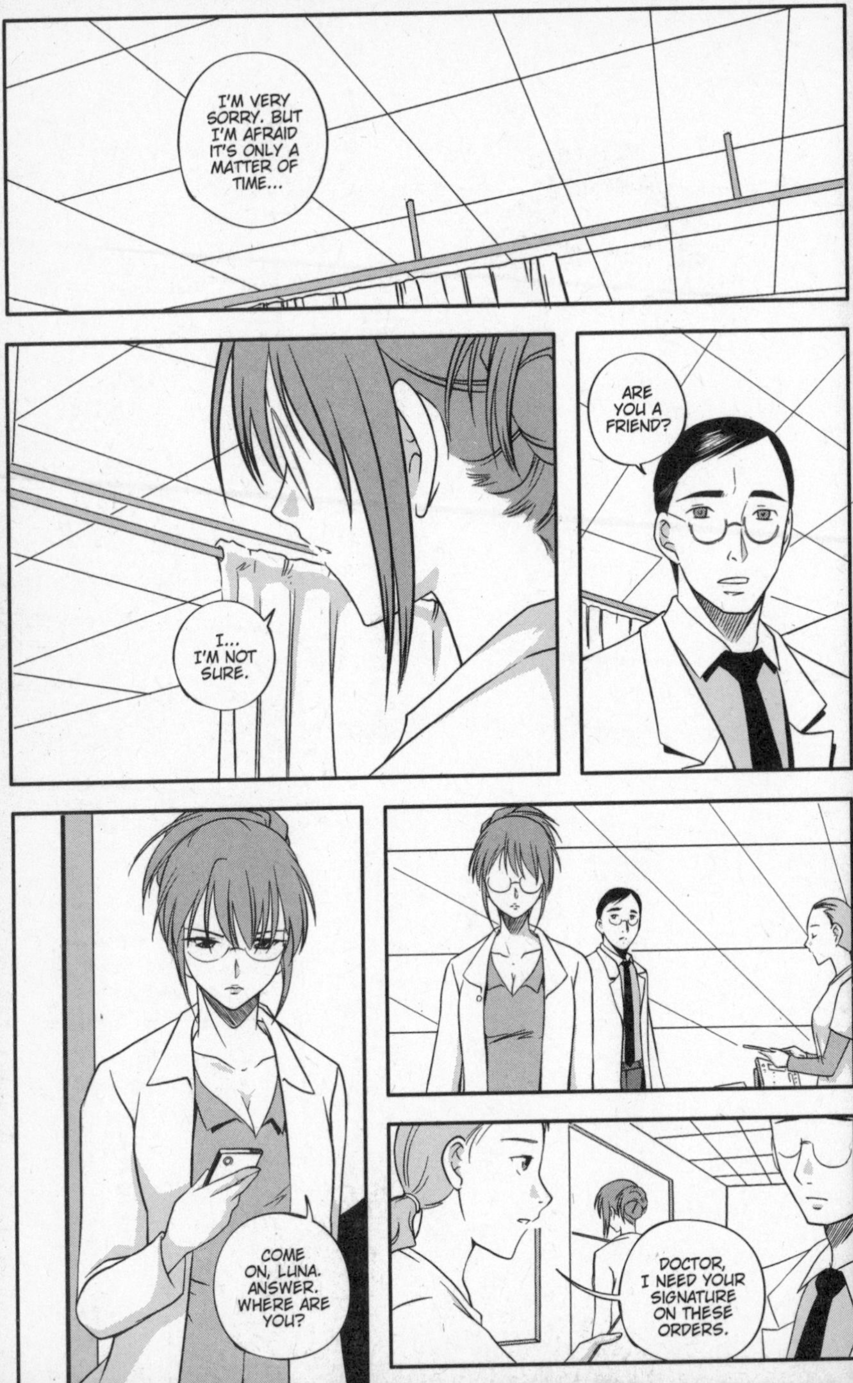
I'M VERY SORRY. BUT I'M AFRAID IT'S ONLY A MATTER OF TIME...
ARE YOU A FRIEND?
I... I'M NOT SURE.
DOCTOR, I NEED YOUR SIGNATURE ON THESE ORDERS.
COME ON, LUNA. ANSWER. WHERE ARE YOU?

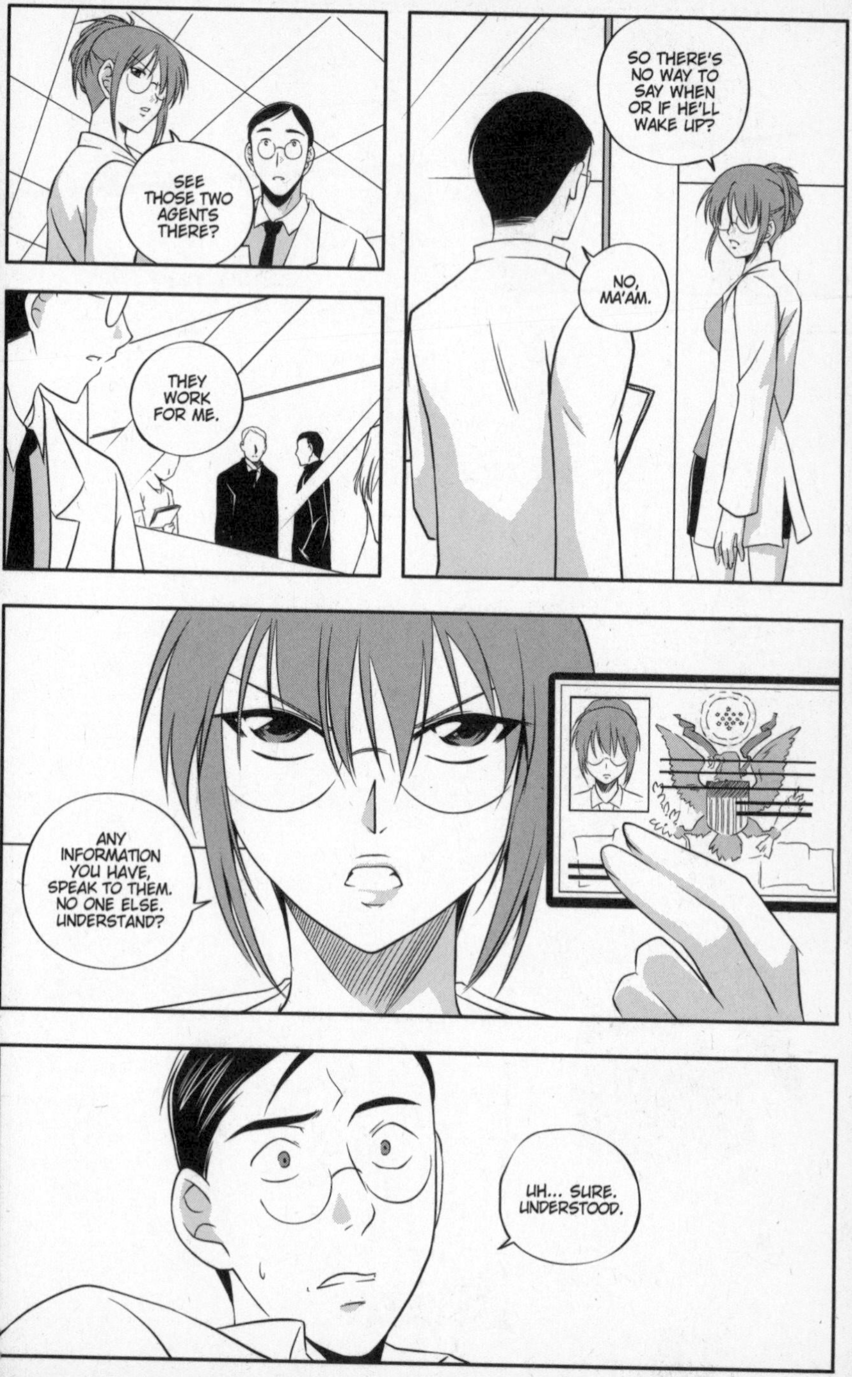
SO THERE'S NO WAY TO SAY WHEN OR IF HE'LL WAKE UP?
NO, MA'AM.
SEE THOSE TWO AGENTS THERE?
THEY WORK FOR ME.
ANY INFORMATION YOU HAVE, SPEAK TO THEM. NO ONE ELSE. UNDERSTAND?
UH... SURE. UNDERSTOOD.

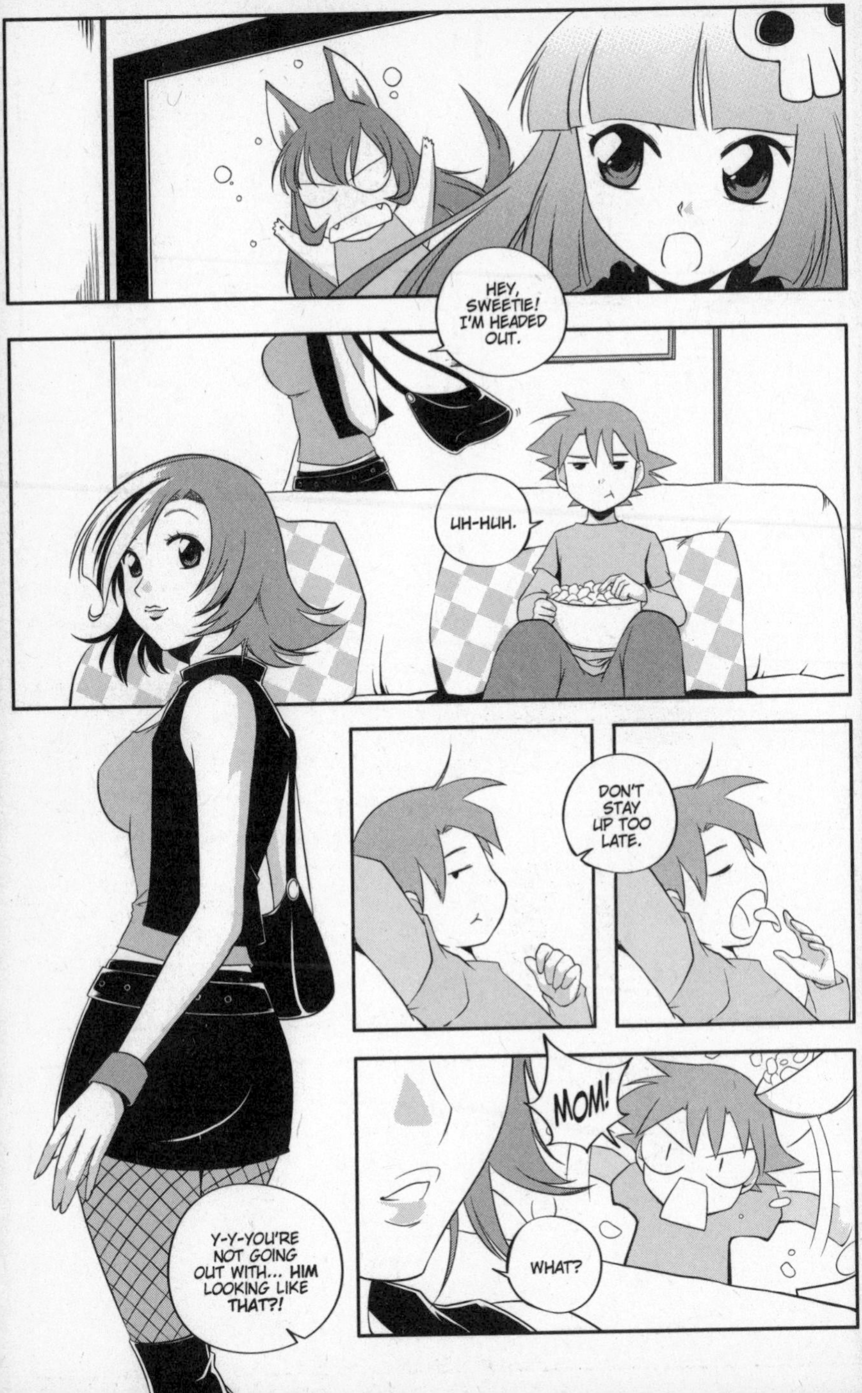
HEY, SWEETIE! I'M HEADED OUT.
UH-HUH.
DON'T STAY UP TOO LATE.
MOM!
WHAT?
Y-Y-YOU'RE NOT GOING OUT WITH... HIM LOOKING LIKE THAT?!

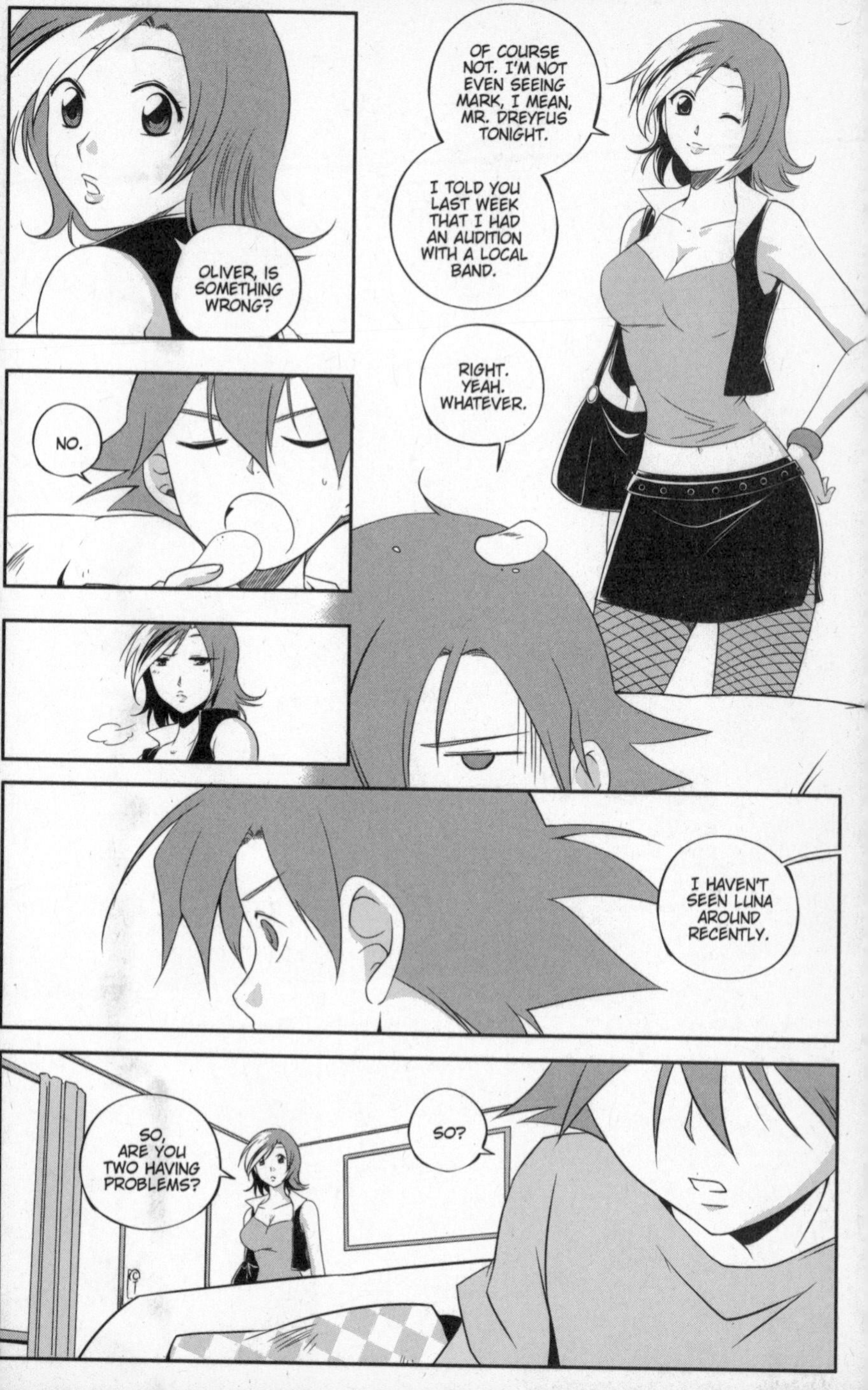
OF COURSE NOT. I'M NOT EVEN SEEING MARK, I MEAN, MR. DREYFUS TONIGHT.
I TOLD YOU LAST WEEK THAT I HAD AN AUDITION WITH A LOCAL BAND.
RIGHT. YEAH. WHATEVER.
OLIVER, IS SOMETHING WRONG?
NO.
I HAVEN'T SEEN LUNA AROUND RECENTLY.
SO?
SO, ARE YOU TWO HAVING PROBLEMS?

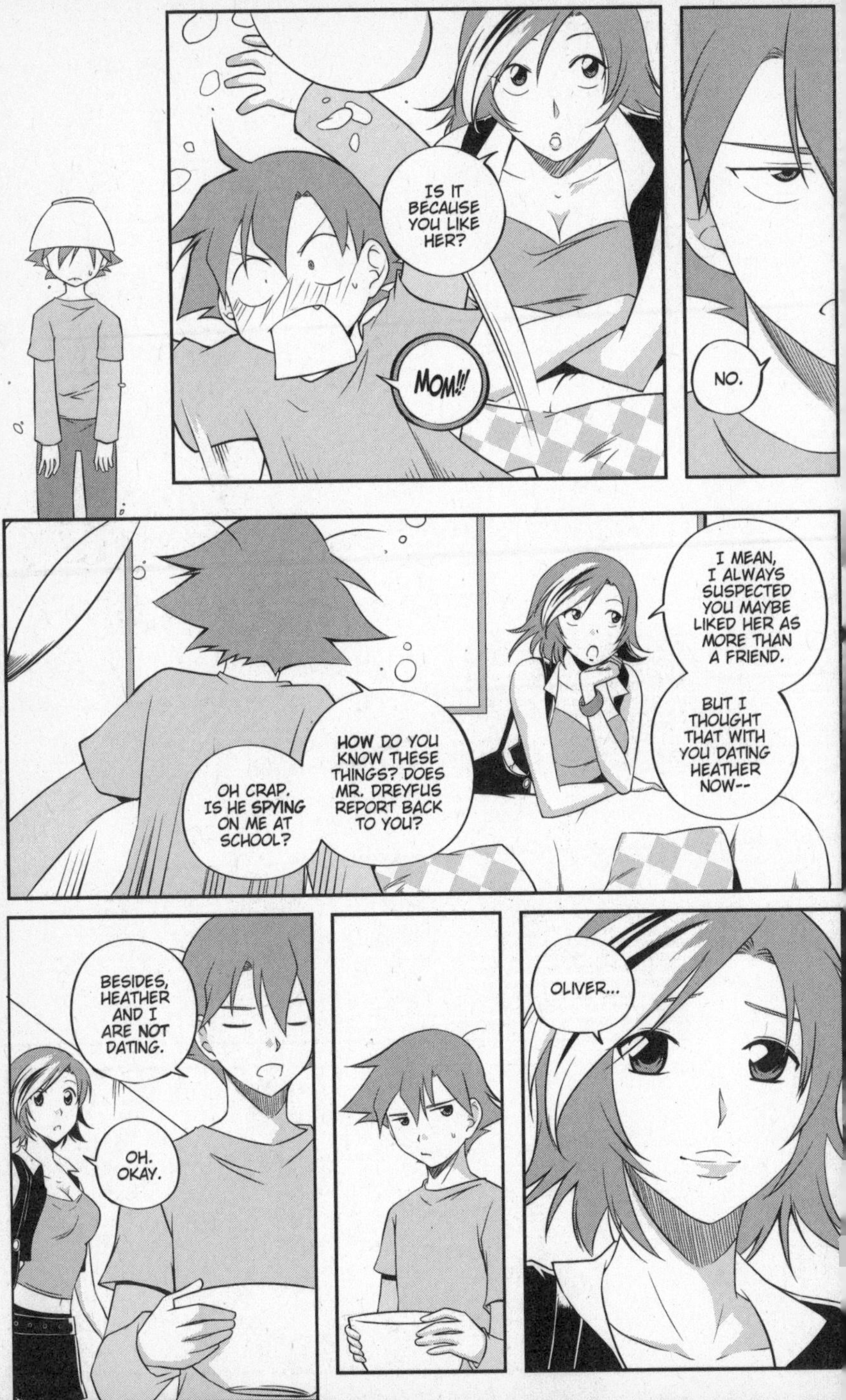
IS IT BECAUSE YOU LIKE HER?
MOM!!!
NO.
OH CRAP. IS HE SPYING ON ME AT SCHOOL?
HOW DO YOU KNOW THESE THINGS? DOES MR. DREYFUS REPORT BACK TO YOU?
I MEAN, I ALWAYS SUSPECTED YOU MAYBE LIKED HER AS MORE THAN A FRIEND.
BUT I THOUGHT THAT WITH YOU DATING HEATHER NOW--
BESIDES, HEATHER AND I ARE NOT DATING.
OH. OKAY.
OLIVER...

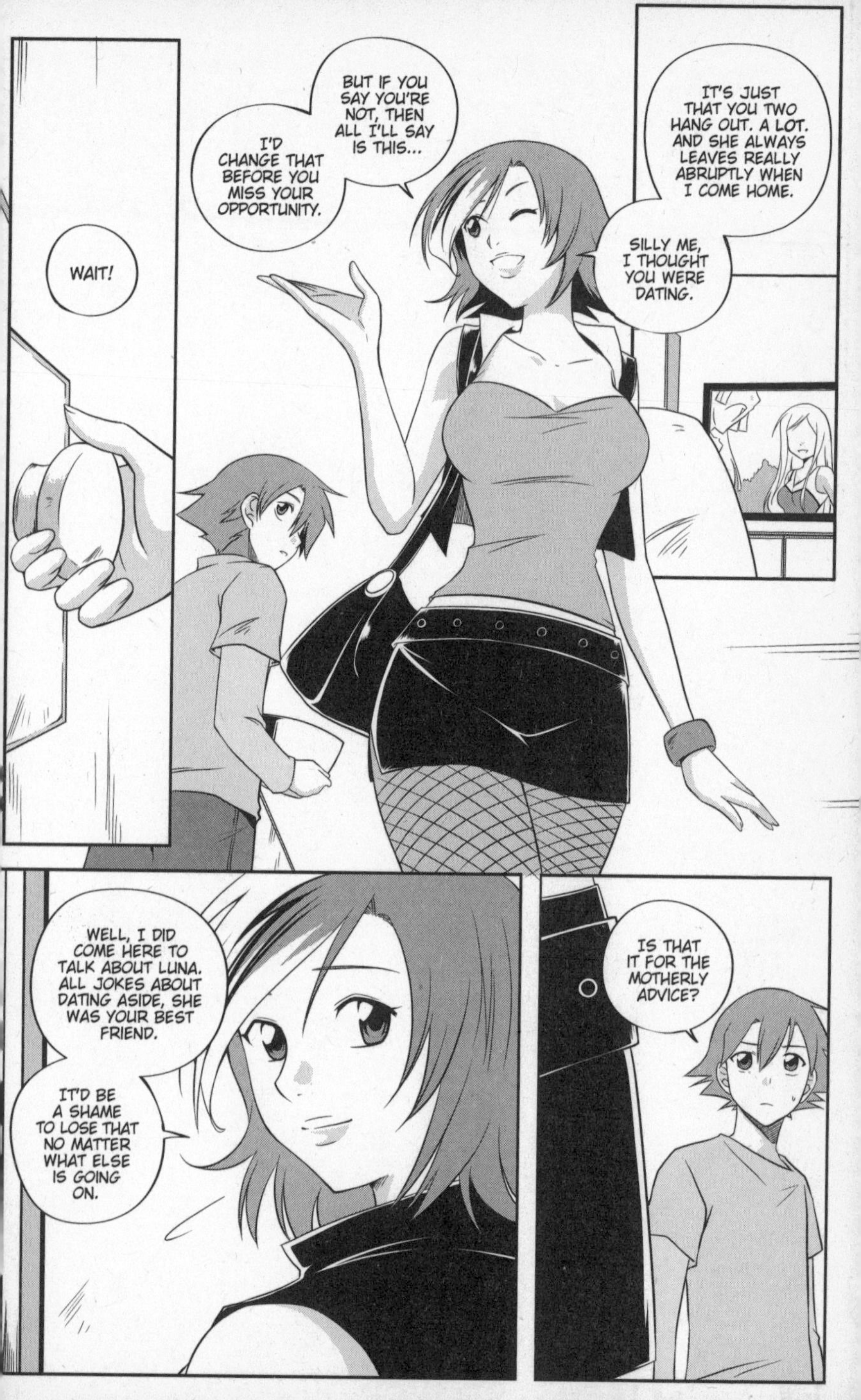
IT'S JUST THAT YOU TWO HANG OUT. A LOT. AND SHE ALWAYS LEAVES REALLY ABRUPTLY WHEN I COME HOME.
SILLY ME, I THOUGHT YOU WERE DATING.
BUT IF YOU SAY YOU'RE NOT, THEN ALL I'LL SAY IS THIS...
I'D CHANGE THAT BEFORE YOU MISS YOUR OPPORTUNITY.
WAIT!
IS THAT IT FOR THE MOTHERLY ADVICE?
WELL, I DID COME HERE TO TALK ABOUT LUNA. ALL JOKES ABOUT DATING ASIDE, SHE WAS YOUR BEST FRIEND.
IT'D BE A SHAME TO LOSE THAT NO MATTER WHAT ELSE IS GOING ON.

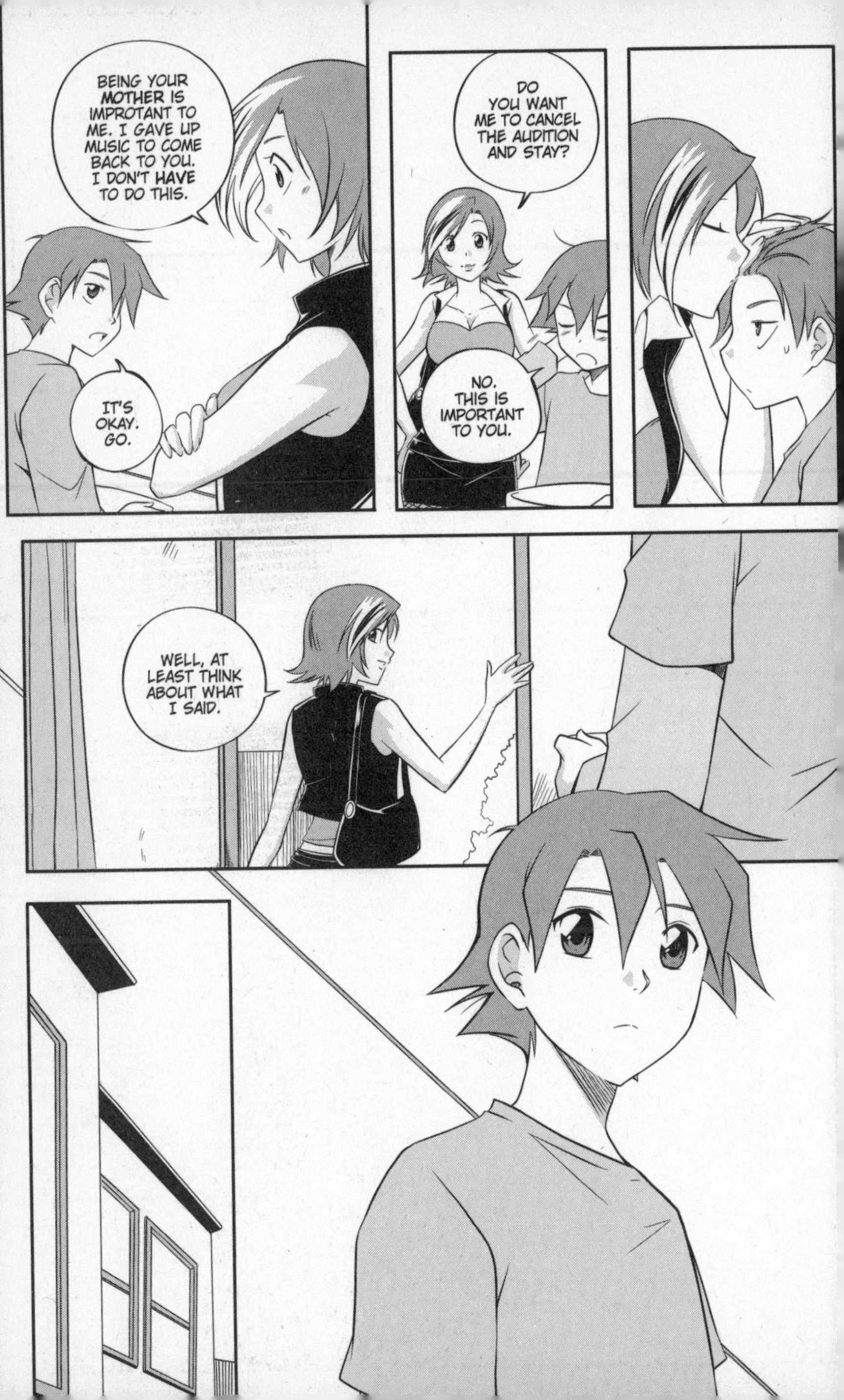
DO YOU WANT ME TO CANCEL THE AUDITION AND STAY?
NO. THIS IS IMPORTANT TO YOU.
BEING YOUR MOTHER IS IMPROTANT TO ME. I GAVE UP MUSIC TO COME BACK TO YOU. I DON'T HAVE TO DO THIS.
IT'S OKAY. GO.
WELL, AT LEAST THINK ABOUT WHAT I SAID.

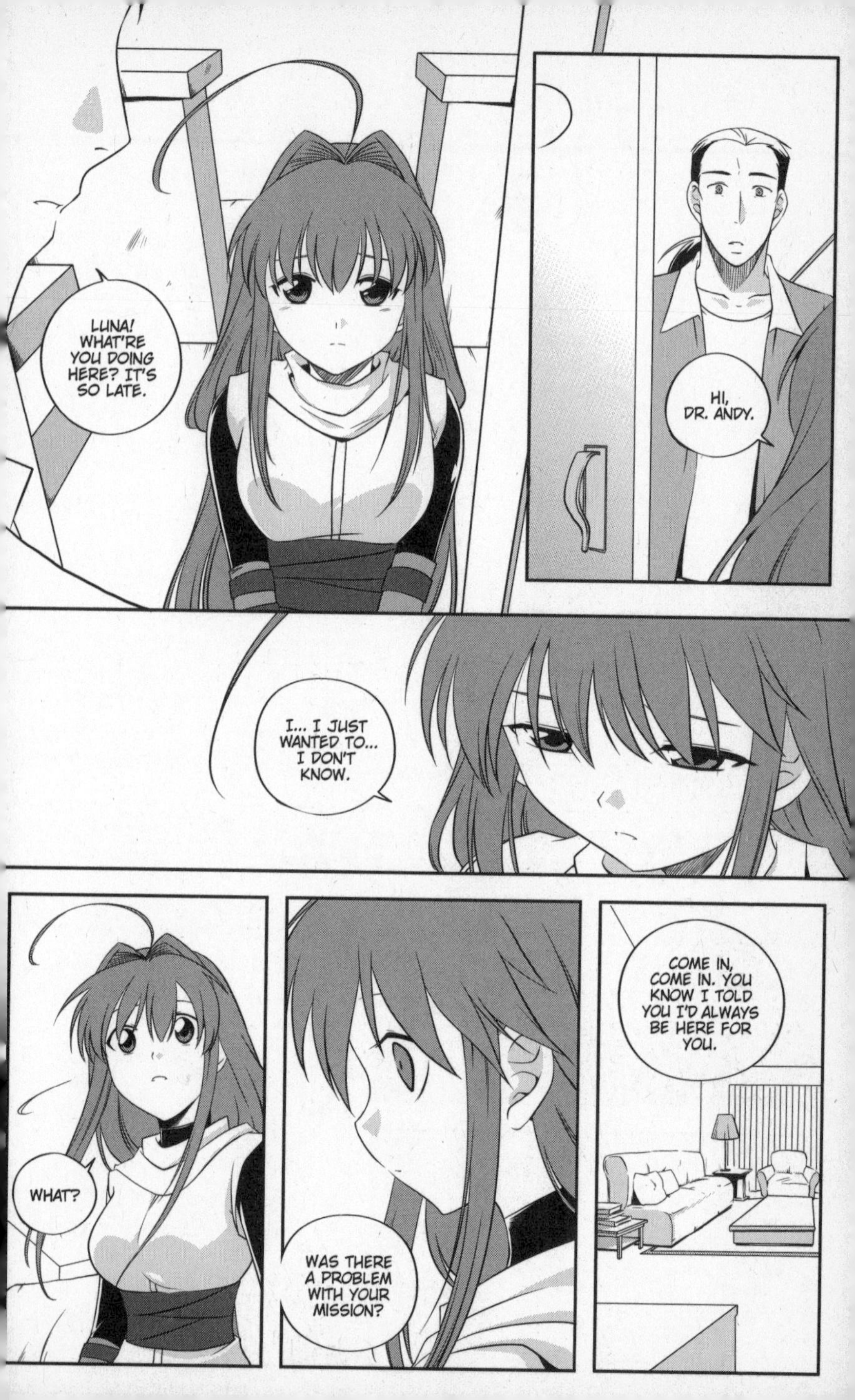
HI, DR. ANDY.
LUNA! WHAT'RE YOU DOING HERE? IT'S SO LATE.
I... I JUST WANTED TO... I DON'T KNOW.
COME IN, COME IN. YOU KNOW I TOLD YOU I'D ALWAYS BE HERE FOR YOU.
WAS THERE A PROBLEM WITH YOUR MISSION?
WHAT?

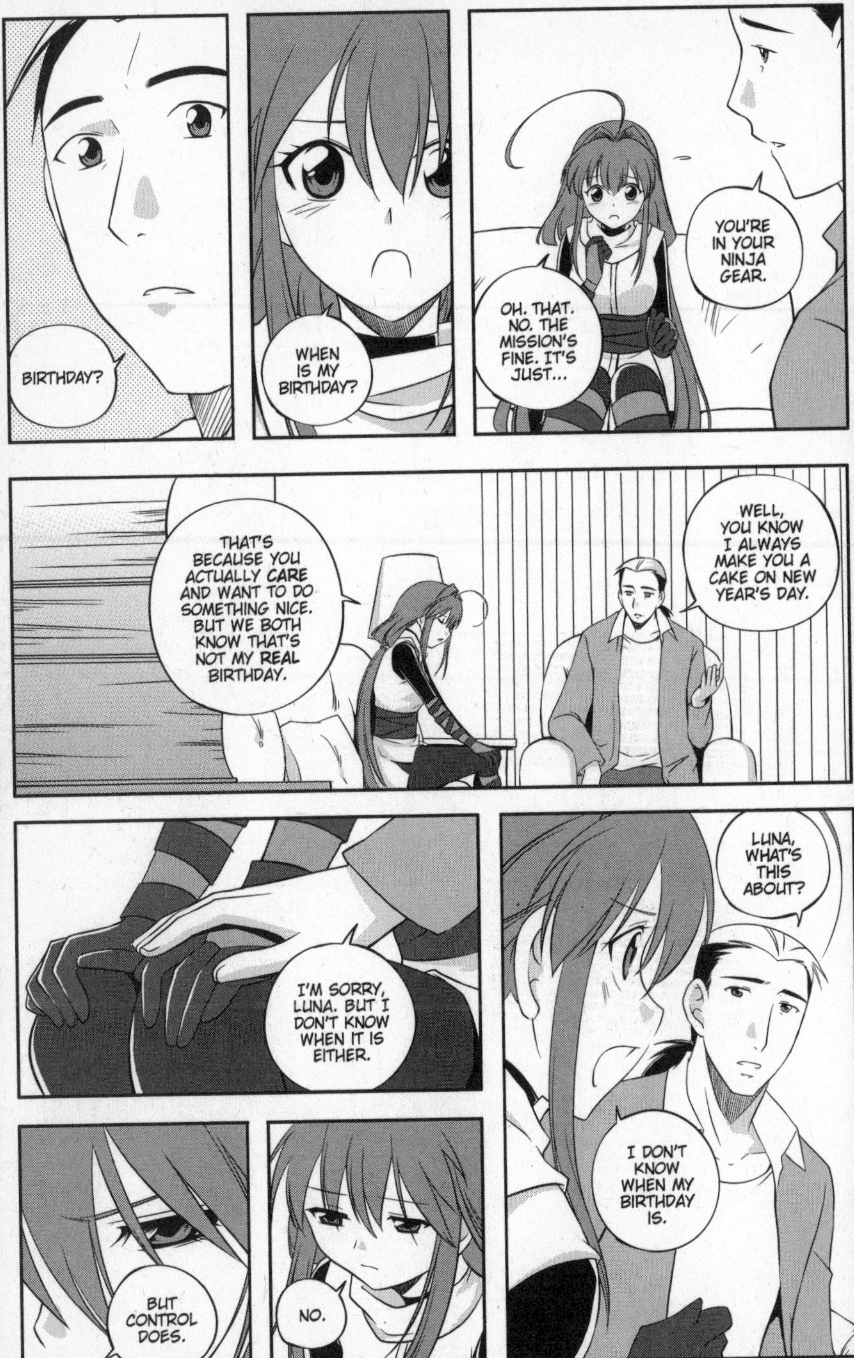
YOU'RE IN YOUR NINJA GEAR.
OH. THAT. NO. THE MISSION'S FINE. IT'S JUST...
WHEN IS MY BIRTHDAY?
BIRTHDAY?
WELL, YOU KNOW I ALWAYS MAKE YOU A CAKE ON NEW YEAR'S DAY.
THAT'S BECAUSE YOU ACTUALLY **CARE** AND WANT TO DO SOMETHING NICE. BUT WE BOTH KNOW THAT'S NOT MY **REAL** BIRTHDAY.
LUNA, WHAT'S THIS ABOUT?
I DON'T KNOW WHEN MY BIRTHDAY IS.
I'M SORRY, LUNA. BUT I DON'T KNOW WHEN IT IS EITHER.
NO.
BUT CONTROL DOES.

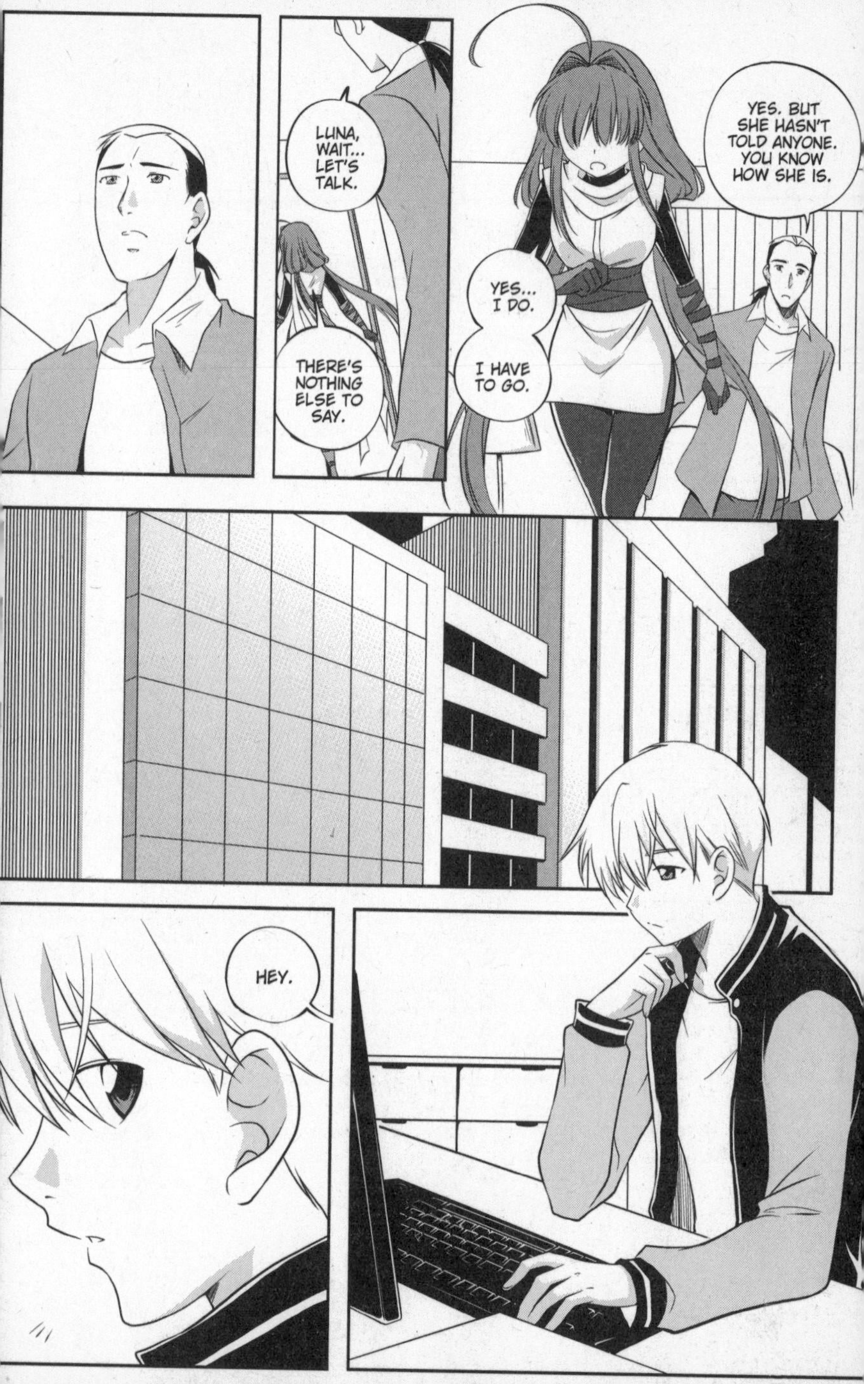
YES. BUT SHE HASN'T TOLD ANYONE. YOU KNOW HOW SHE IS.
YES... I DO.
I HAVE TO GO.
LUNA, WAIT... LET'S TALK.
THERE'S NOTHING ELSE TO SAY.
HEY.

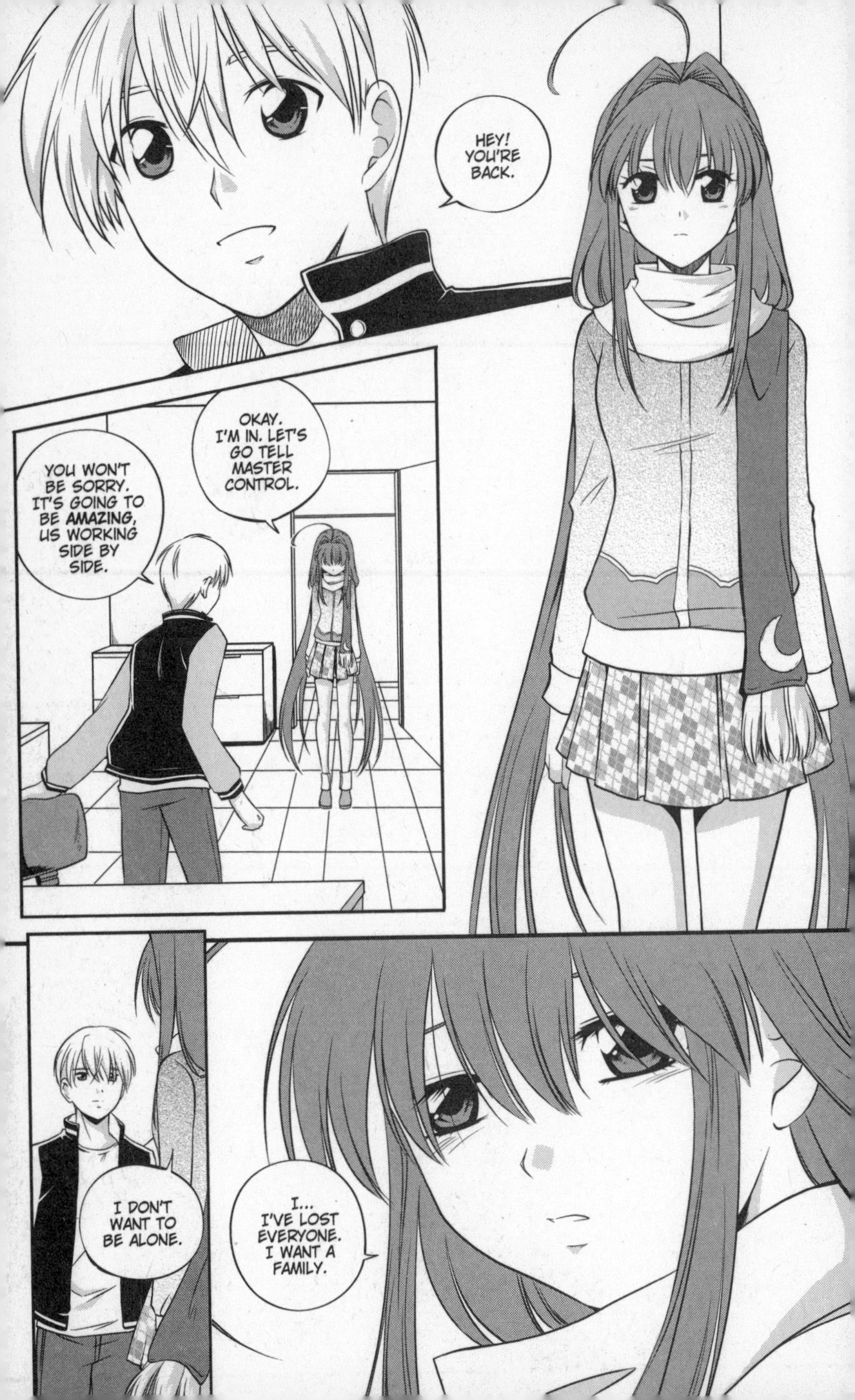
HEY! YOU'RE BACK.
OKAY. I'M IN. LET'S GO TELL MASTER CONTROL.
YOU WON'T BE SORRY. IT'S GOING TO BE **AMAZING**, US WORKING SIDE BY SIDE.
I... I'VE LOST EVERYONE. I WANT A FAMILY.
I DON'T WANT TO BE ALONE.

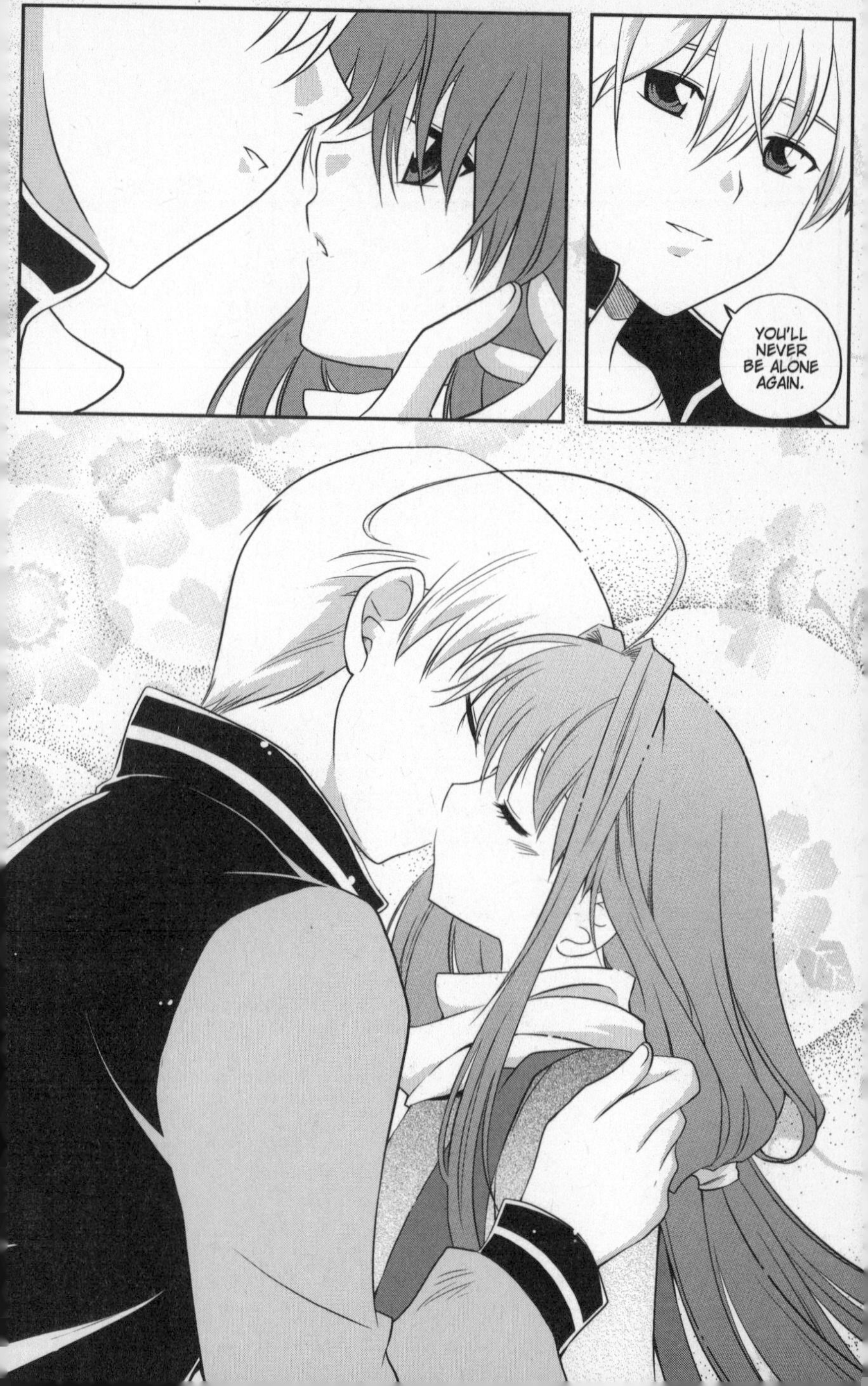
YOU'LL NEVER BE ALONE AGAIN.

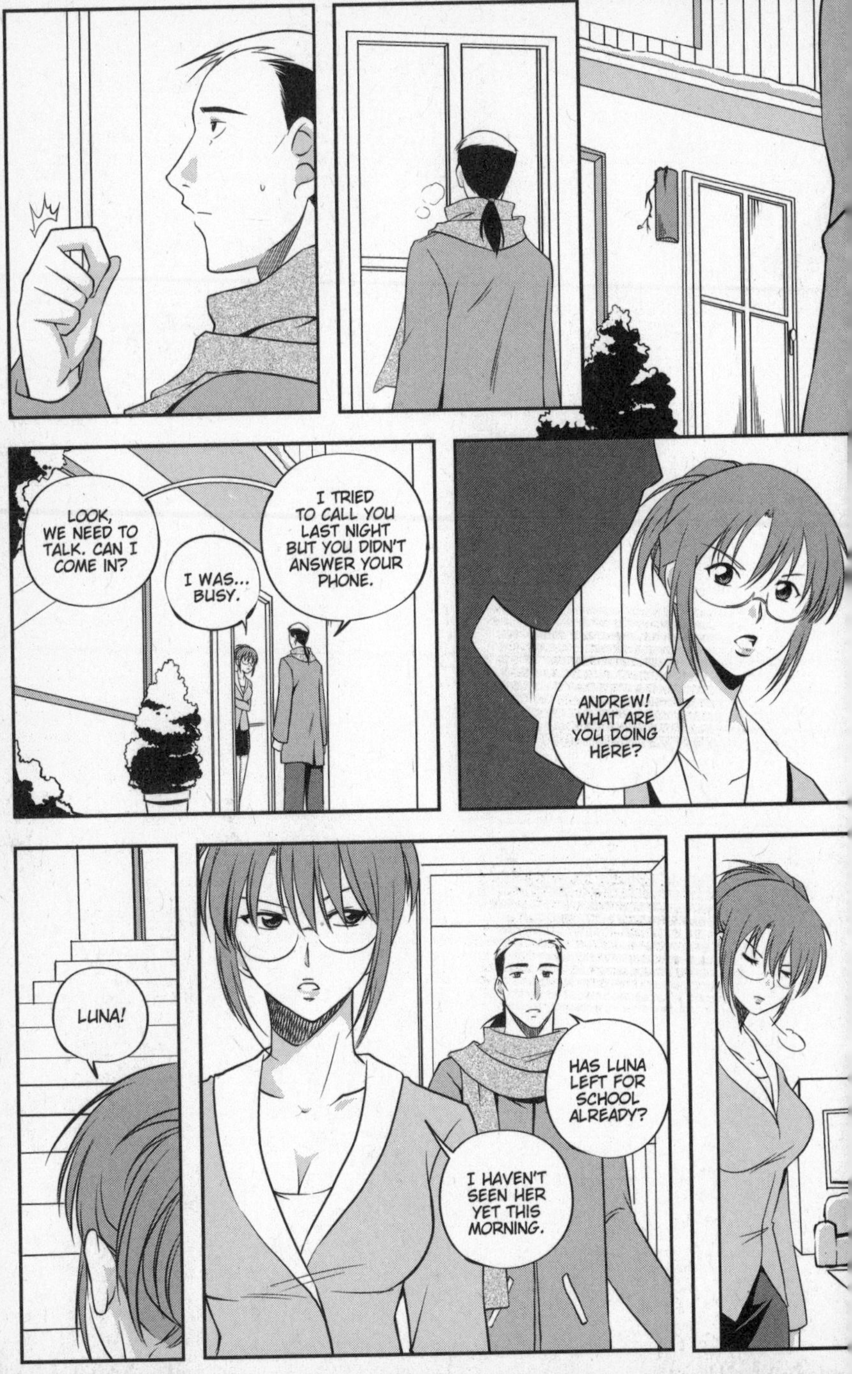
ANDREW! WHAT ARE YOU DOING HERE?
I TRIED TO CALL YOU LAST NIGHT BUT YOU DIDN'T ANSWER YOUR PHONE.
I WAS... BUSY.
LOOK, WE NEED TO TALK. CAN I COME IN?
HAS LUNA LEFT FOR SCHOOL ALREADY?
I HAVEN'T SEEN HER YET THIS MORNING.
LUNA!

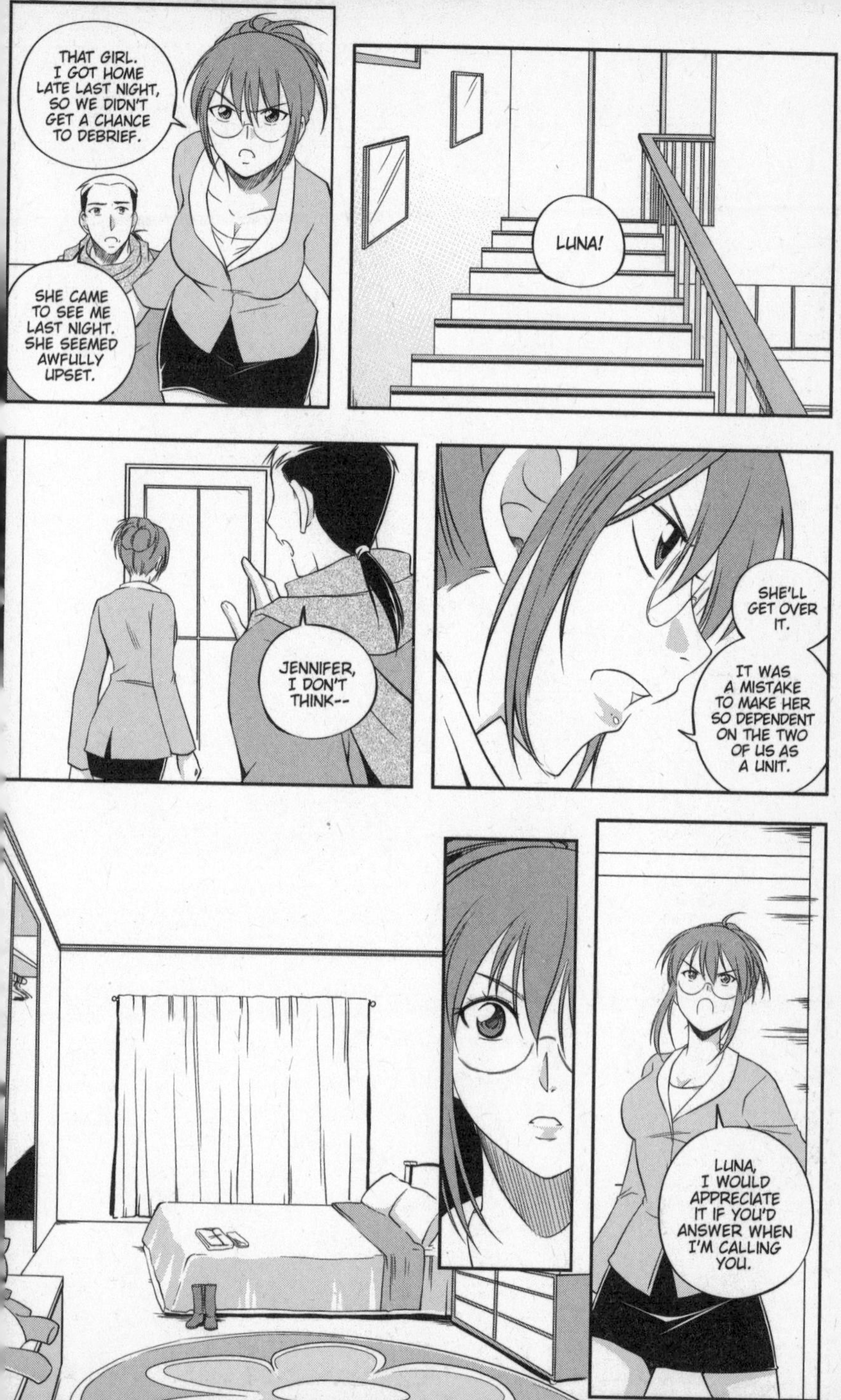
THAT GIRL. I GOT HOME LATE LAST NIGHT, SO WE DIDN'T GET A CHANCE TO DEBRIEF.
SHE CAME TO SEE ME LAST NIGHT. SHE SEEMED AWFULLY UPSET.
LUNA!
JENNIFER, I DON'T THINK--
SHE'LL GET OVER IT.
IT WAS A MISTAKE TO MAKE HER SO DEPENDENT ON THE TWO OF US AS A UNIT.
LUNA, I WOULD APPRECIATE IT IF YOU'D ANSWER WHEN I'M CALLING YOU.

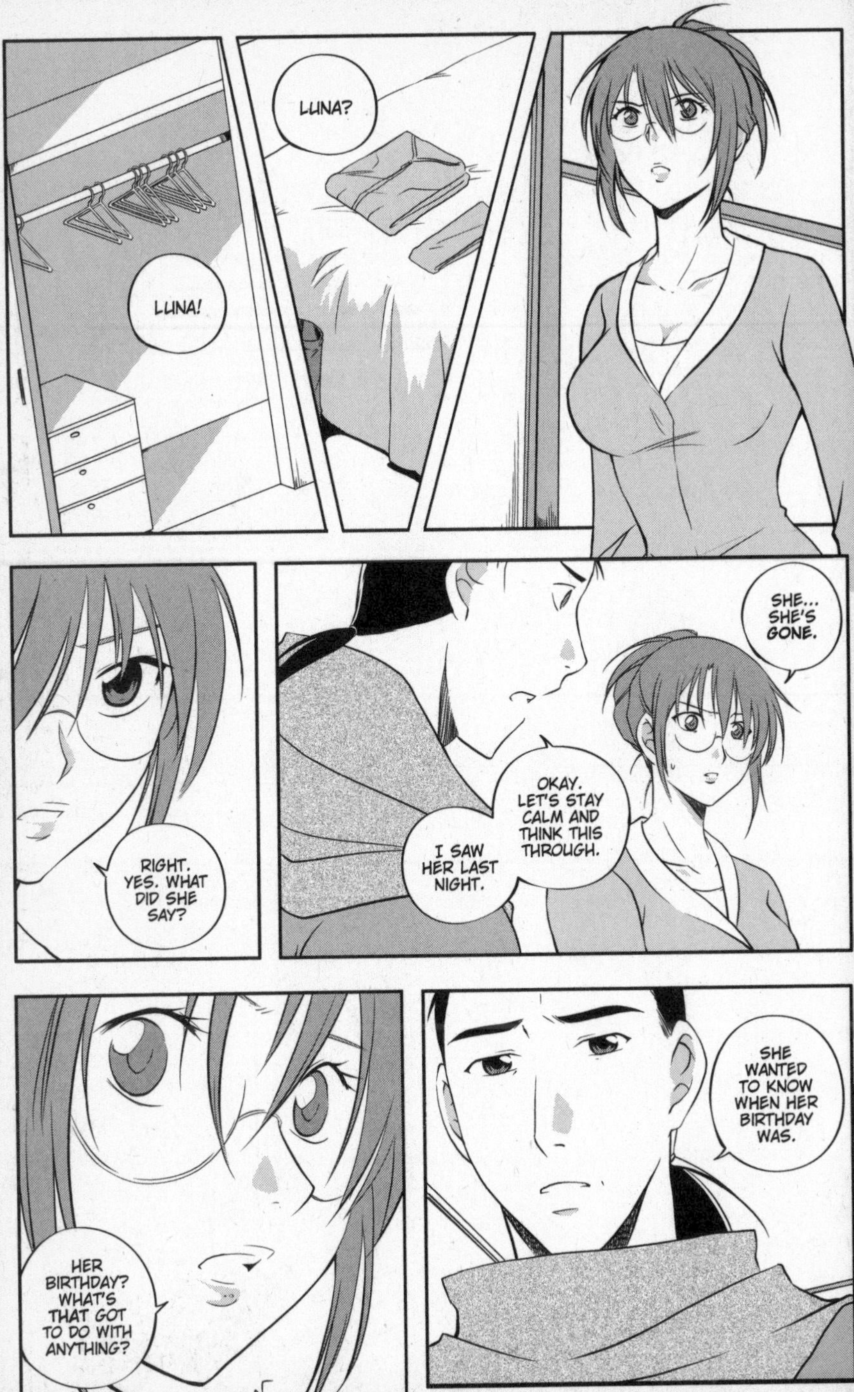

LUNA?
LUNA!
SHE... SHE'S GONE.
OKAY. LET'S STAY CALM AND THINK THIS THROUGH.
I SAW HER LAST NIGHT.
RIGHT. YES. WHAT DID SHE SAY?
SHE WANTED TO KNOW WHEN HER BIRTHDAY WAS.
HER BIRTHDAY? WHAT'S THAT GOT TO DO WITH ANYTHING?

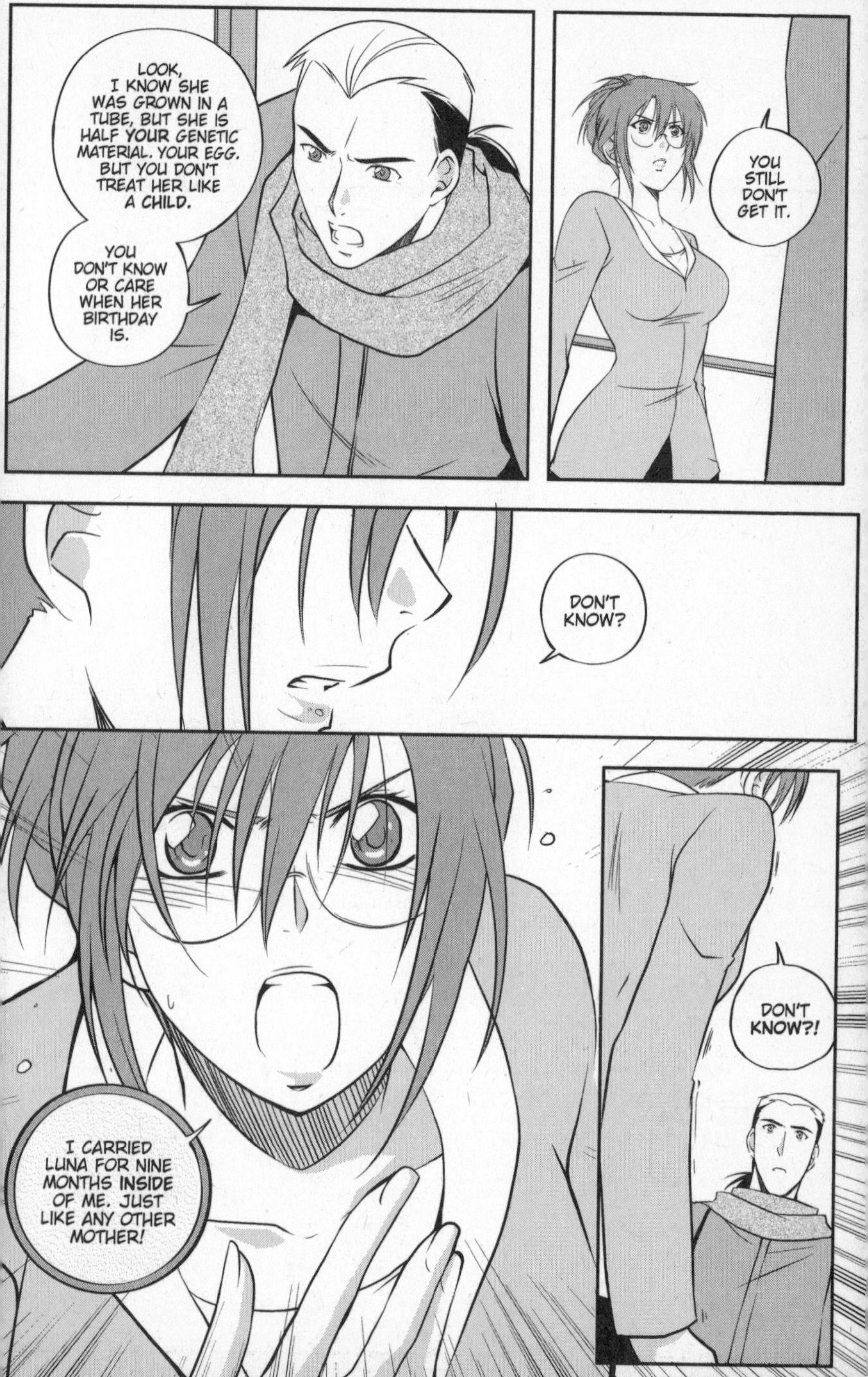
YOU STILL DON'T GET IT.
LOOK, I KNOW SHE WAS GROWN IN A TUBE, BUT SHE IS HALF YOUR GENETIC MATERIAL. YOUR EGG. BUT YOU DON'T TREAT HER LIKE A CHILD.
YOU DON'T KNOW OR CARE WHEN HER BIRTHDAY IS.
DON'T KNOW?
DON'T KNOW?!
I CARRIED LUNA FOR NINE MONTHS INSIDE OF ME. JUST LIKE ANY OTHER MOTHER!

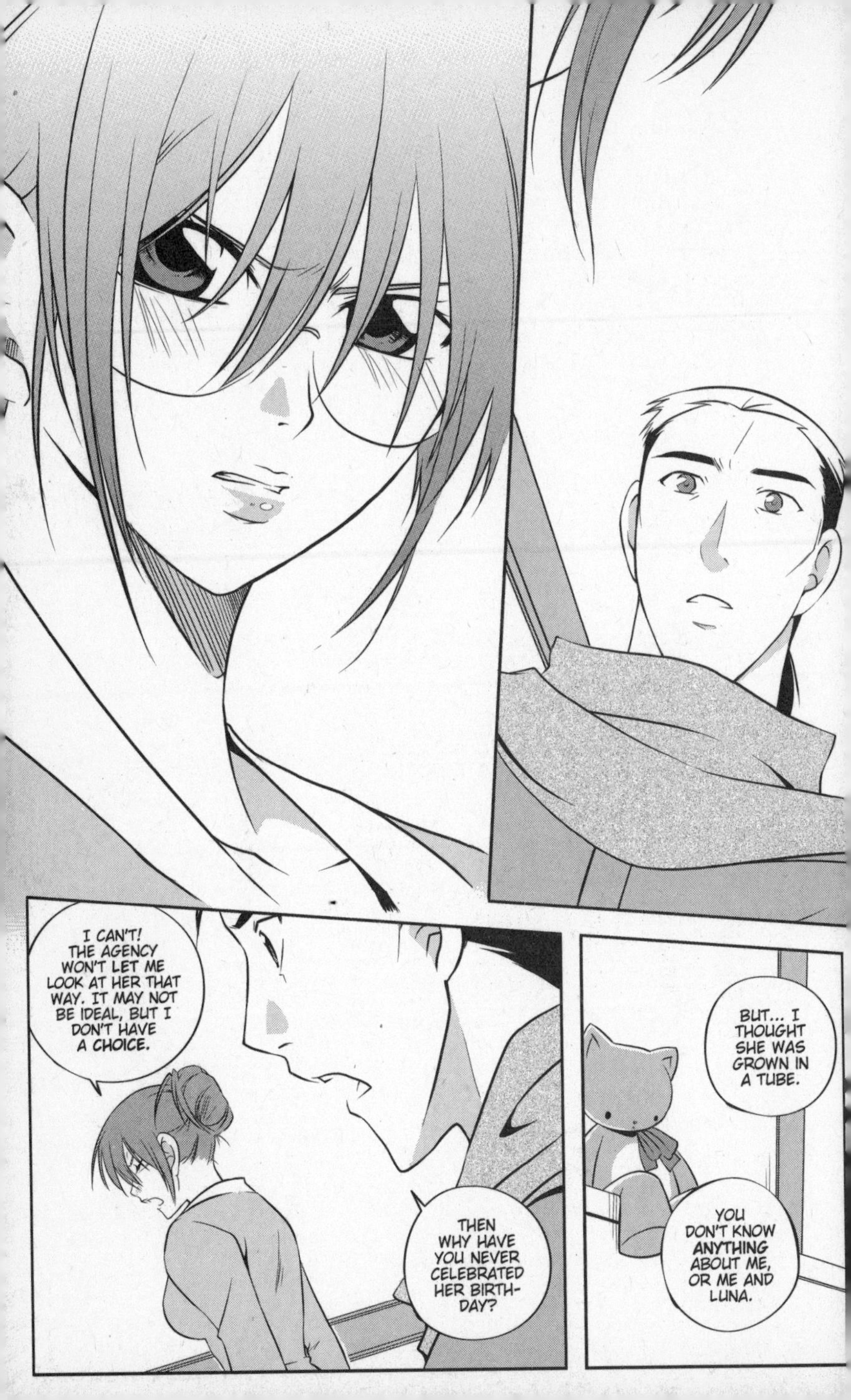
BUT... I THOUGHT SHE WAS GROWN IN A TUBE.
YOU DON'T KNOW ANYTHING ABOUT ME, OR ME AND LUNA.
THEN WHY HAVE YOU NEVER CELEBRATED HER BIRTH-DAY?
I CAN'T! THE AGENCY WON'T LET ME LOOK AT HER THAT WAY. IT MAY NOT BE IDEAL, BUT I DON'T HAVE A CHOICE.

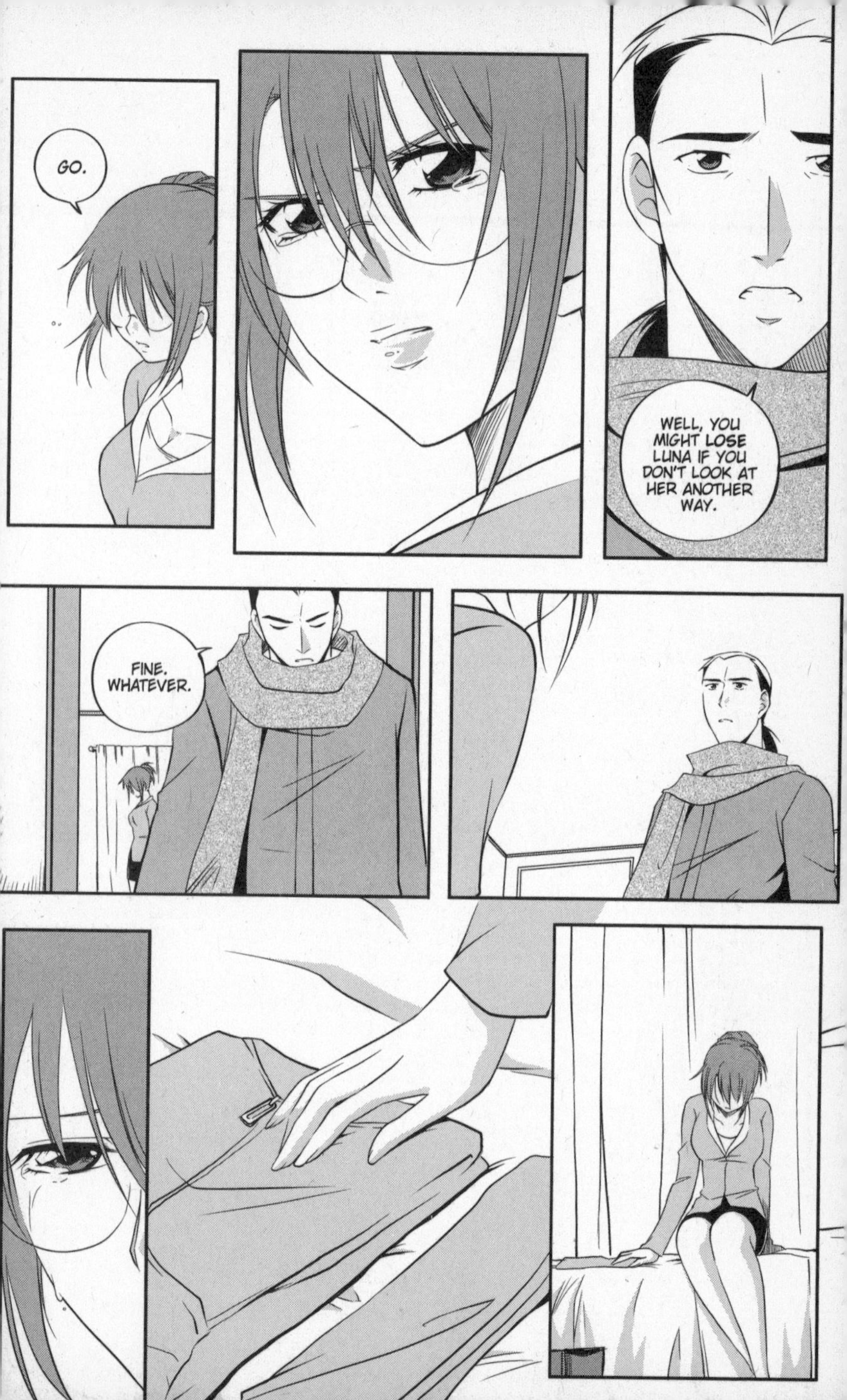
WELL, YOU MIGHT LOSE LUNA IF YOU DON'T LOOK AT HER ANOTHER WAY.
GO.
FINE. WHATEVER.

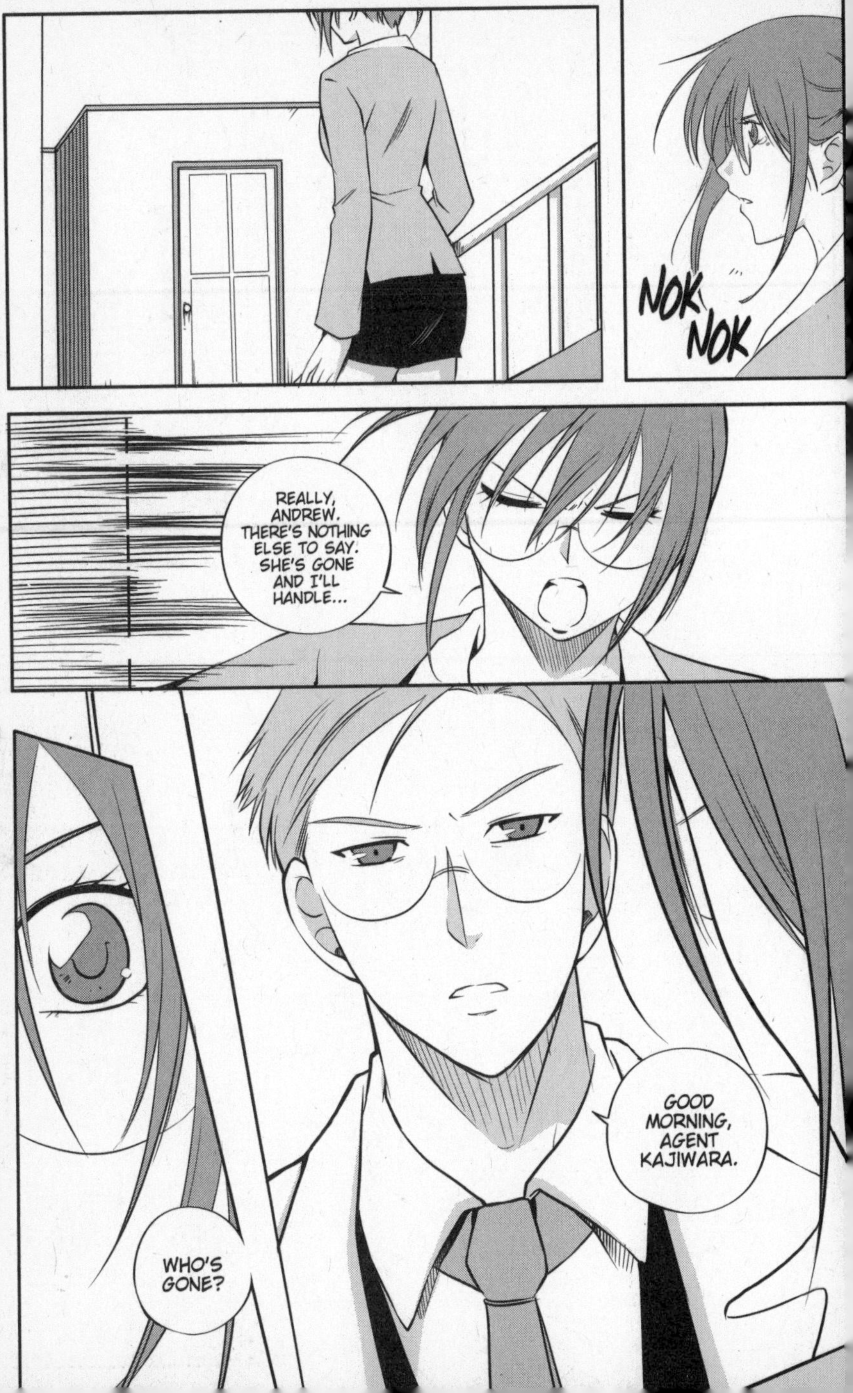
NOK NOK
REALLY, ANDREW. THERE'S NOTHING ELSE TO SAY. SHE'S GONE AND I'LL HANDLE...
GOOD MORNING, AGENT KAJIWARA.
WHO'S GONE?

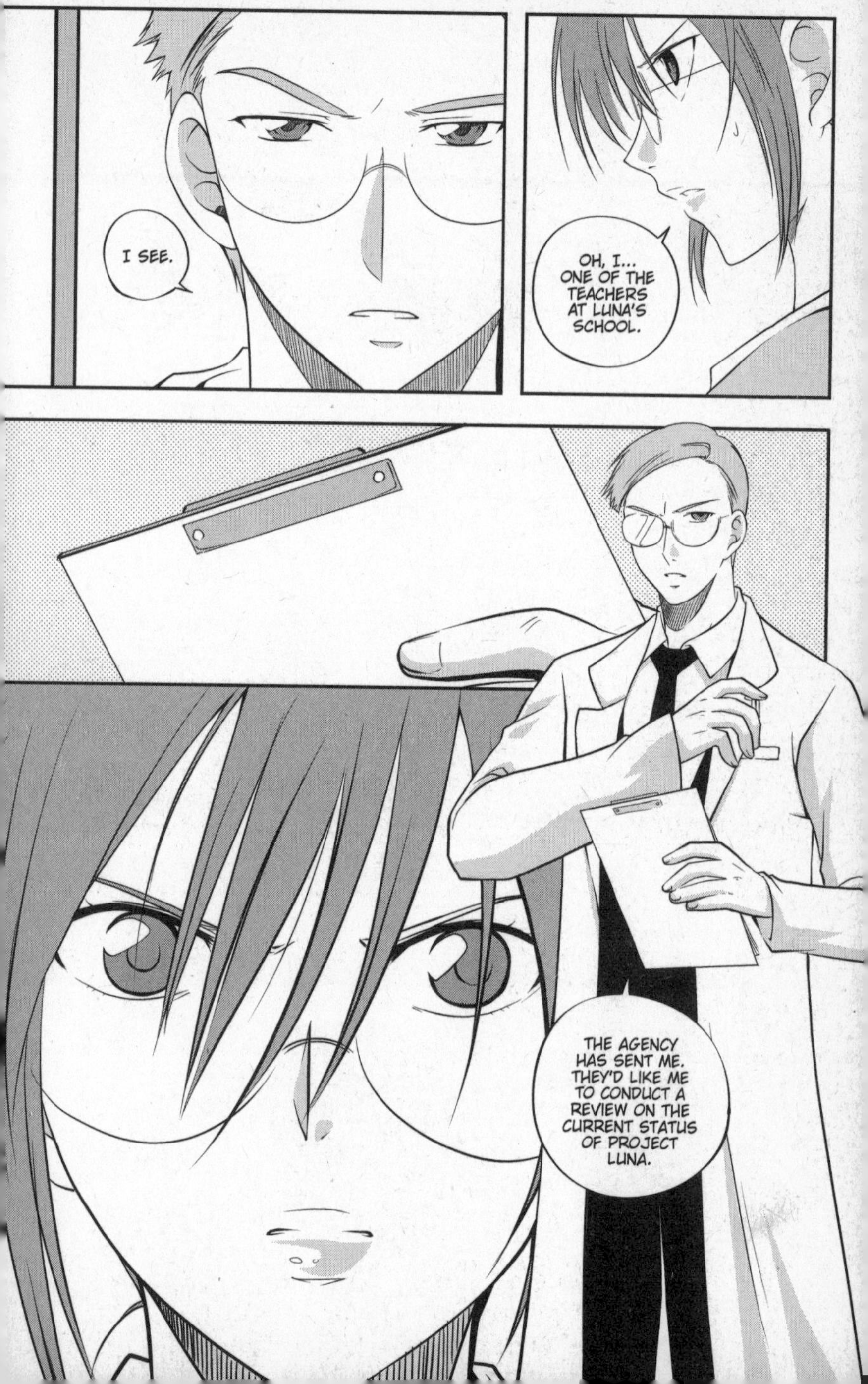
OH, I... ONE OF THE TEACHERS AT LUNA'S SCHOOL.
I SEE.
THE AGENCY HAS SENT ME. THEY'D LIKE ME TO CONDUCT A REVIEW ON THE CURRENT STATUS OF PROJECT LUNA.

File 46
MOTHER ISSUES

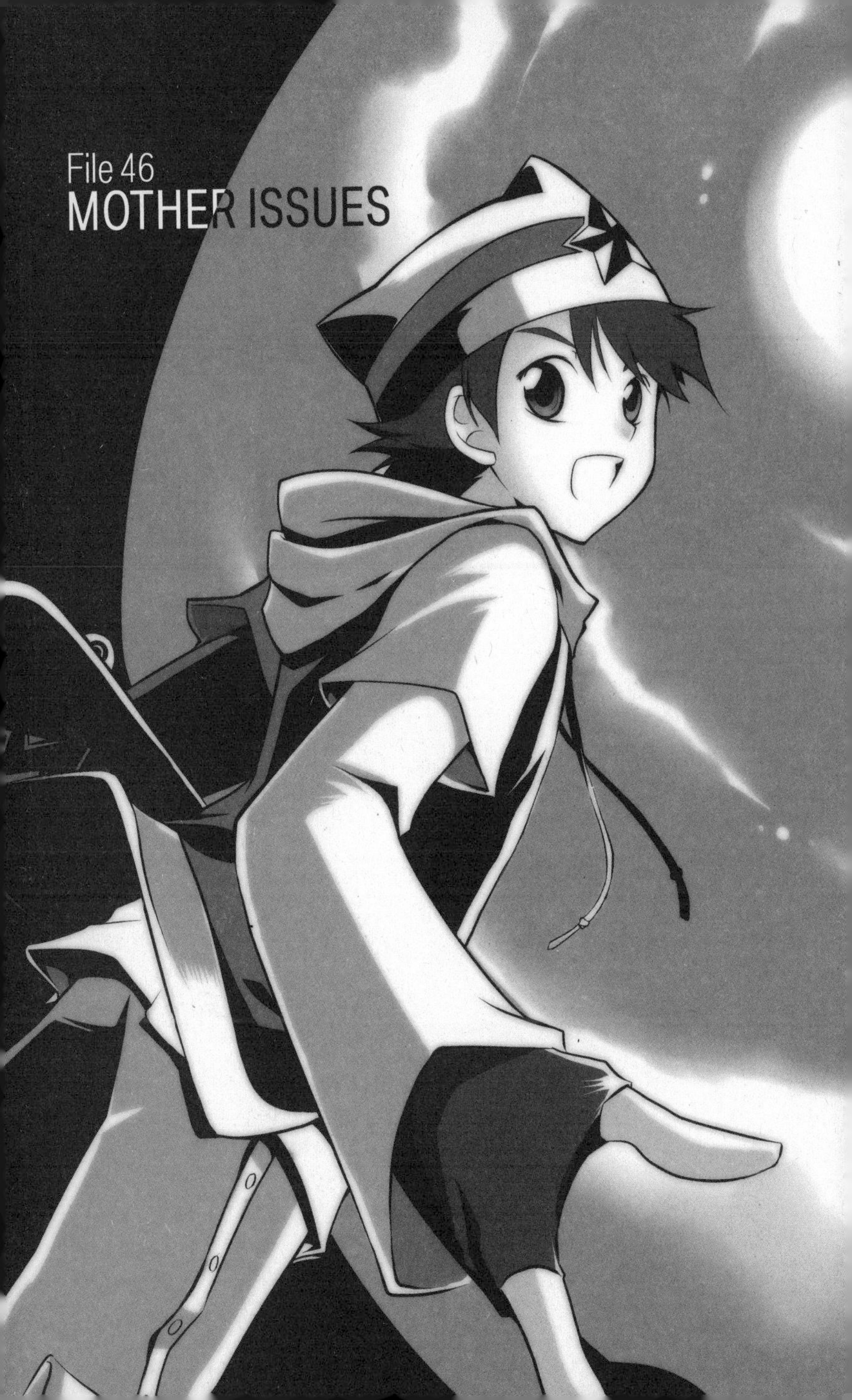

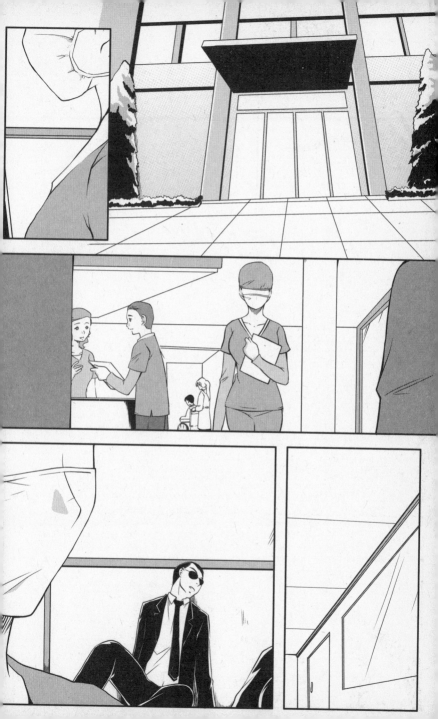

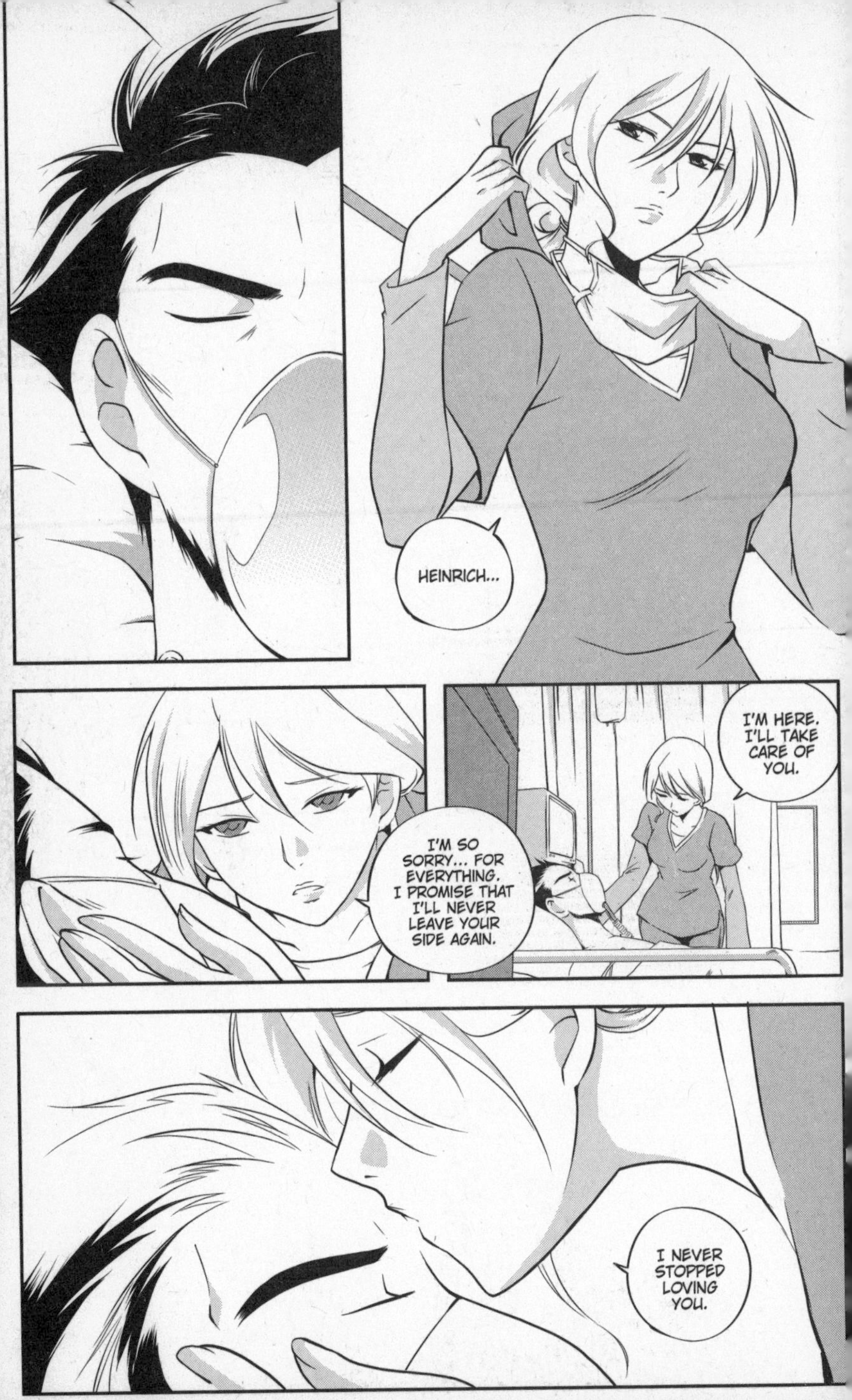
HEINRICH...
I'M HERE. I'LL TAKE CARE OF YOU.
I'M SO SORRY... FOR EVERYTHING. I PROMISE THAT I'LL NEVER LEAVE YOUR SIDE AGAIN.
I NEVER STOPPED LOVING YOU.

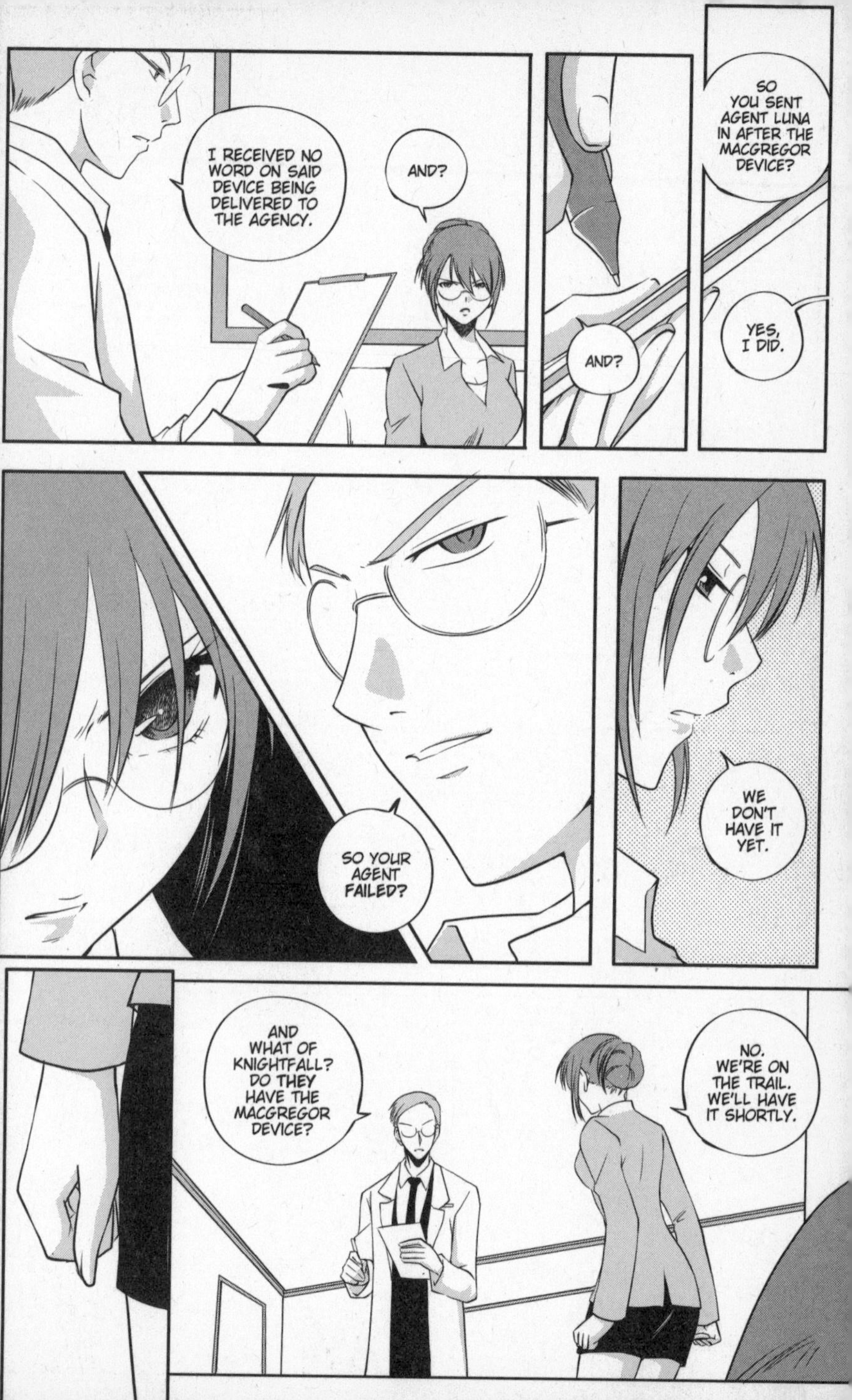
SO YOU SENT AGENT LUNA IN AFTER THE MACGREGOR DEVICE?
YES, I DID.
AND?
AND?
I RECEIVED NO WORD ON SAID DEVICE BEING DELIVERED TO THE AGENCY.
WE DON'T HAVE IT YET.
SO YOUR AGENT FAILED?
NO. WE'RE ON THE TRAIL. WE'LL HAVE IT SHORTLY.
AND WHAT OF KNIGHTFALL? DO THEY HAVE THE MACGREGOR DEVICE?

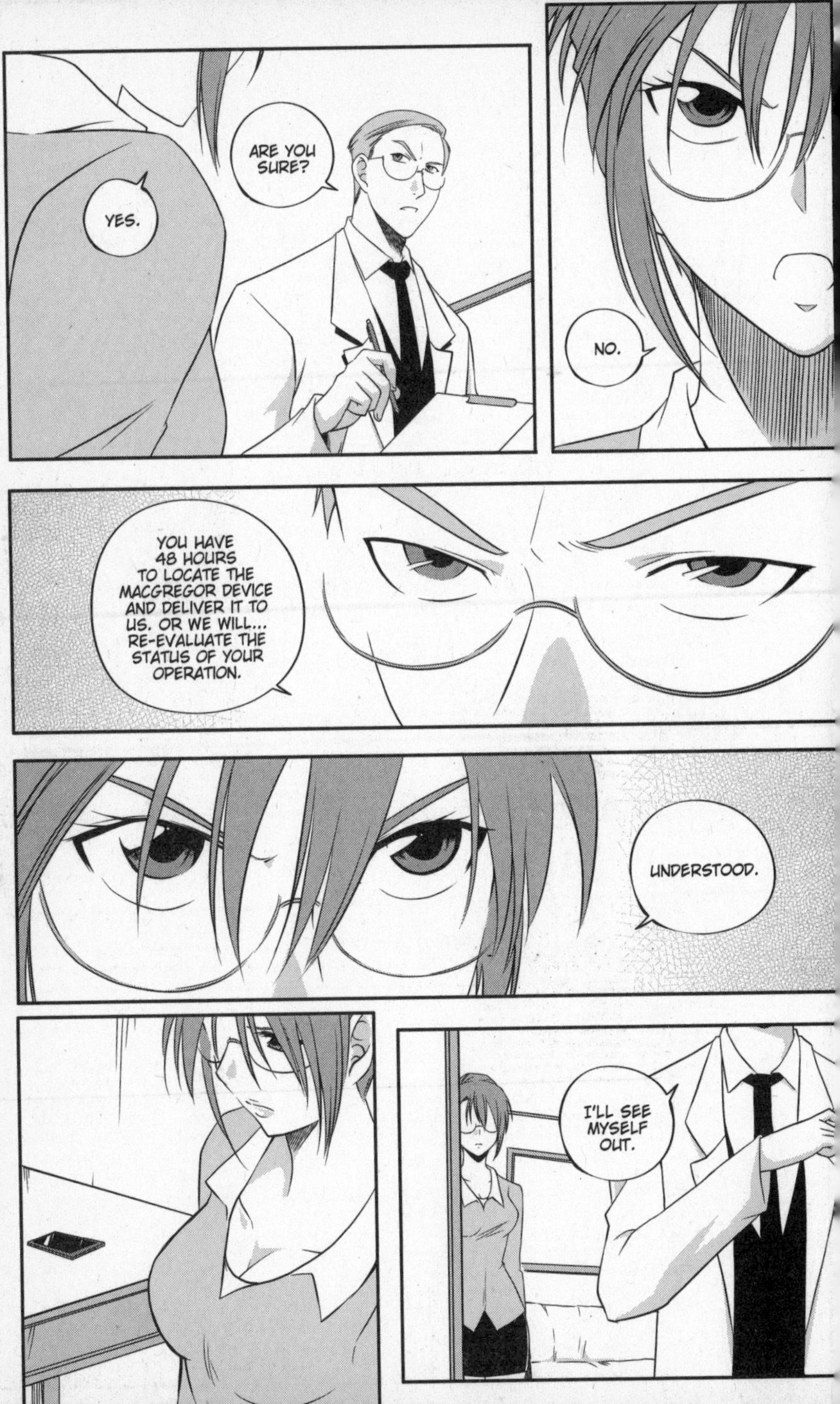
NO.
ARE YOU SURE?
YES.
YOU HAVE 48 HOURS TO LOCATE THE MACGREGOR DEVICE AND DELIVER IT TO US. OR WE WILL... RE-EVALUATE THE STATUS OF YOUR OPERATION.
UNDERSTOOD.
I'LL SEE MYSELF OUT.

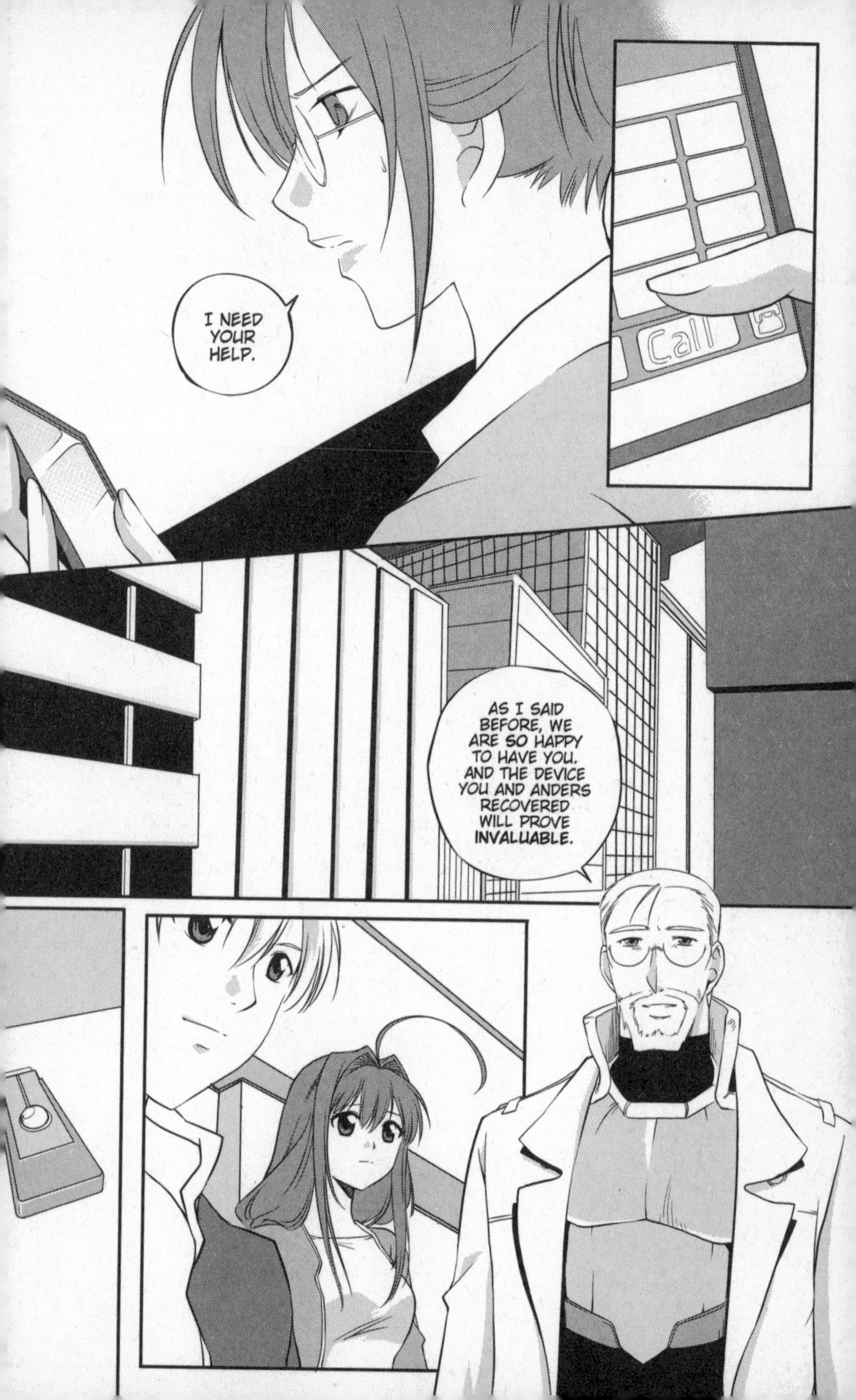
Call
I NEED YOUR HELP.
AS I SAID BEFORE, WE ARE SO HAPPY TO HAVE YOU. AND THE DEVICE YOU AND ANDERS RECOVERED WILL PROVE **INVALUABLE.**

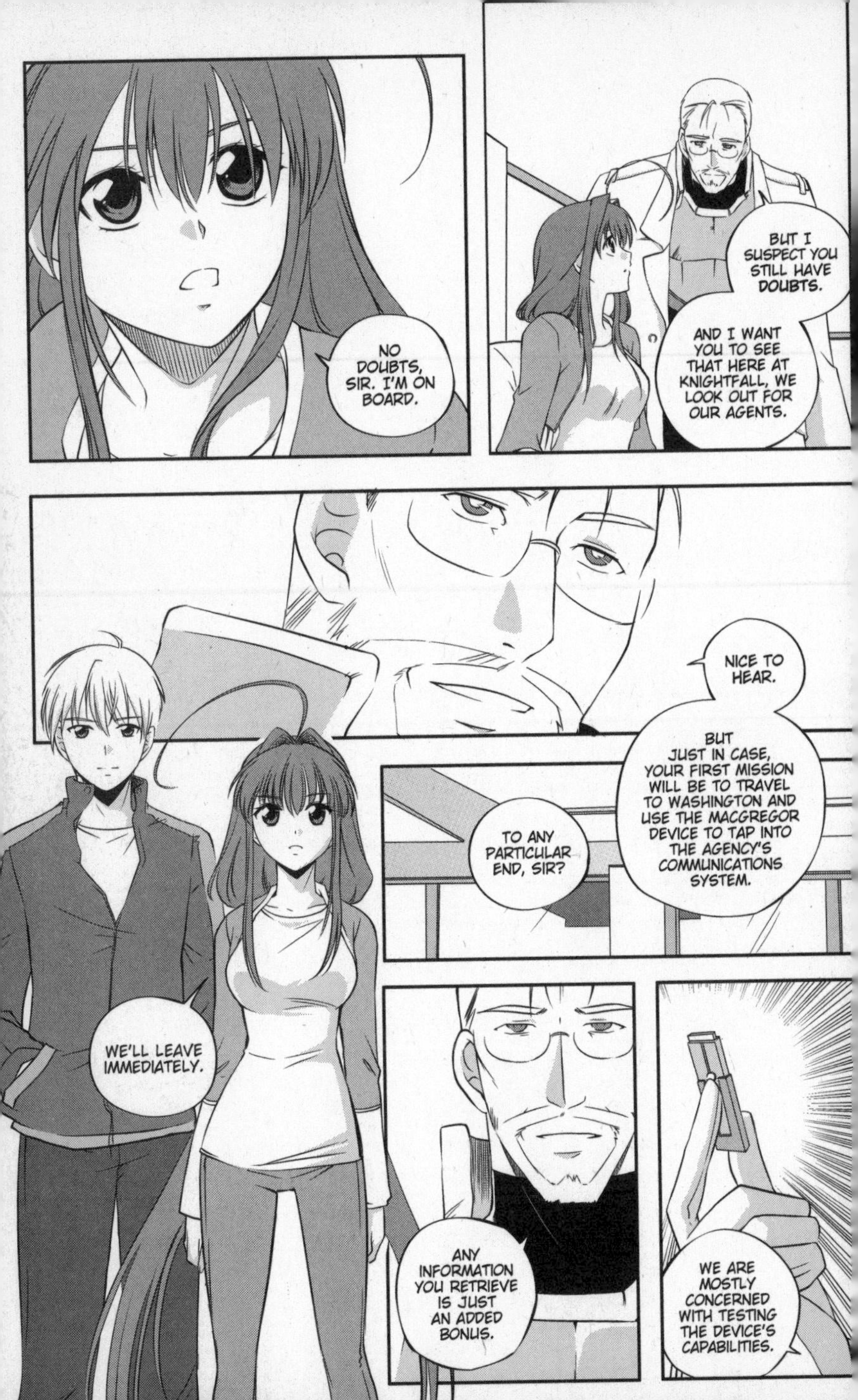
BUT I SUSPECT YOU STILL HAVE DOUBTS.
AND I WANT YOU TO SEE THAT HERE AT KNIGHTFALL, WE LOOK OUT FOR OUR AGENTS.
NO DOUBTS, SIR. I'M ON BOARD.
NICE TO HEAR.
BUT JUST IN CASE, YOUR FIRST MISSION WILL BE TO TRAVEL TO WASHINGTON AND USE THE MACGREGOR DEVICE TO TAP INTO THE AGENCY'S COMMUNICATIONS SYSTEM.
TO ANY PARTICULAR END, SIR?
WE ARE MOSTLY CONCERNED WITH TESTING THE DEVICE'S CAPABILITIES.
ANY INFORMATION YOU RETRIEVE IS JUST AN ADDED BONUS.
WE'LL LEAVE IMMEDIATELY.

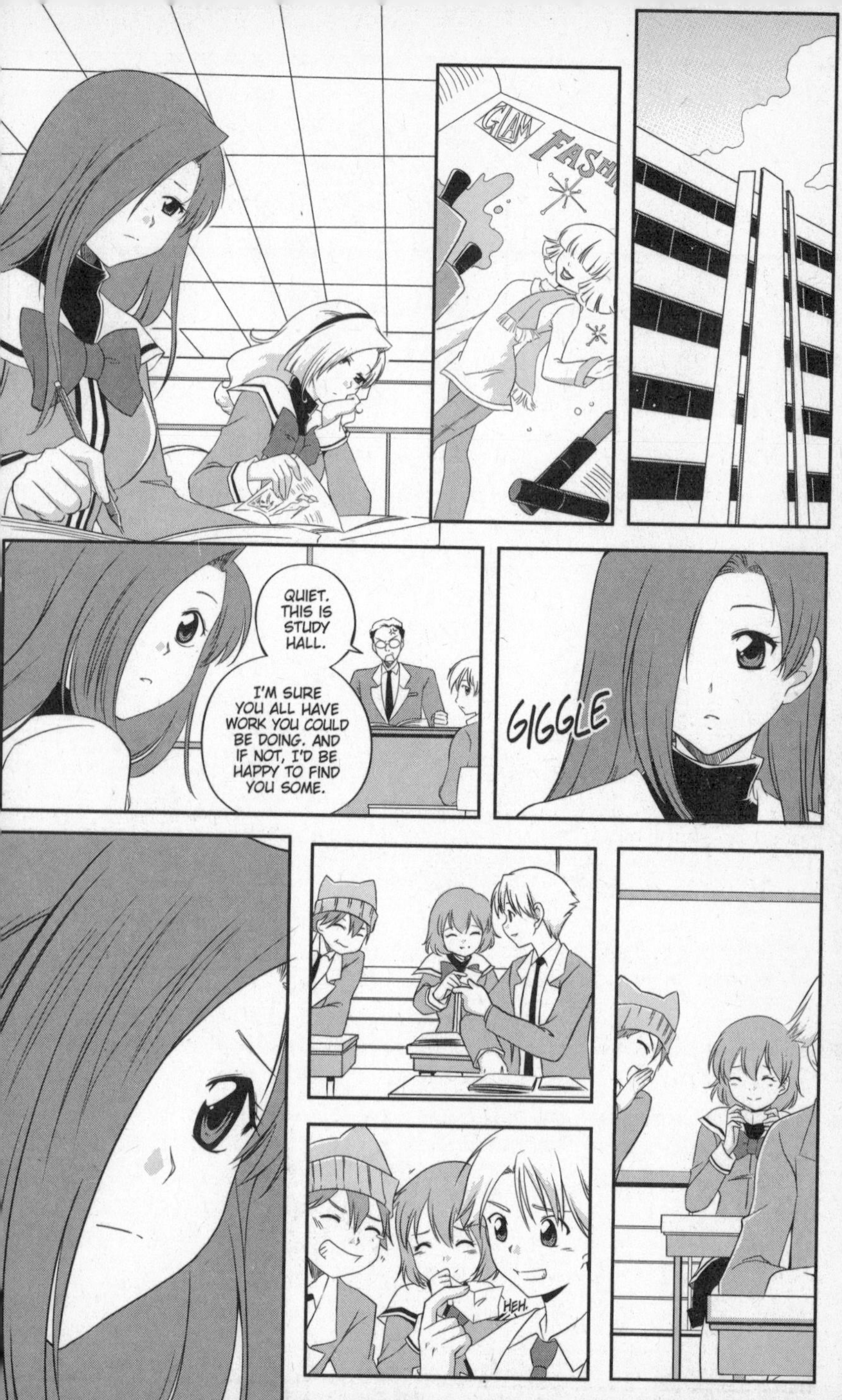
GLAM
GIGGLE
QUIET. THIS IS STUDY HALL.
I'M SURE YOU ALL HAVE WORK YOU COULD BE DOING. AND IF NOT, I'D BE HAPPY TO FIND YOU SOME.
HEH.

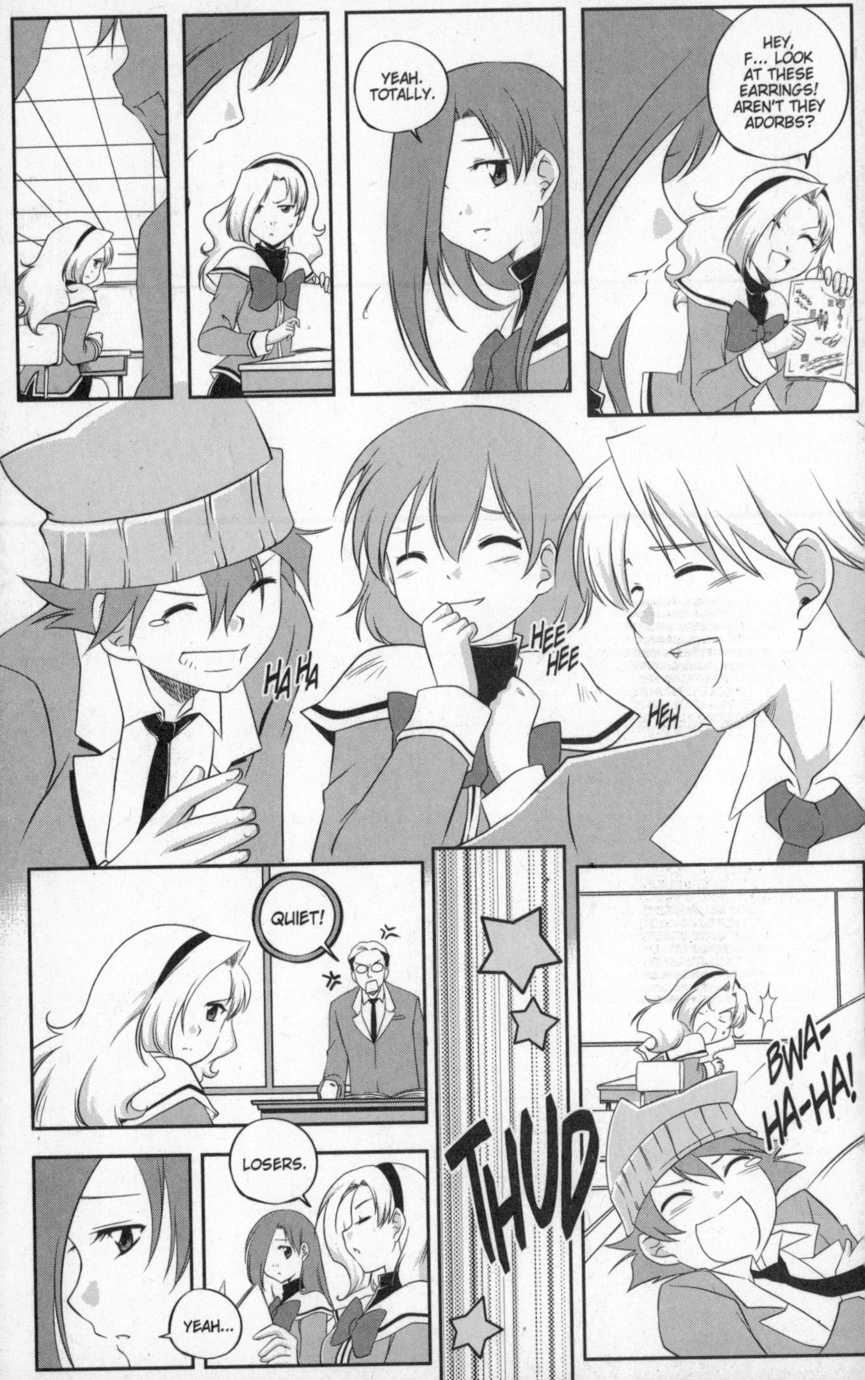
HEY, F... LOOK AT THESE EARRINGS! AREN'T THEY ADORBS?
YEAH. TOTALLY.
HEH
HEE HEE
HA HA
BWA-HA-HA!
THUD
QUIET!
LOSERS.
YEAH...

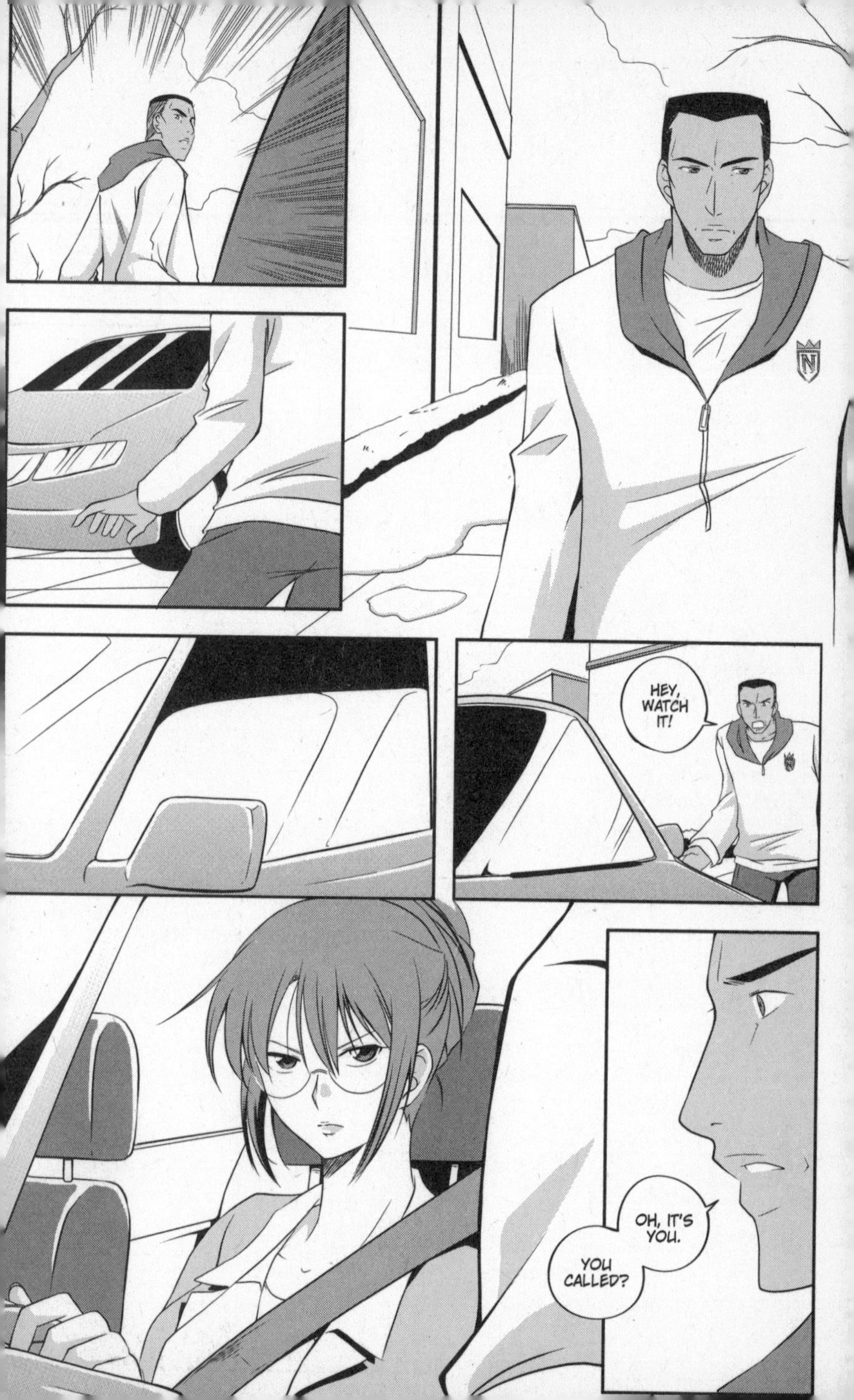
HEY, WATCH IT!
OH, IT'S YOU.
YOU CALLED?

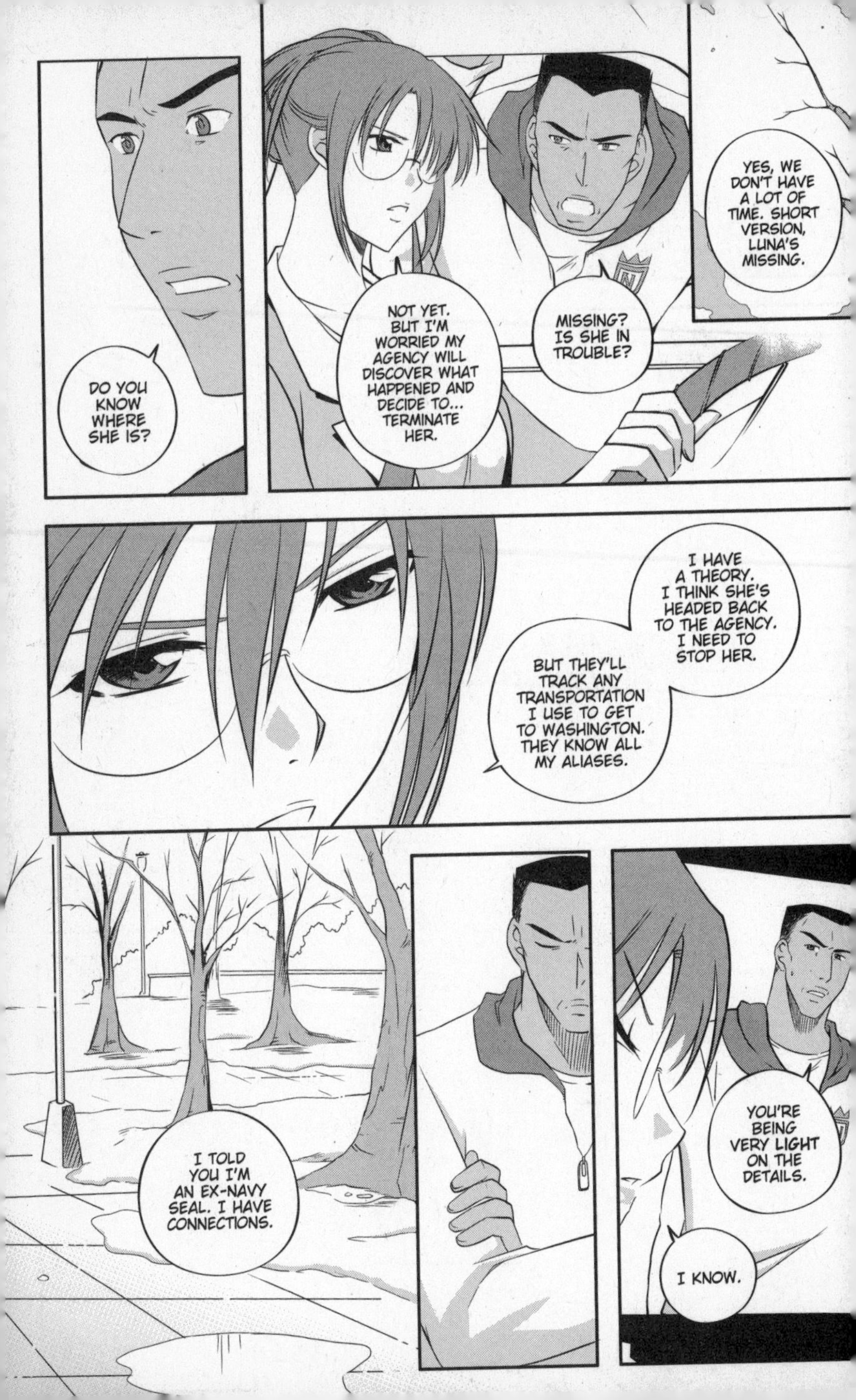
YES, WE DON'T HAVE A LOT OF TIME. SHORT VERSION, LUNA'S MISSING.
MISSING? IS SHE IN TROUBLE?
NOT YET. BUT I'M WORRIED MY AGENCY WILL DISCOVER WHAT HAPPENED AND DECIDE TO... TERMINATE HER.
DO YOU KNOW WHERE SHE IS?
I HAVE A THEORY. I THINK SHE'S HEADED BACK TO THE AGENCY. I NEED TO STOP HER.
BUT THEY'LL TRACK ANY TRANSPORTATION I USE TO GET TO WASHINGTON. THEY KNOW ALL MY ALIASES.
YOU'RE BEING VERY LIGHT ON THE DETAILS.
I KNOW.
I TOLD YOU I'M AN EX-NAVY SEAL. I HAVE CONNECTIONS.

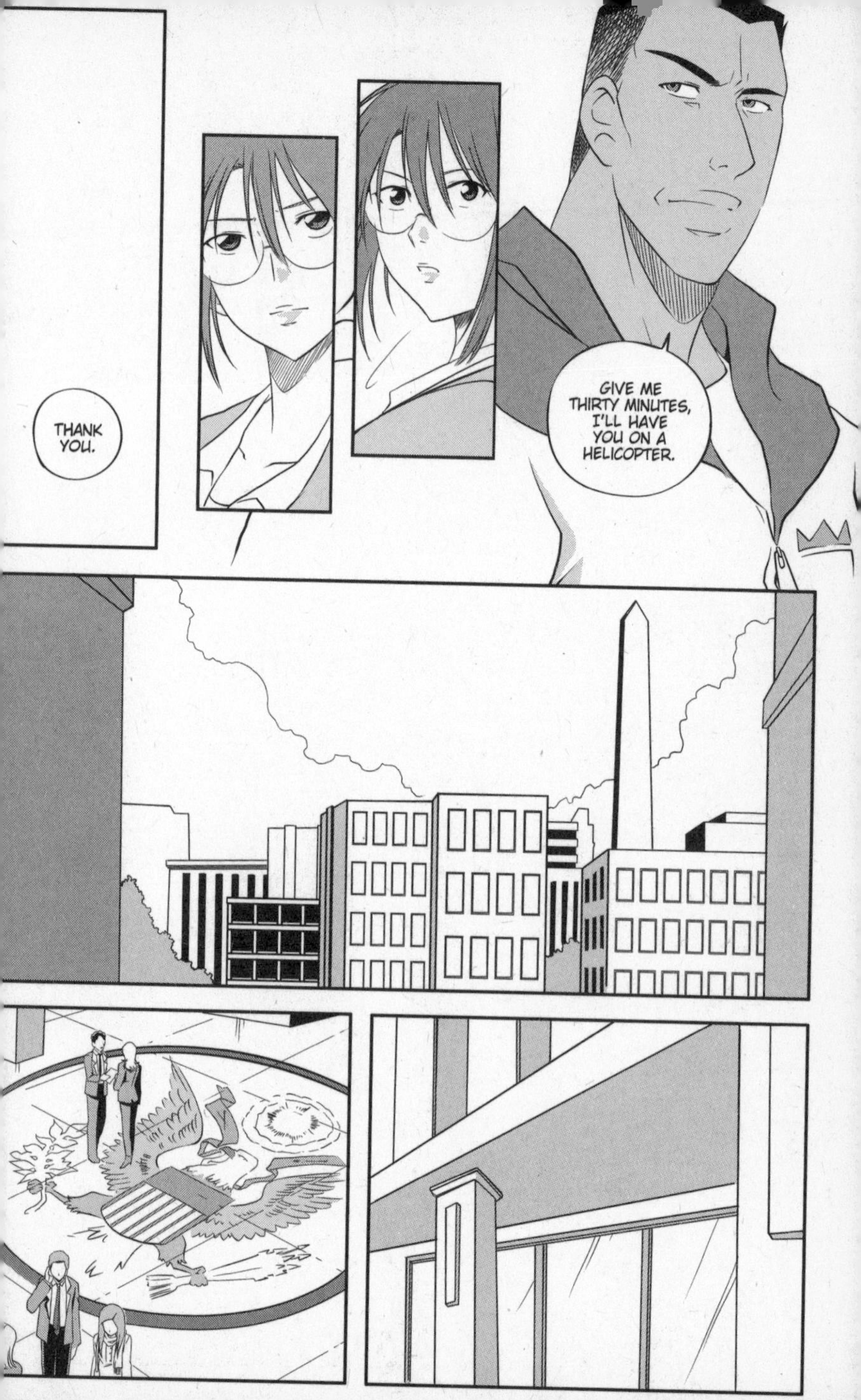
GIVE ME THIRTY MINUTES, I'LL HAVE YOU ON A HELICOPTER.
THANK YOU.

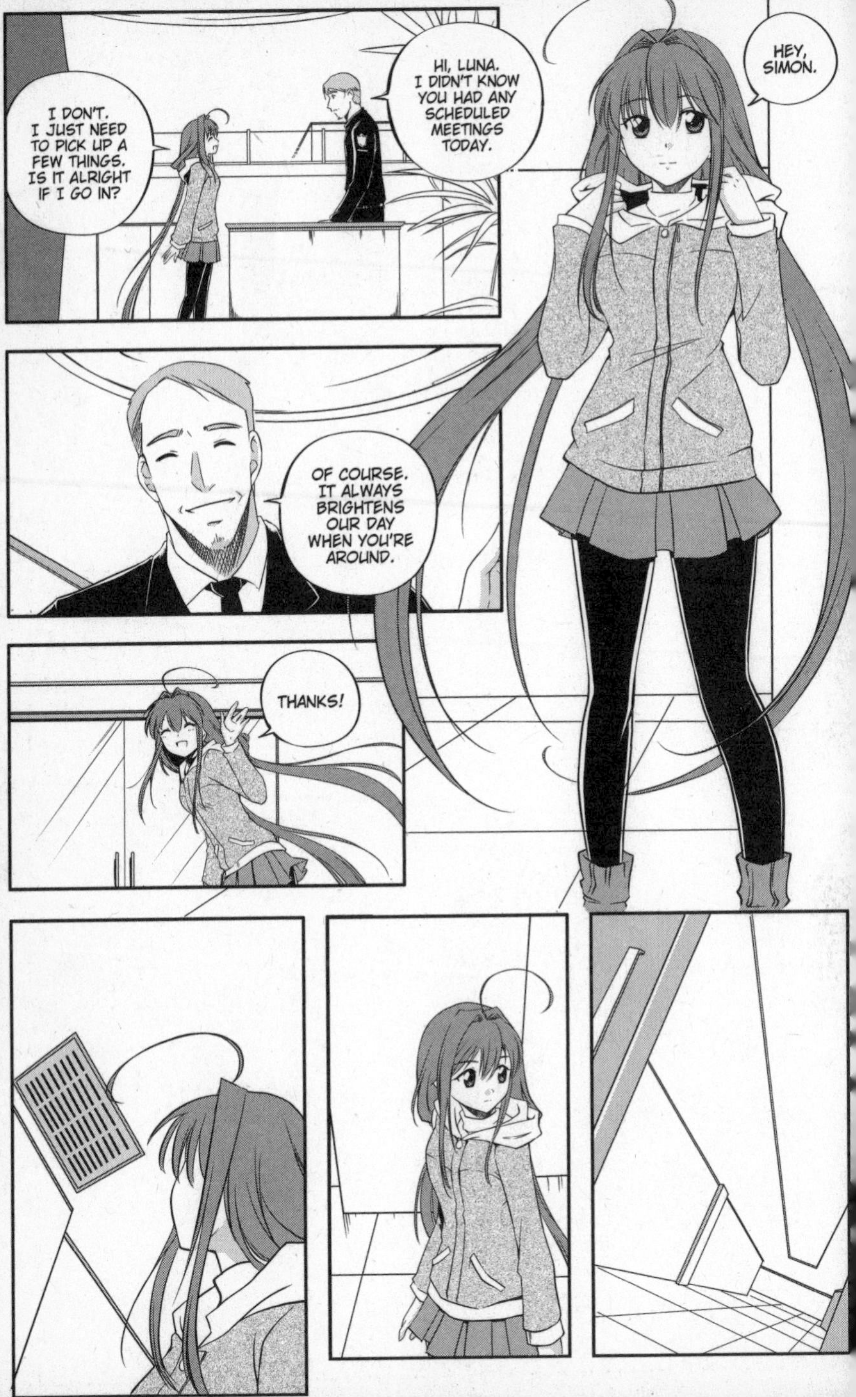
HEY, SIMON.
HI, LUNA. I DIDN'T KNOW YOU HAD ANY SCHEDULED MEETINGS TODAY.
I DON'T. I JUST NEED TO PICK UP A FEW THINGS. IS IT ALRIGHT IF I GO IN?
OF COURSE. IT ALWAYS BRIGHTENS OUR DAY WHEN YOU'RE AROUND.
THANKS!

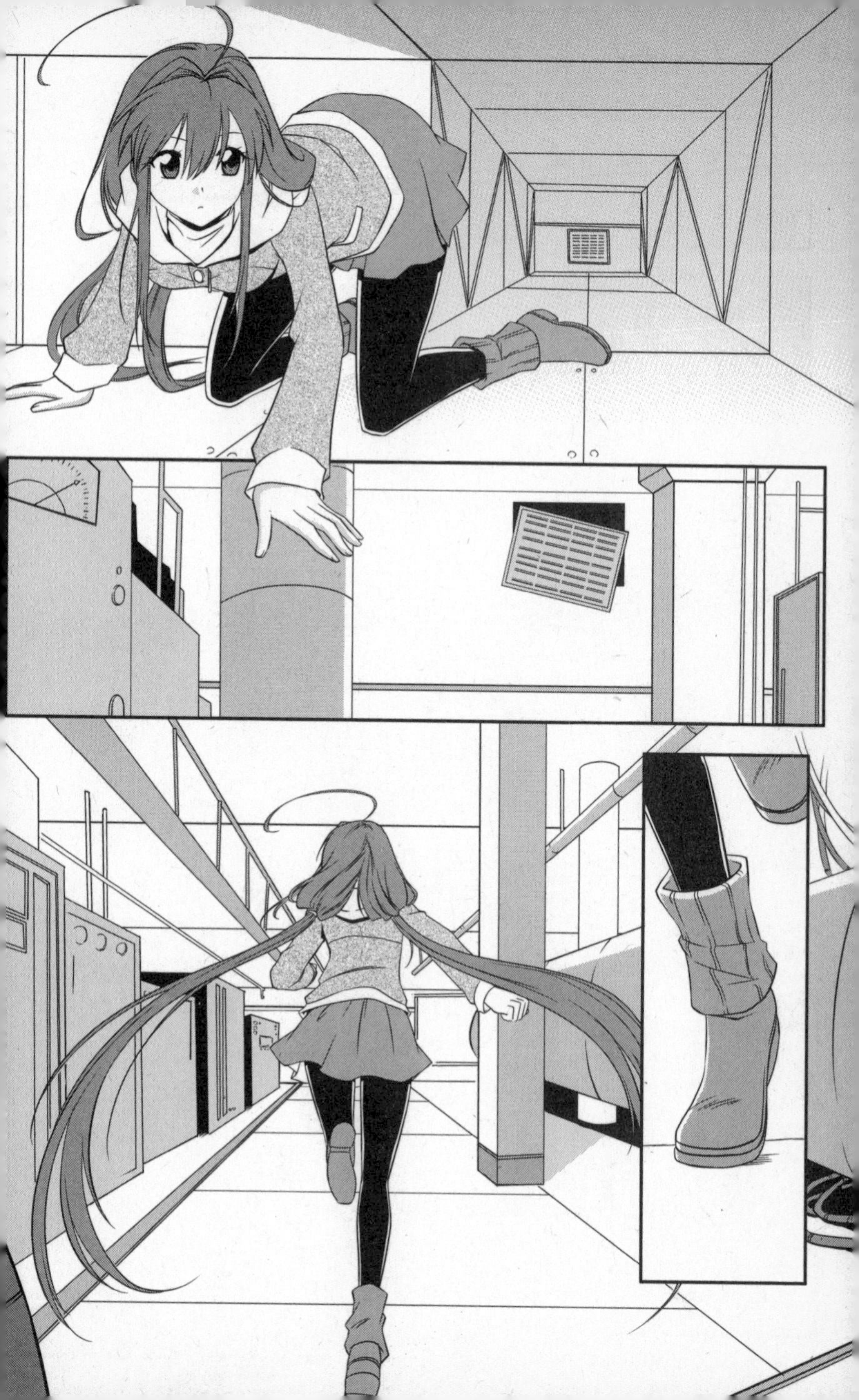

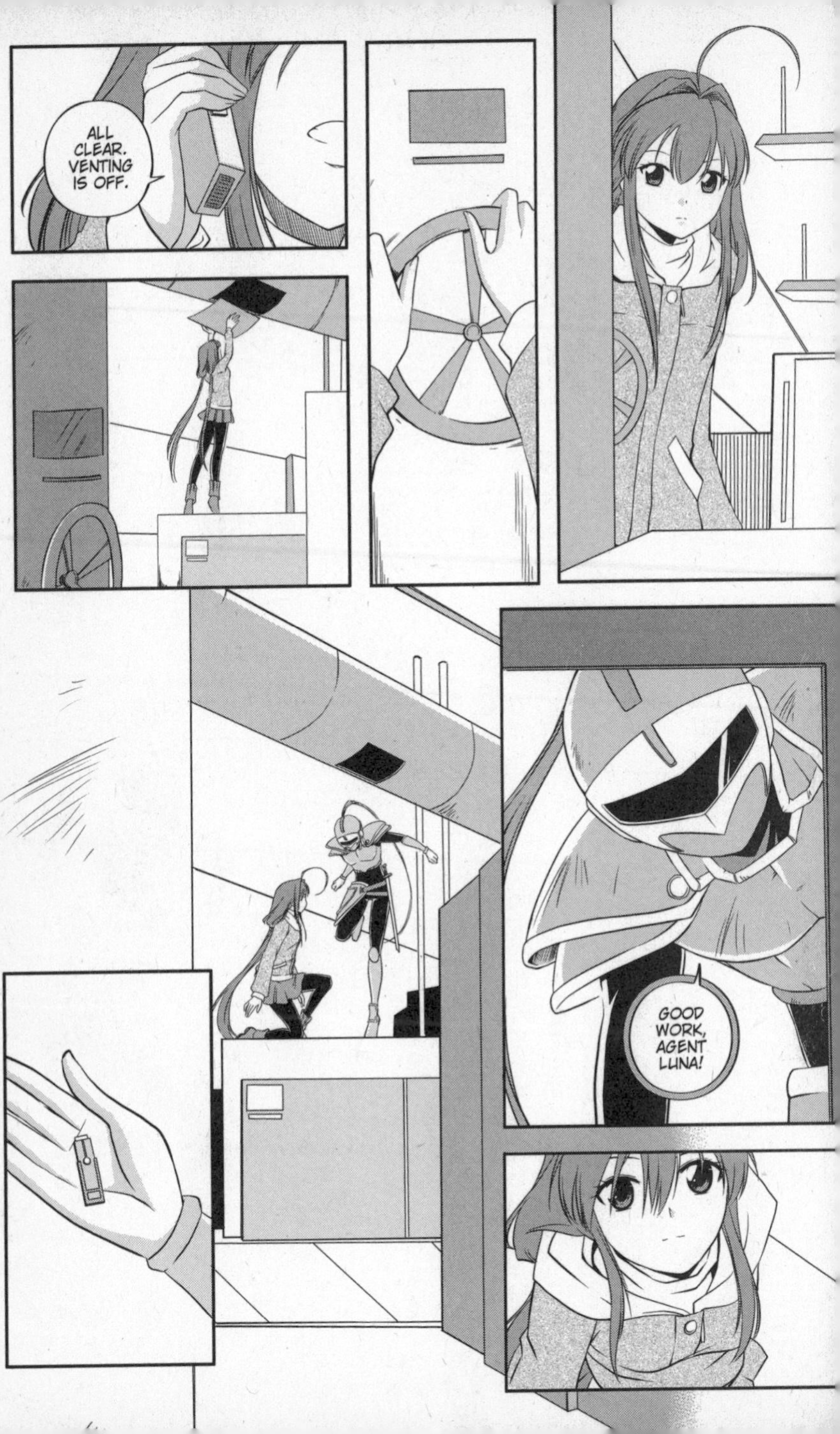
ALL CLEAR. VENTING IS OFF.
GOOD WORK, AGENT LUNA!

WILL IT WORK?

COME ON. THIS WAY.

BUT MASTER CONTROL HAD ONE OF THE SCIENCE TECHS SHOW ME HOW TO HOOK IT UP.

DON'T KNOW YET.

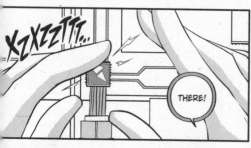

XZXZZTT...

THERE!

JUST... ONE... MORE... MINUTE...

IT'S ALL STATIC-Y.

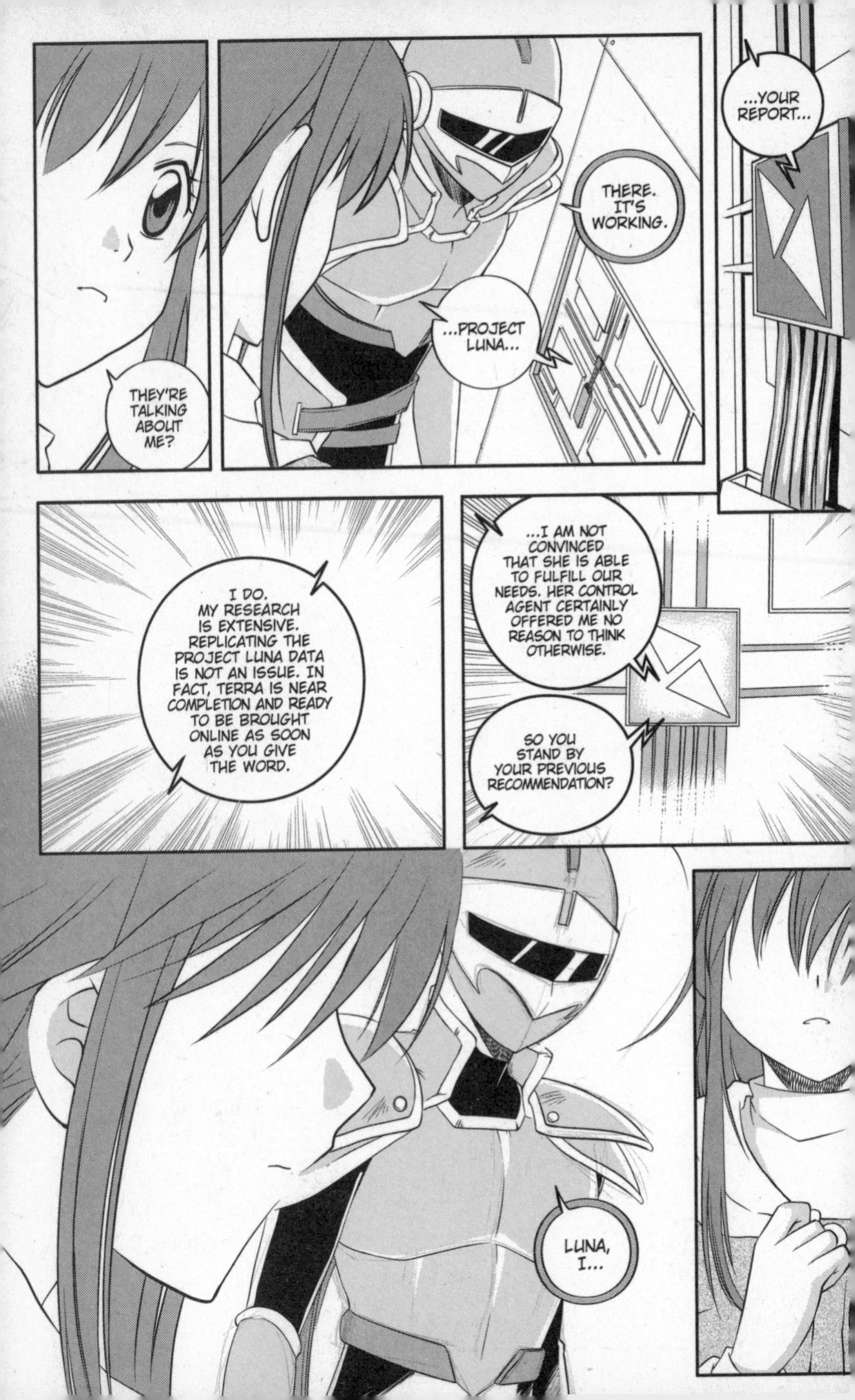
...YOUR REPORT...
THERE. IT'S WORKING.
...PROJECT LUNA...
THEY'RE TALKING ABOUT ME?
...I AM NOT CONVINCED THAT SHE IS ABLE TO FULFILL OUR NEEDS. HER CONTROL AGENT CERTAINLY OFFERED ME NO REASON TO THINK OTHERWISE.
SO YOU STAND BY YOUR PREVIOUS RECOMMENDATION?
I DO. MY RESEARCH IS EXTENSIVE. REPLICATING THE PROJECT LUNA DATA IS NOT AN ISSUE. IN FACT, TERRA IS NEAR COMPLETION AND READY TO BE BROUGHT ONLINE AS SOON AS YOU GIVE THE WORD.
LUNA, I...

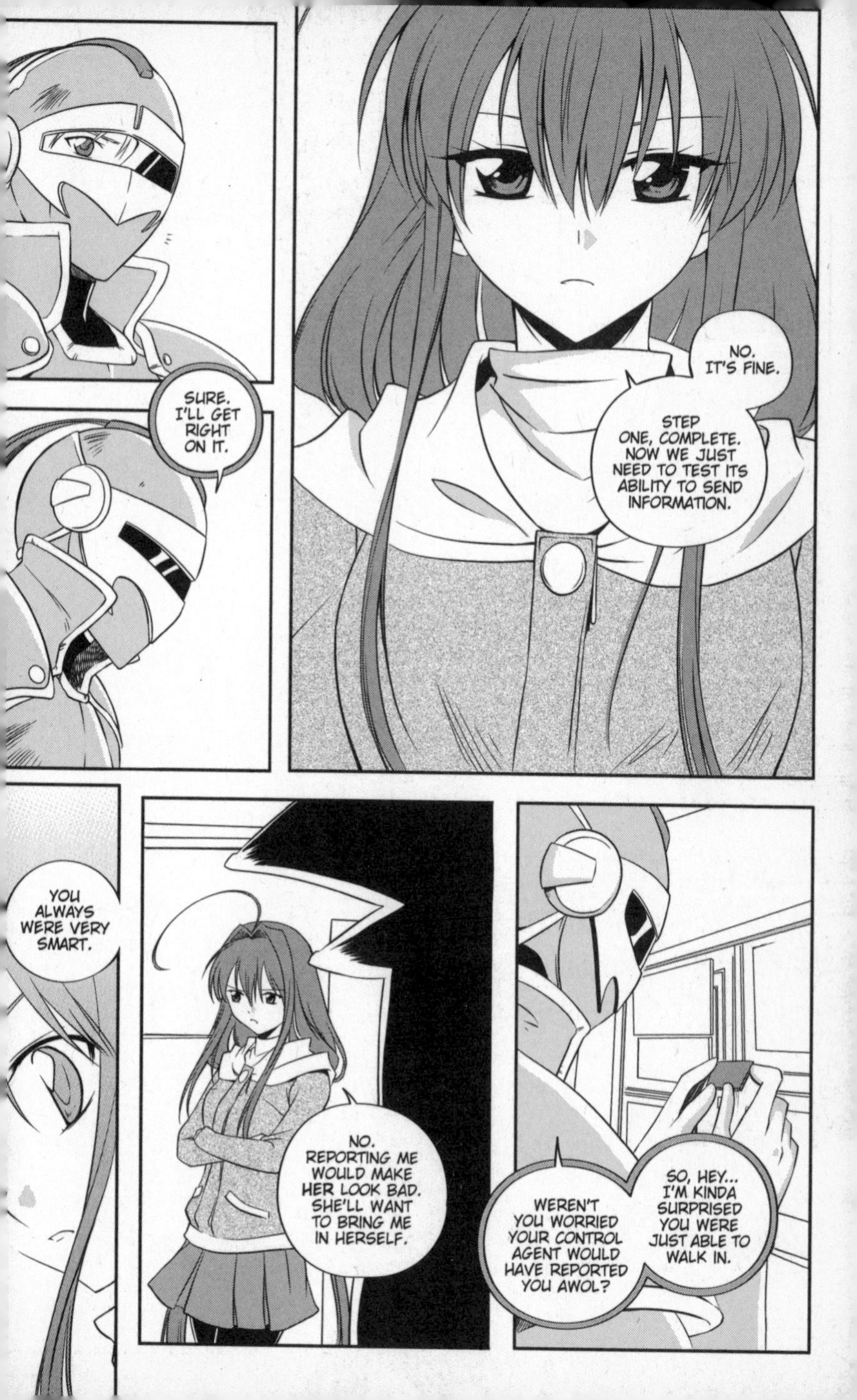
NO. IT'S FINE.
STEP ONE, COMPLETE. NOW WE JUST NEED TO TEST ITS ABILITY TO SEND INFORMATION.
SURE. I'LL GET RIGHT ON IT.
SO, HEY... I'M KINDA SURPRISED YOU WERE JUST ABLE TO WALK IN.
WEREN'T YOU WORRIED YOUR CONTROL AGENT WOULD HAVE REPORTED YOU AWOL?
NO. REPORTING ME WOULD MAKE **HER** LOOK BAD. SHE'LL WANT TO BRING ME IN HERSELF.
YOU ALWAYS WERE VERY SMART.

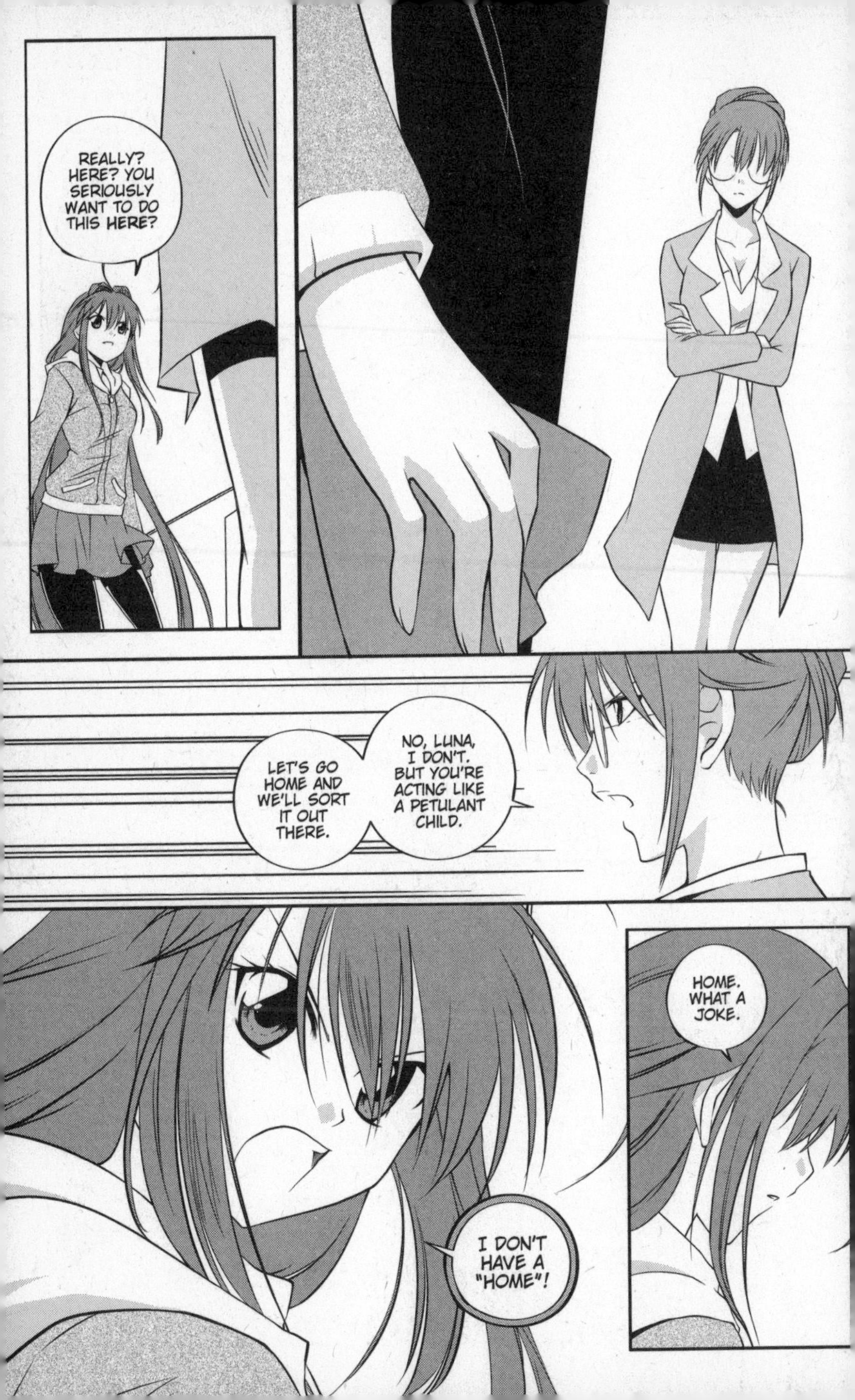
REALLY? HERE? YOU SERIOUSLY WANT TO DO THIS HERE?
NO, LUNA, I DON'T. BUT YOU'RE ACTING LIKE A PETULANT CHILD.
LET'S GO HOME AND WE'LL SORT IT OUT THERE.
HOME. WHAT A JOKE.
I DON'T HAVE A "HOME"!

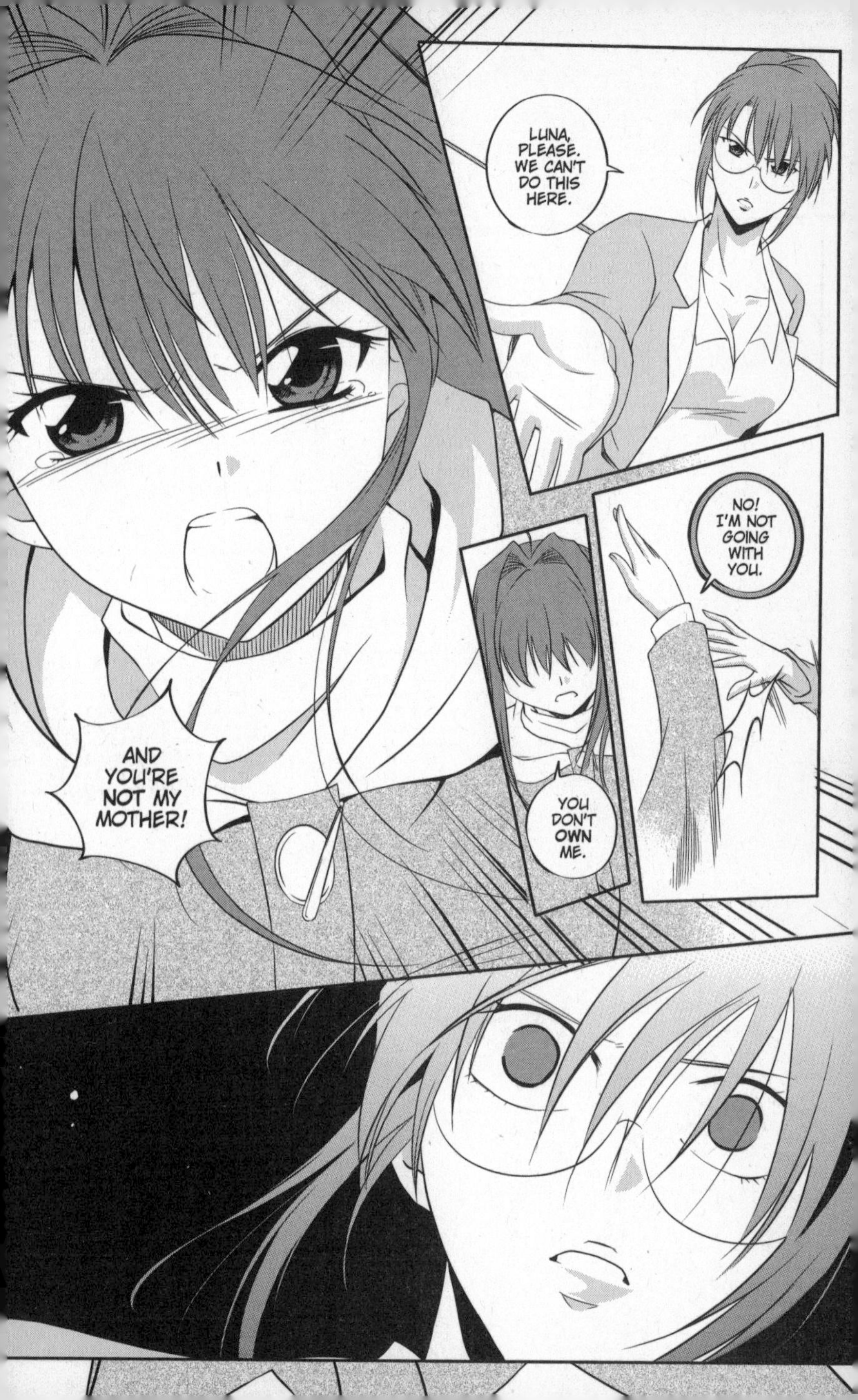
LUNA, PLEASE. WE CAN'T DO THIS HERE.
NO! I'M NOT GOING WITH YOU.
YOU DON'T OWN ME.
AND YOU'RE NOT MY MOTHER!

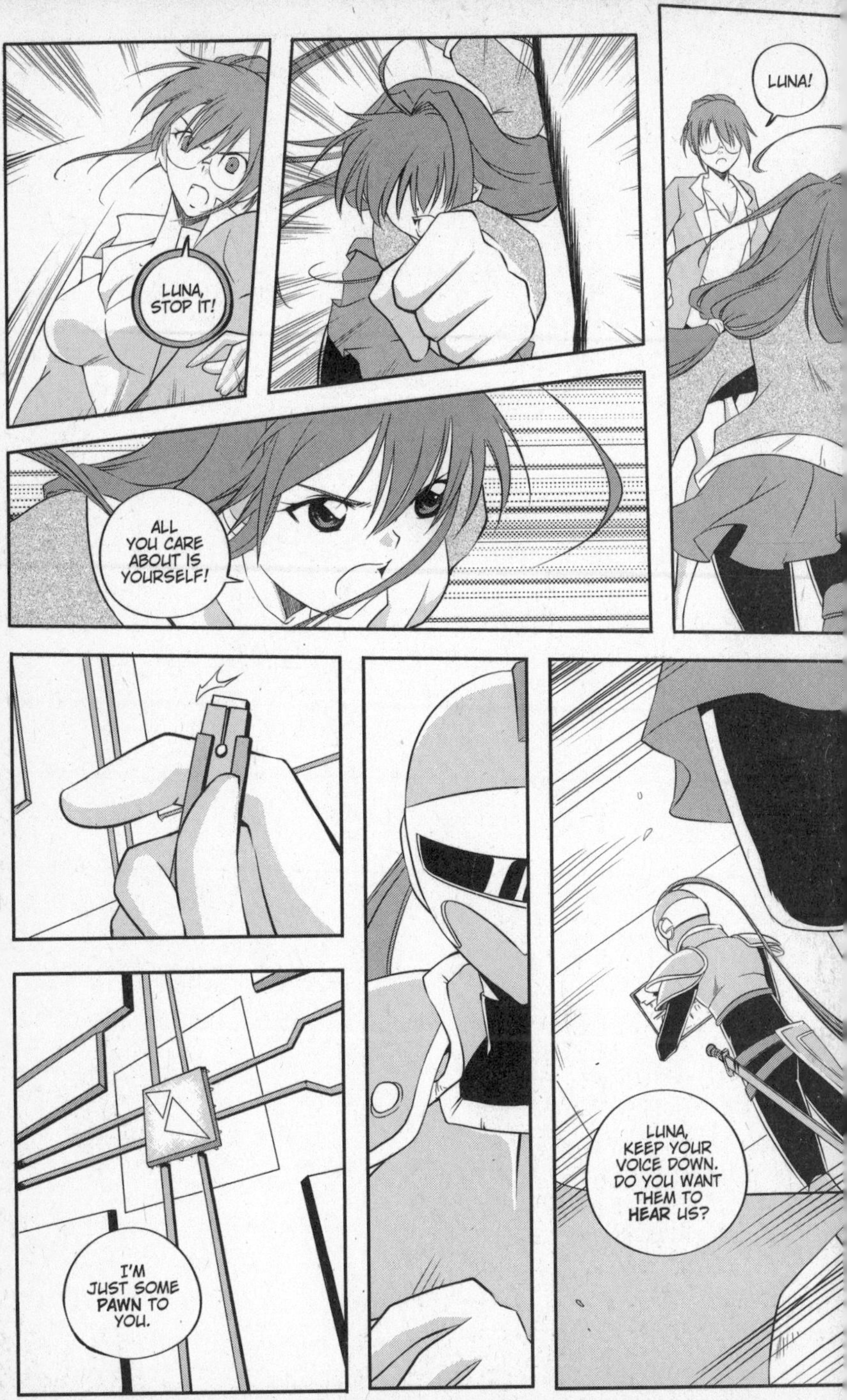
LUNA!
LUNA, STOP IT!
ALL YOU CARE ABOUT IS YOURSELF!
LUNA, KEEP YOUR VOICE DOWN. DO YOU WANT THEM TO HEAR US?
I'M JUST SOME PAWN TO YOU.

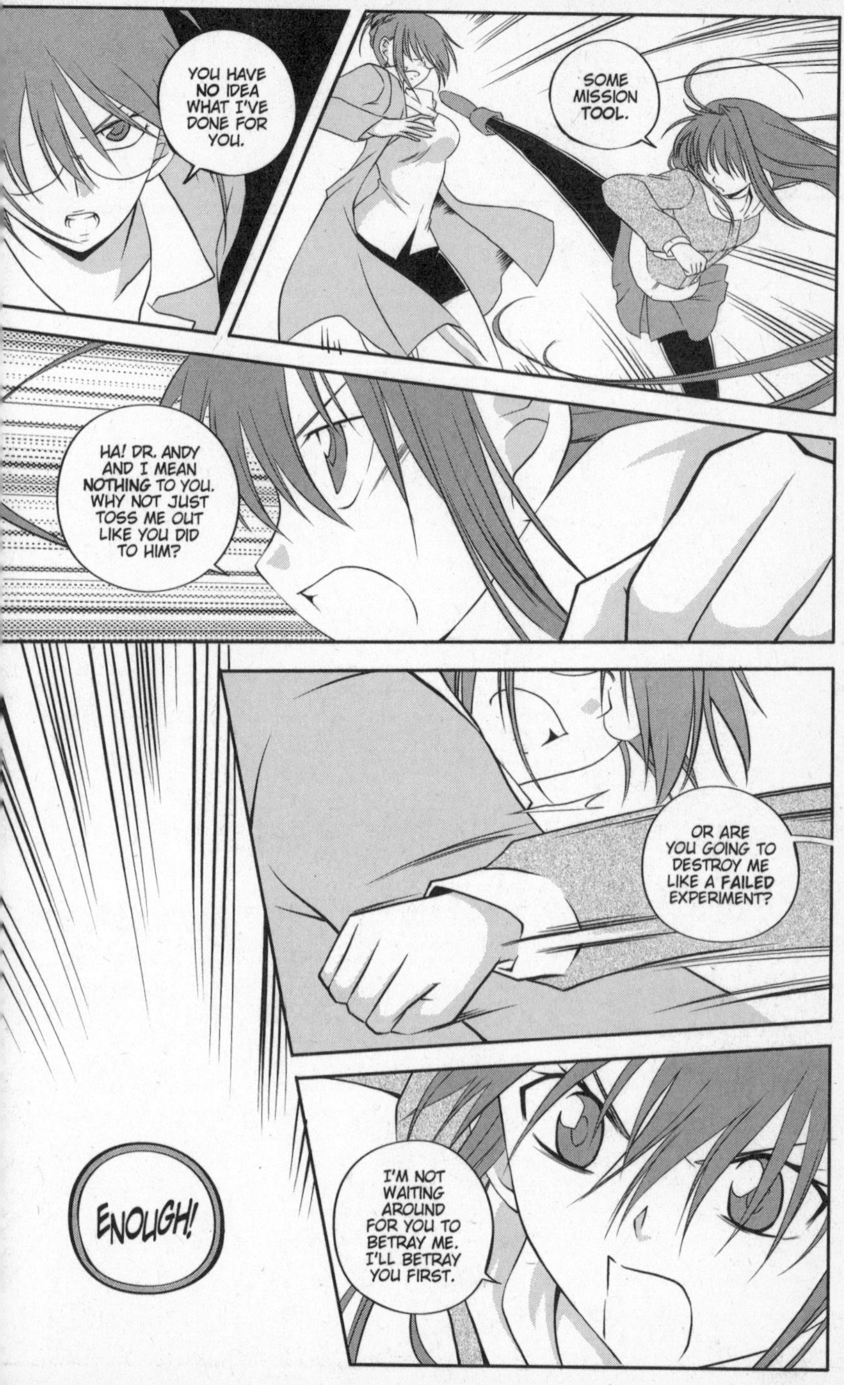
SOME MISSION TOOL.
YOU HAVE NO IDEA WHAT I'VE DONE FOR YOU.
HA! DR. ANDY AND I MEAN NOTHING TO YOU. WHY NOT JUST TOSS ME OUT LIKE YOU DID TO HIM?
OR ARE YOU GOING TO DESTROY ME LIKE A FAILED EXPERIMENT?
I'M NOT WAITING AROUND FOR YOU TO BETRAY ME. I'LL BETRAY YOU FIRST.
ENOUGH!

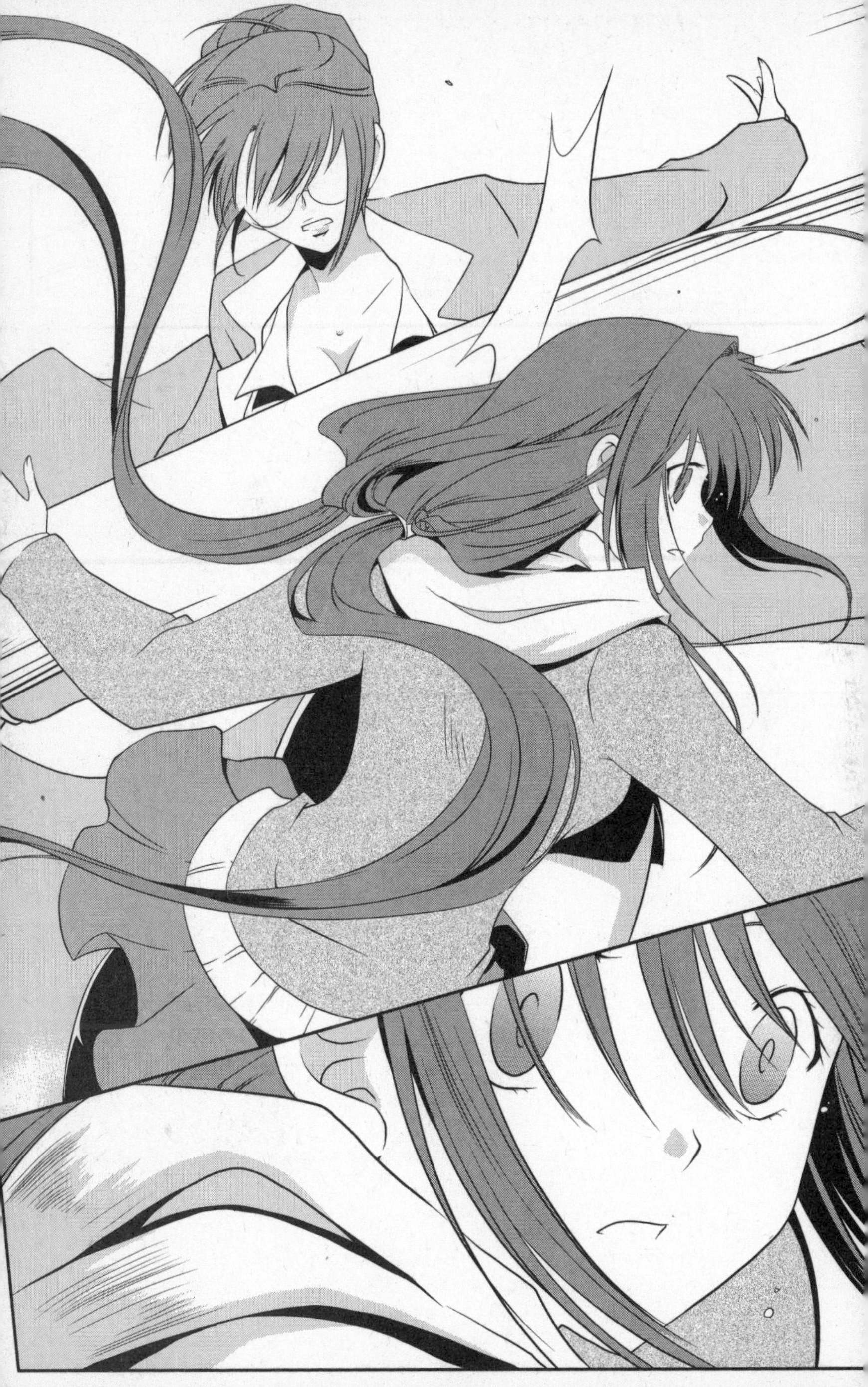

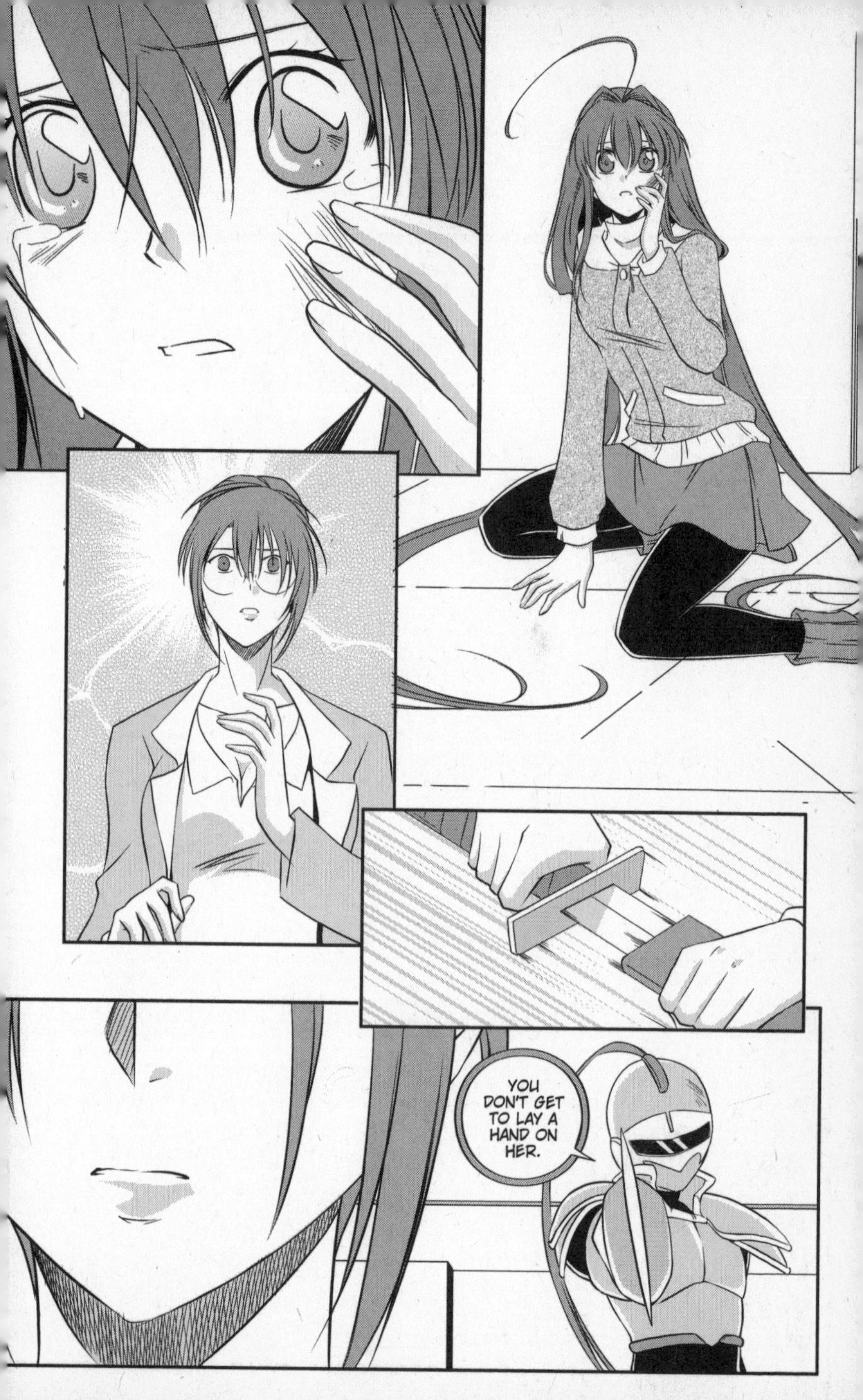
YOU DON'T GET TO LAY A HAND ON HER.

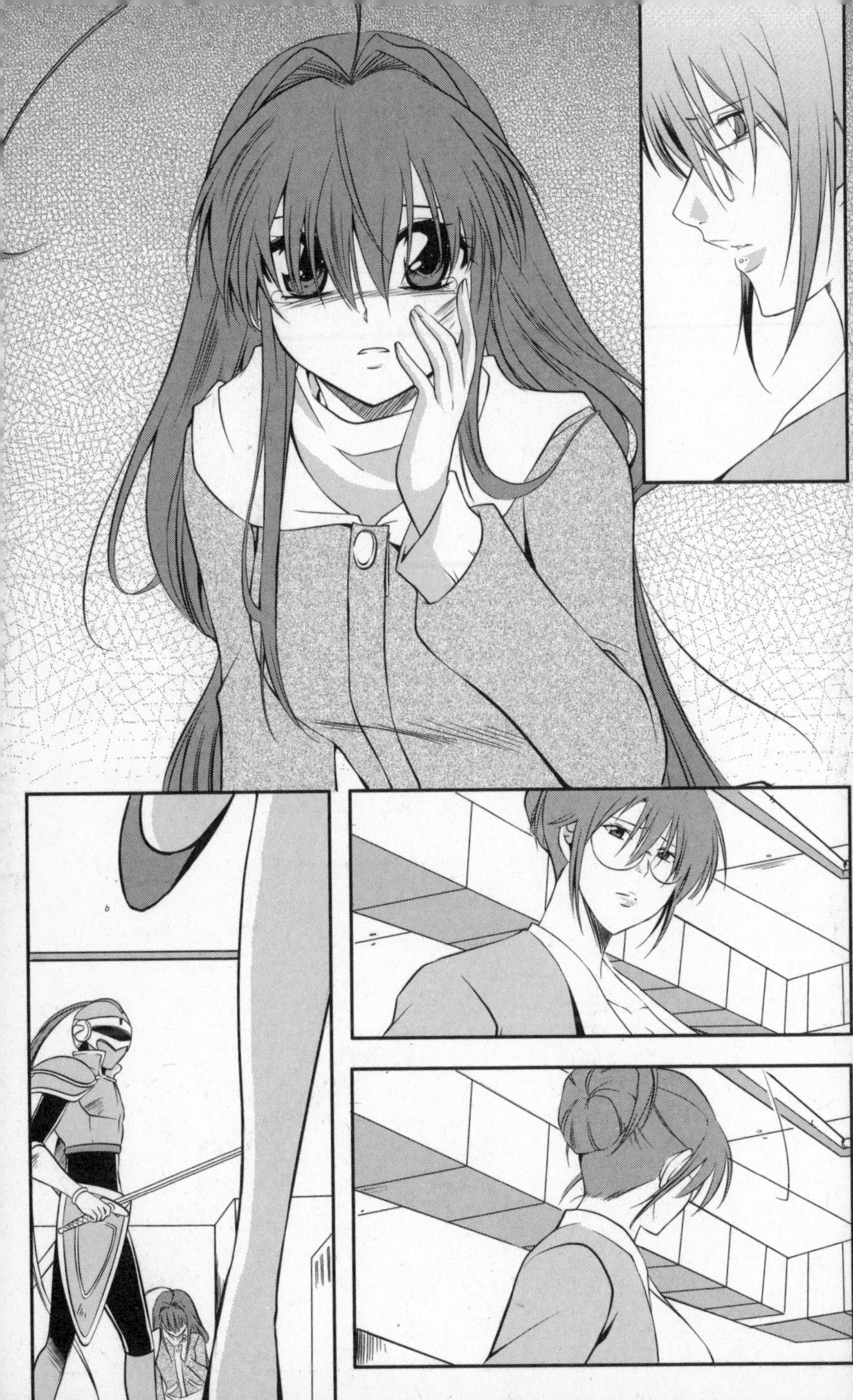

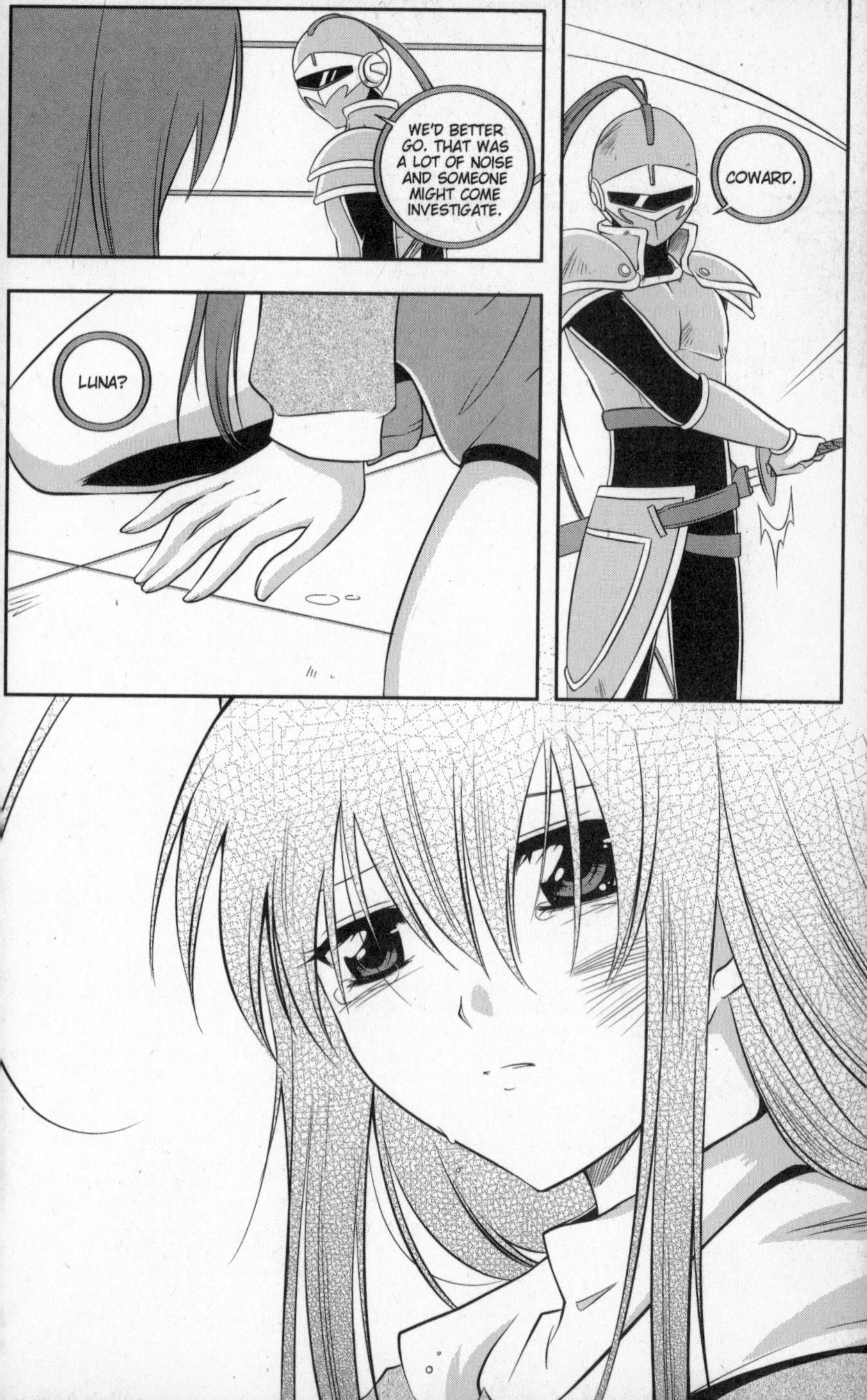
COWARD.
WE'D BETTER GO. THAT WAS A LOT OF NOISE AND SOMEONE MIGHT COME INVESTIGATE.
LUNA?

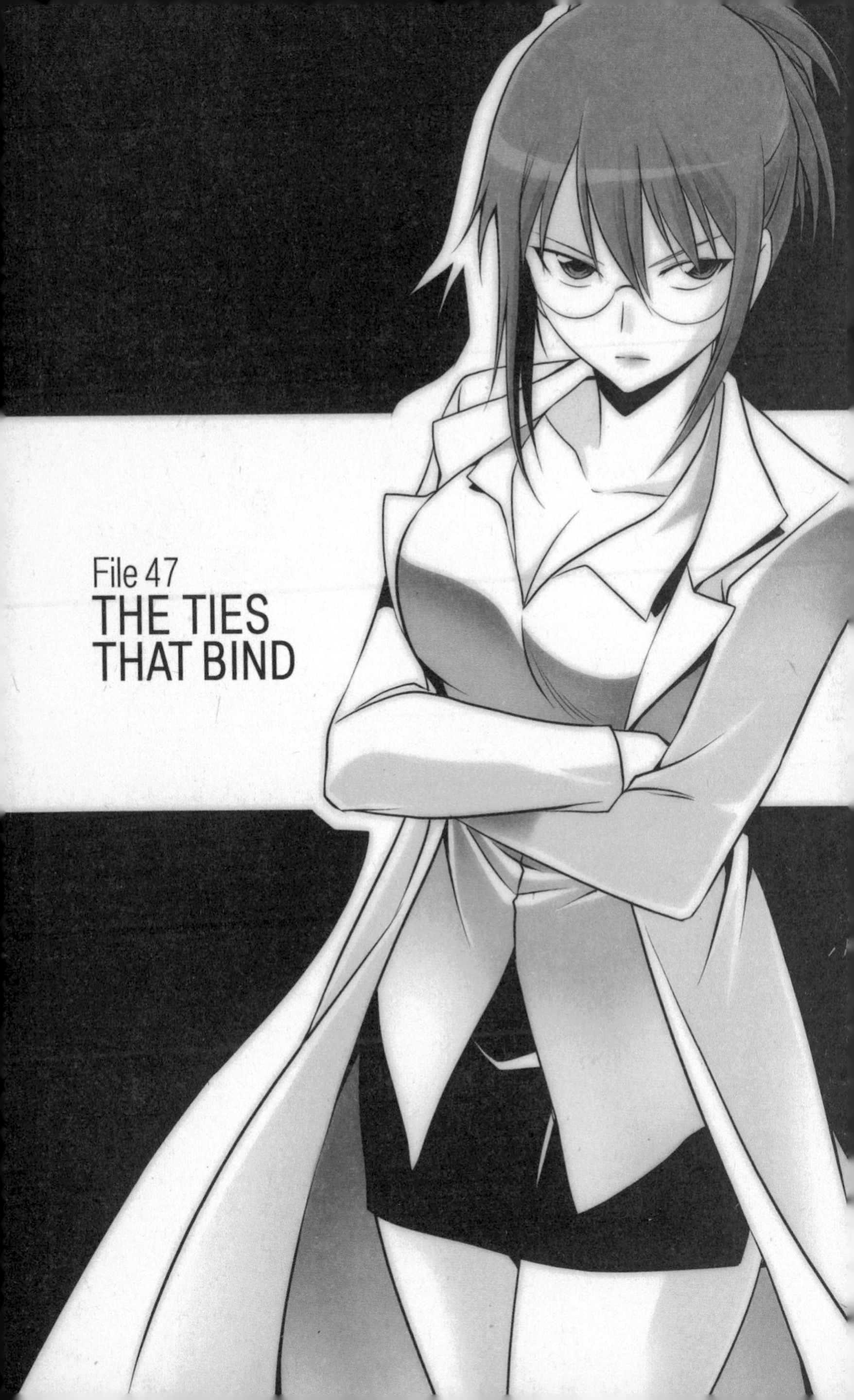

File 47
THE TIES THAT BIND

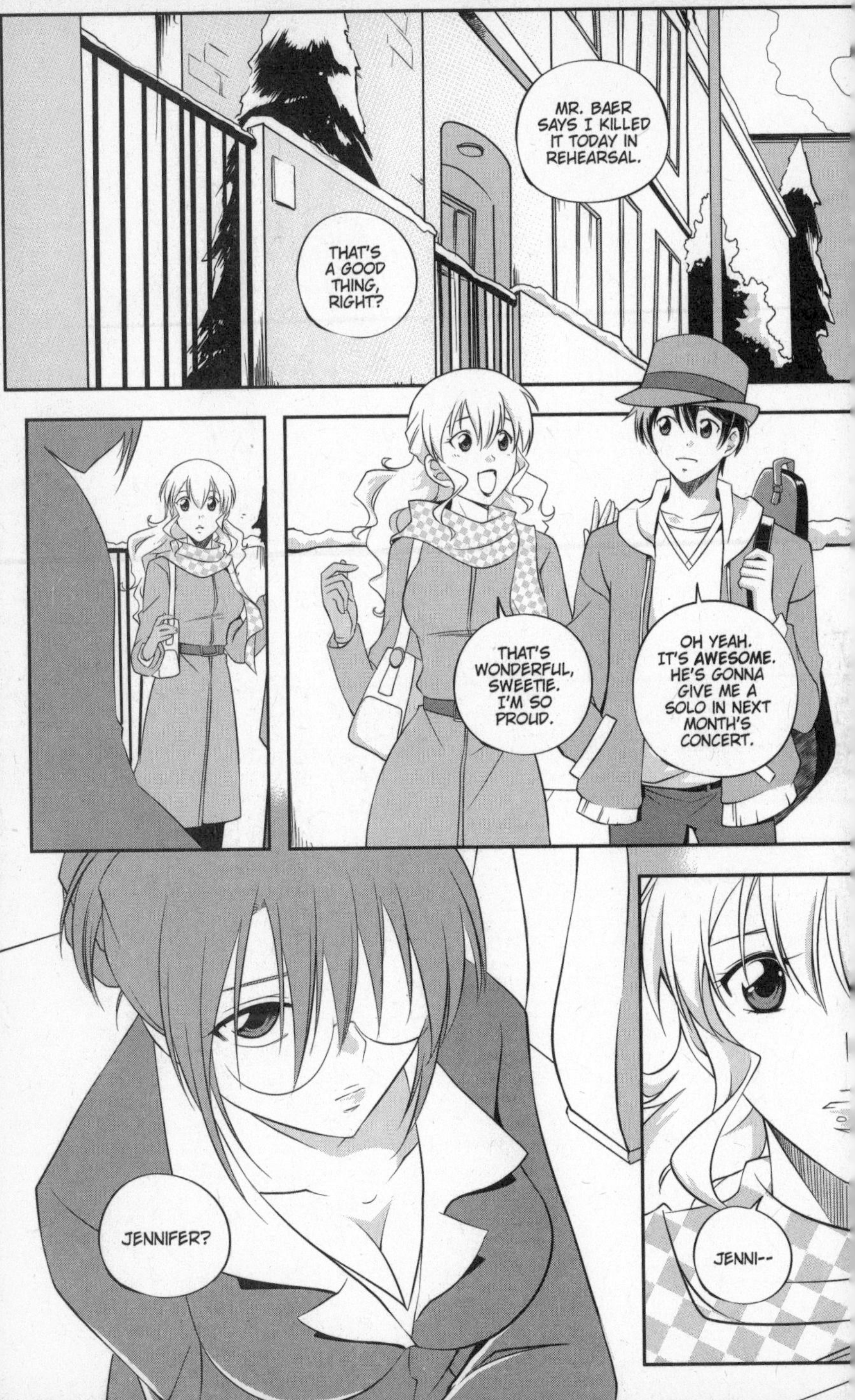
MR. BAER SAYS I KILLED IT TODAY IN REHEARSAL.
THAT'S A GOOD THING, RIGHT?
OH YEAH. IT'S AWESOME. HE'S GONNA GIVE ME A SOLO IN NEXT MONTH'S CONCERT.
THAT'S WONDERFUL, SWEETIE. I'M SO PROUD.
JENNI--
JENNIFER?

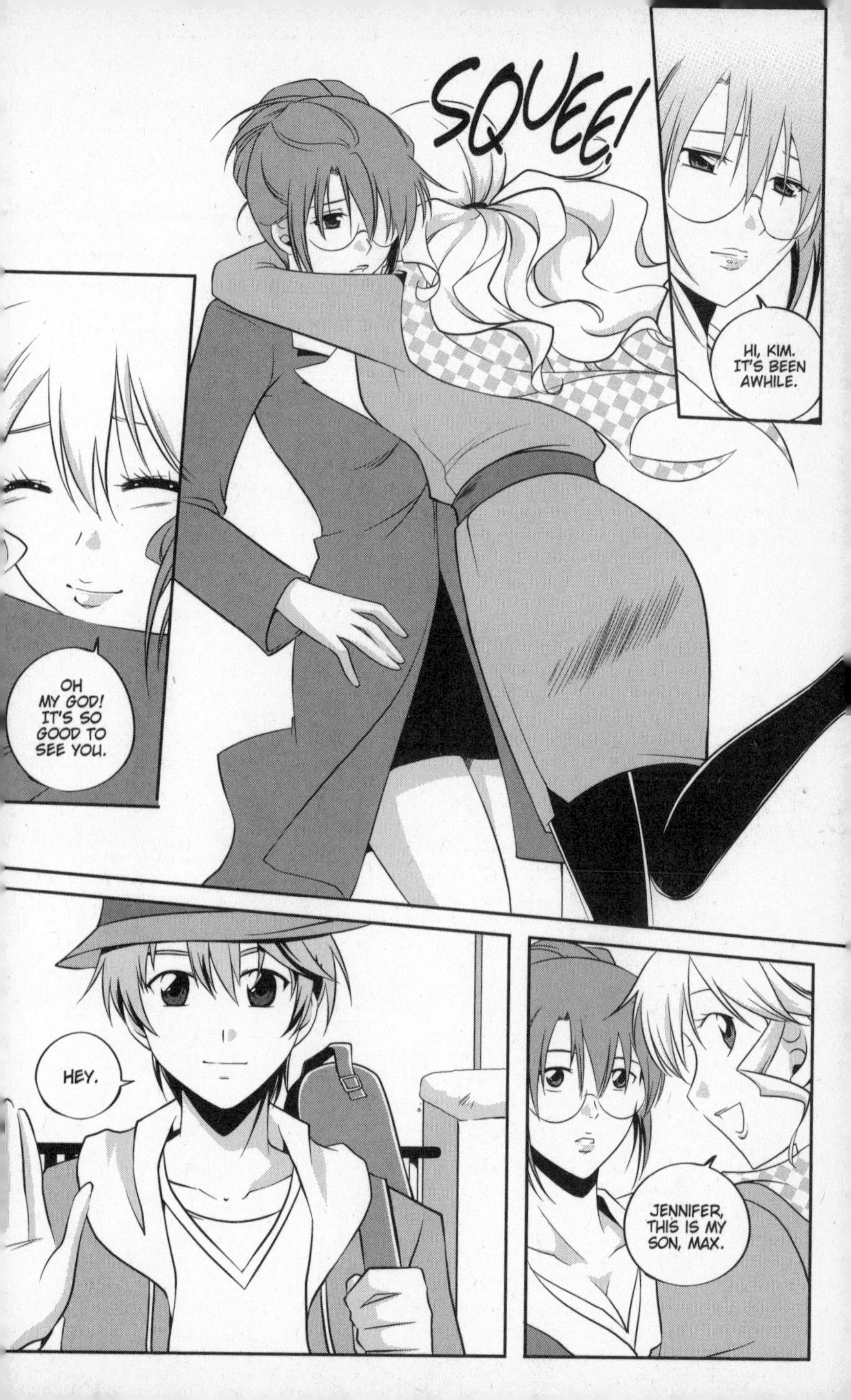
HI, KIM. IT'S BEEN AWHILE.
SQUEE!
OH MY GOD! IT'S SO GOOD TO SEE YOU.
JENNIFER, THIS IS MY SON, MAX.
HEY.

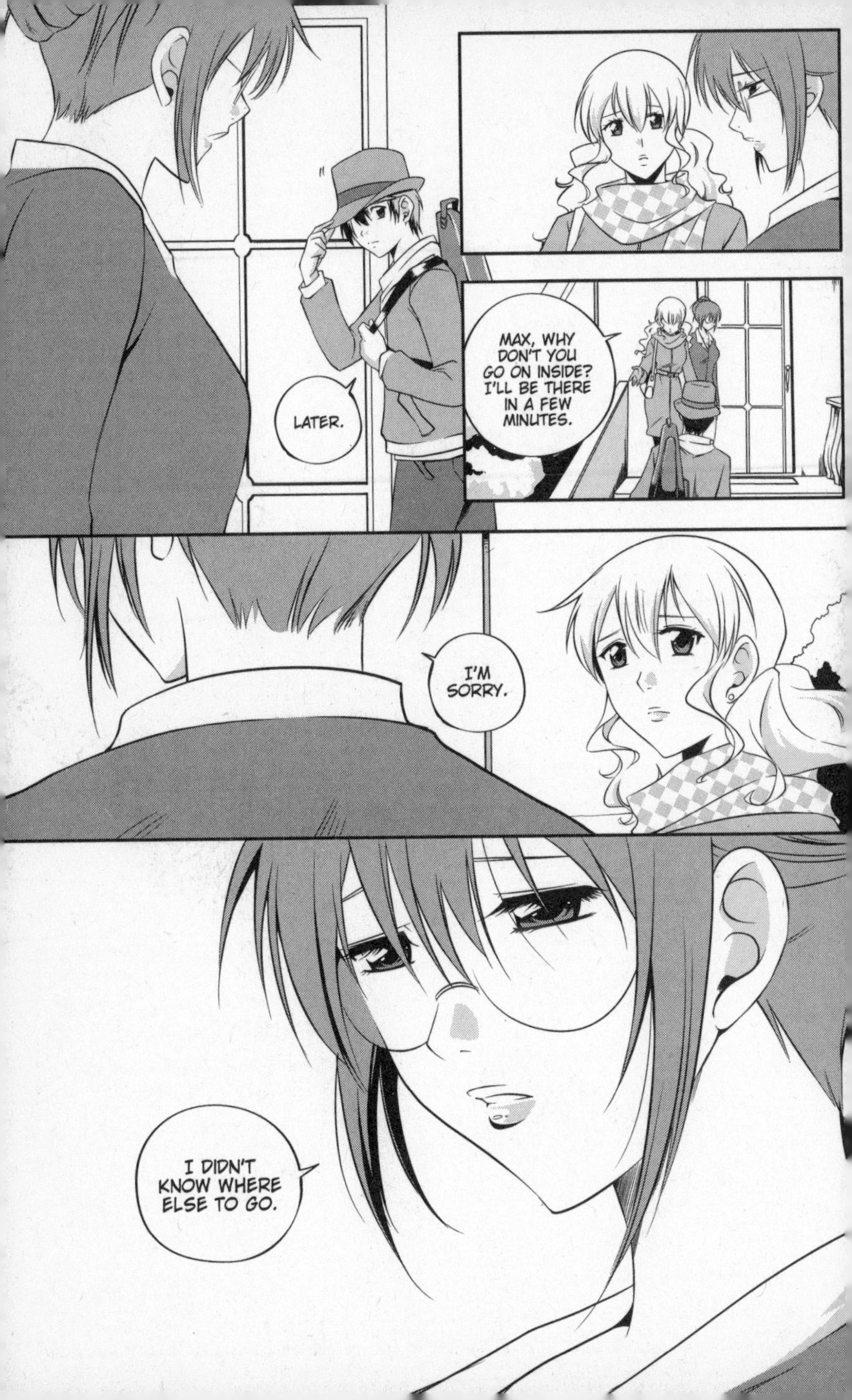
MAX, WHY DON'T YOU GO ON INSIDE? I'LL BE THERE IN A FEW MINUTES.
LATER.
I'M SORRY.
I DIDN'T KNOW WHERE ELSE TO GO.

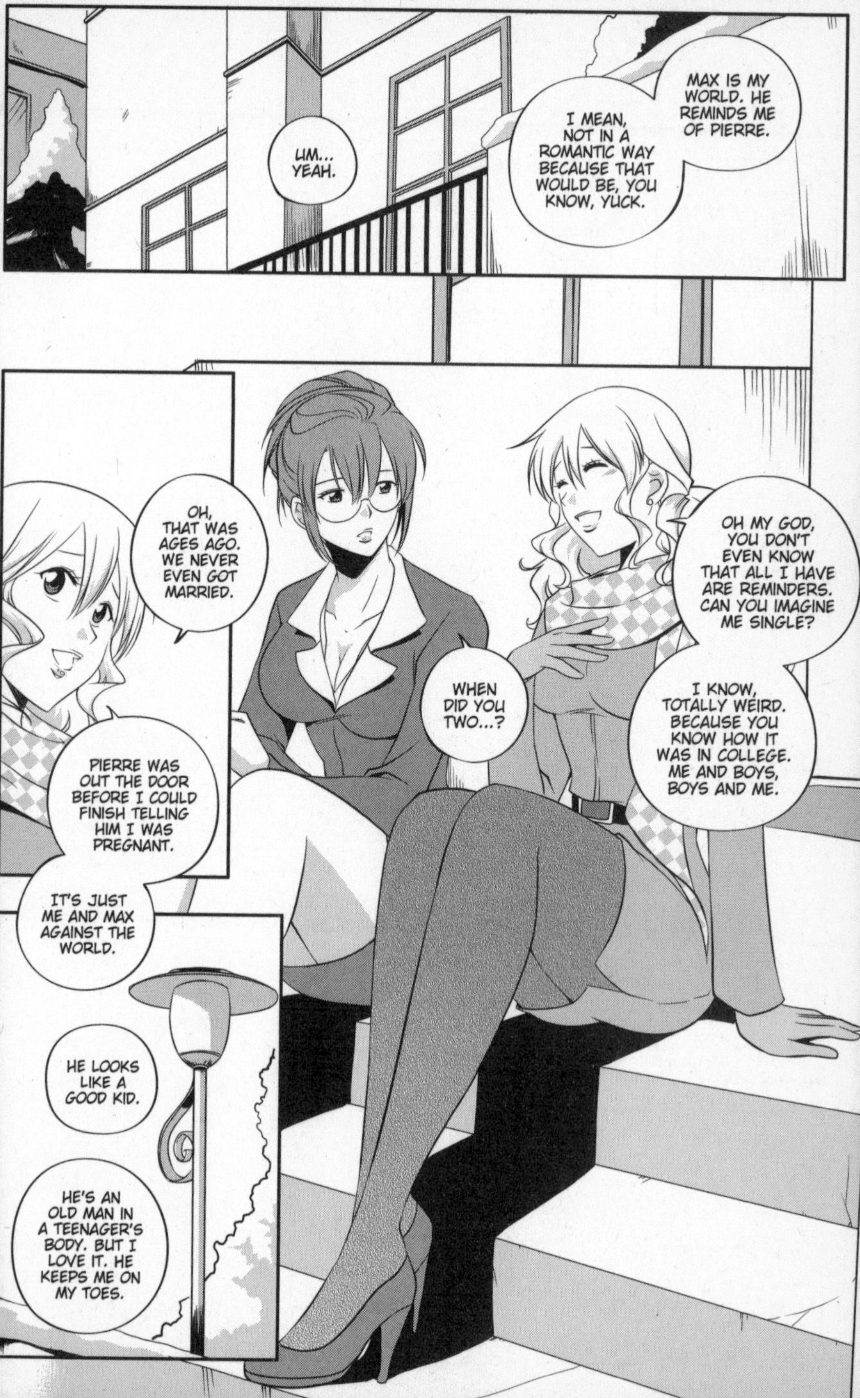
MAX IS MY WORLD. HE REMINDS ME OF PIERRE.
I MEAN, NOT IN A ROMANTIC WAY BECAUSE THAT WOULD BE, YOU KNOW, YUCK.
UM... YEAH.
OH MY GOD, YOU DON'T EVEN KNOW THAT ALL I HAVE ARE REMINDERS. CAN YOU IMAGINE ME SINGLE?
I KNOW, TOTALLY WEIRD. BECAUSE YOU KNOW HOW IT WAS IN COLLEGE. ME AND BOYS, BOYS AND ME.
WHEN DID YOU TWO...?
OH, THAT WAS AGES AGO. WE NEVER EVEN GOT MARRIED.
PIERRE WAS OUT THE DOOR BEFORE I COULD FINISH TELLING HIM I WAS PREGNANT.
IT'S JUST ME AND MAX AGAINST THE WORLD.
HE LOOKS LIKE A GOOD KID.
HE'S AN OLD MAN IN A TEENAGER'S BODY. BUT I LOVE IT. HE KEEPS ME ON MY TOES.

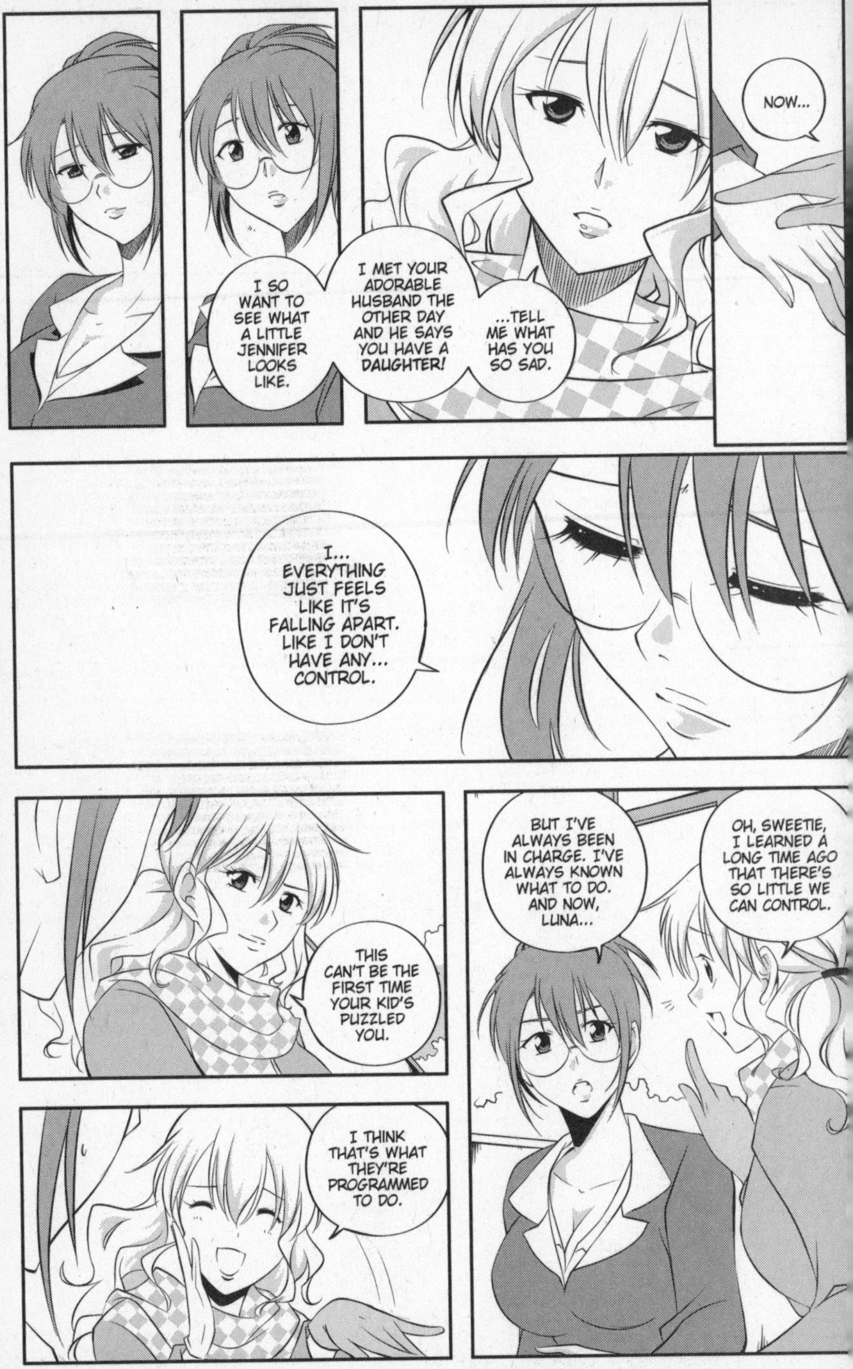
NOW...
...TELL ME WHAT HAS YOU SO SAD.
I MET YOUR ADORABLE HUSBAND THE OTHER DAY AND HE SAYS YOU HAVE A DAUGHTER!
I SO WANT TO SEE WHAT A LITTLE JENNIFER LOOKS LIKE.
I... EVERYTHING JUST FEELS LIKE IT'S FALLING APART. LIKE I DON'T HAVE ANY... CONTROL.
OH, SWEETIE, I LEARNED A LONG TIME AGO THAT THERE'S SO LITTLE WE CAN CONTROL.
BUT I'VE ALWAYS BEEN IN CHARGE. I'VE ALWAYS KNOWN WHAT TO DO. AND NOW, LUNA...
THIS CAN'T BE THE FIRST TIME YOUR KID'S PUZZLED YOU.
I THINK THAT'S WHAT THEY'RE PROGRAMMED TO DO.

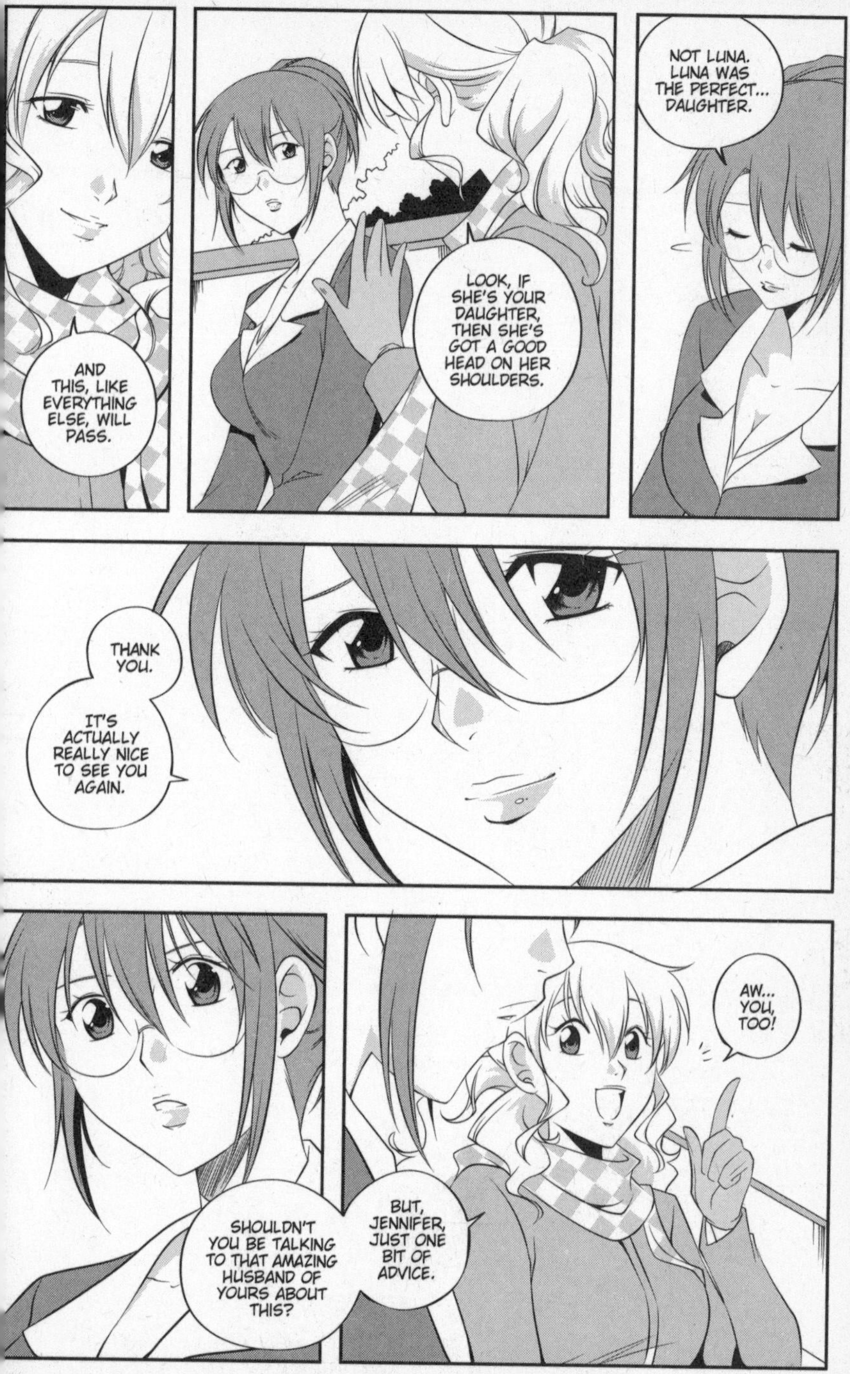
NOT LUNA. LUNA WAS THE PERFECT... DAUGHTER.
LOOK, IF SHE'S YOUR DAUGHTER, THEN SHE'S GOT A GOOD HEAD ON HER SHOULDERS.
AND THIS, LIKE EVERYTHING ELSE, WILL PASS.
THANK YOU.
IT'S ACTUALLY REALLY NICE TO SEE YOU AGAIN.
AW... YOU, TOO!
BUT, JENNIFER, JUST ONE BIT OF ADVICE.
SHOULDN'T YOU BE TALKING TO THAT AMAZING HUSBAND OF YOURS ABOUT THIS?

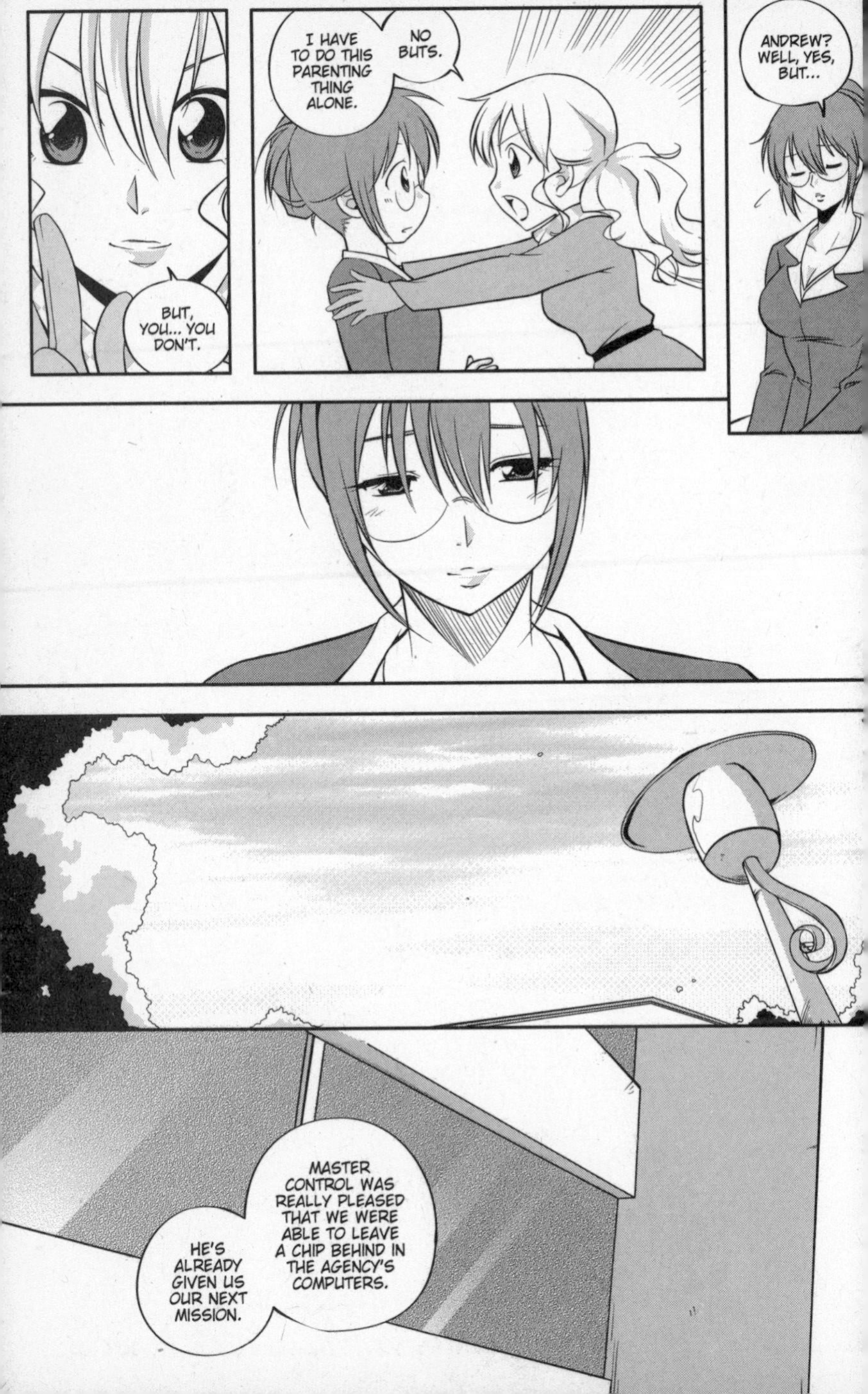
ANDREW? WELL, YES, BUT...
NO BUTS.
I HAVE TO DO THIS PARENTING THING ALONE.
BUT, YOU... YOU DON'T.
MASTER CONTROL WAS REALLY PLEASED THAT WE WERE ABLE TO LEAVE A CHIP BEHIND IN THE AGENCY'S COMPUTERS.
HE'S ALREADY GIVEN US OUR NEXT MISSION.

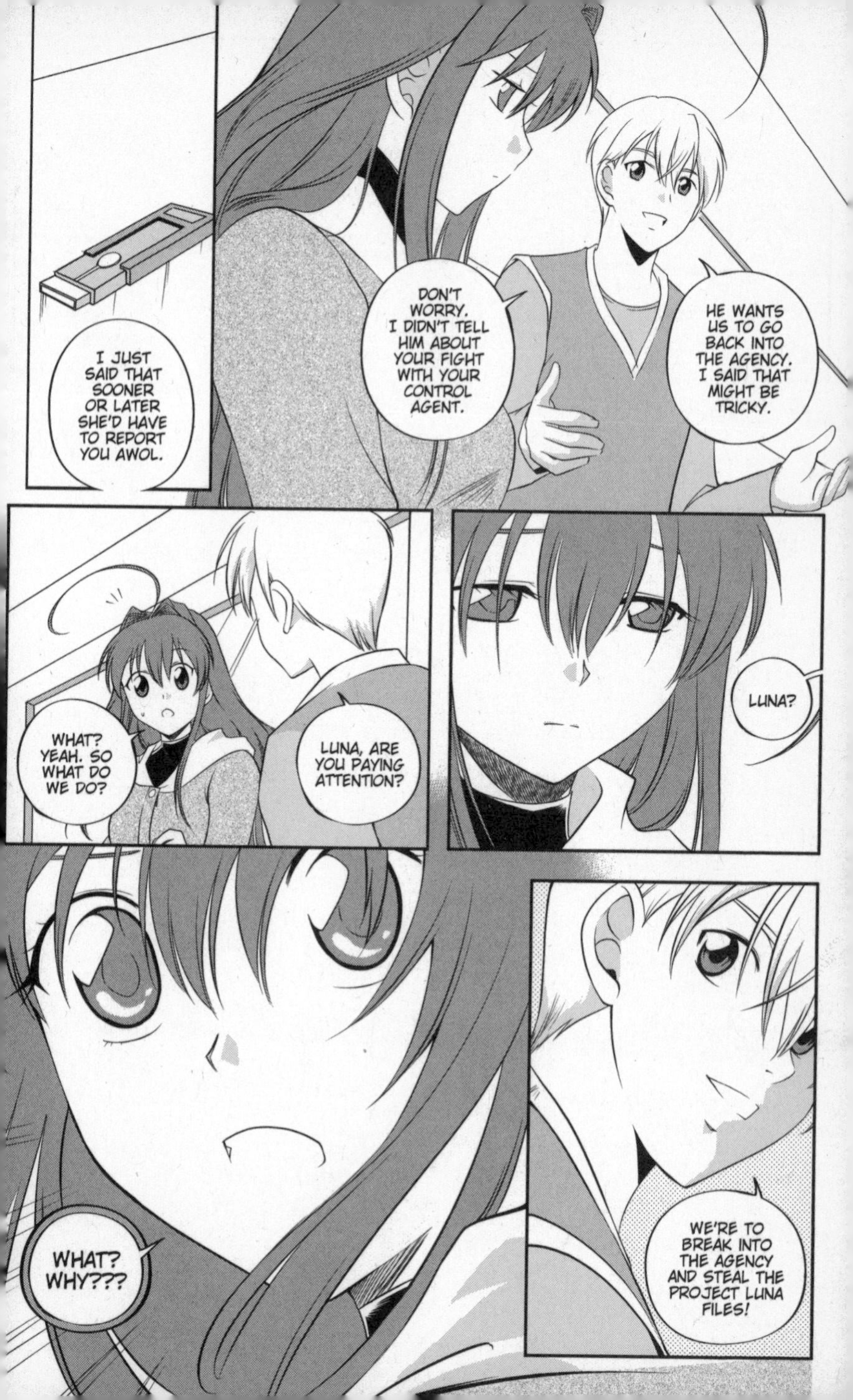
HE WANTS US TO GO BACK INTO THE AGENCY. I SAID THAT MIGHT BE TRICKY.
DON'T WORRY. I DIDN'T TELL HIM ABOUT YOUR FIGHT WITH YOUR CONTROL AGENT.
I JUST SAID THAT SOONER OR LATER SHE'D HAVE TO REPORT YOU AWOL.
LUNA?
LUNA, ARE YOU PAYING ATTENTION?
WHAT? YEAH. SO WHAT DO WE DO?
WE'RE TO BREAK INTO THE AGENCY AND STEAL THE PROJECT LUNA FILES!
WHAT? WHY???

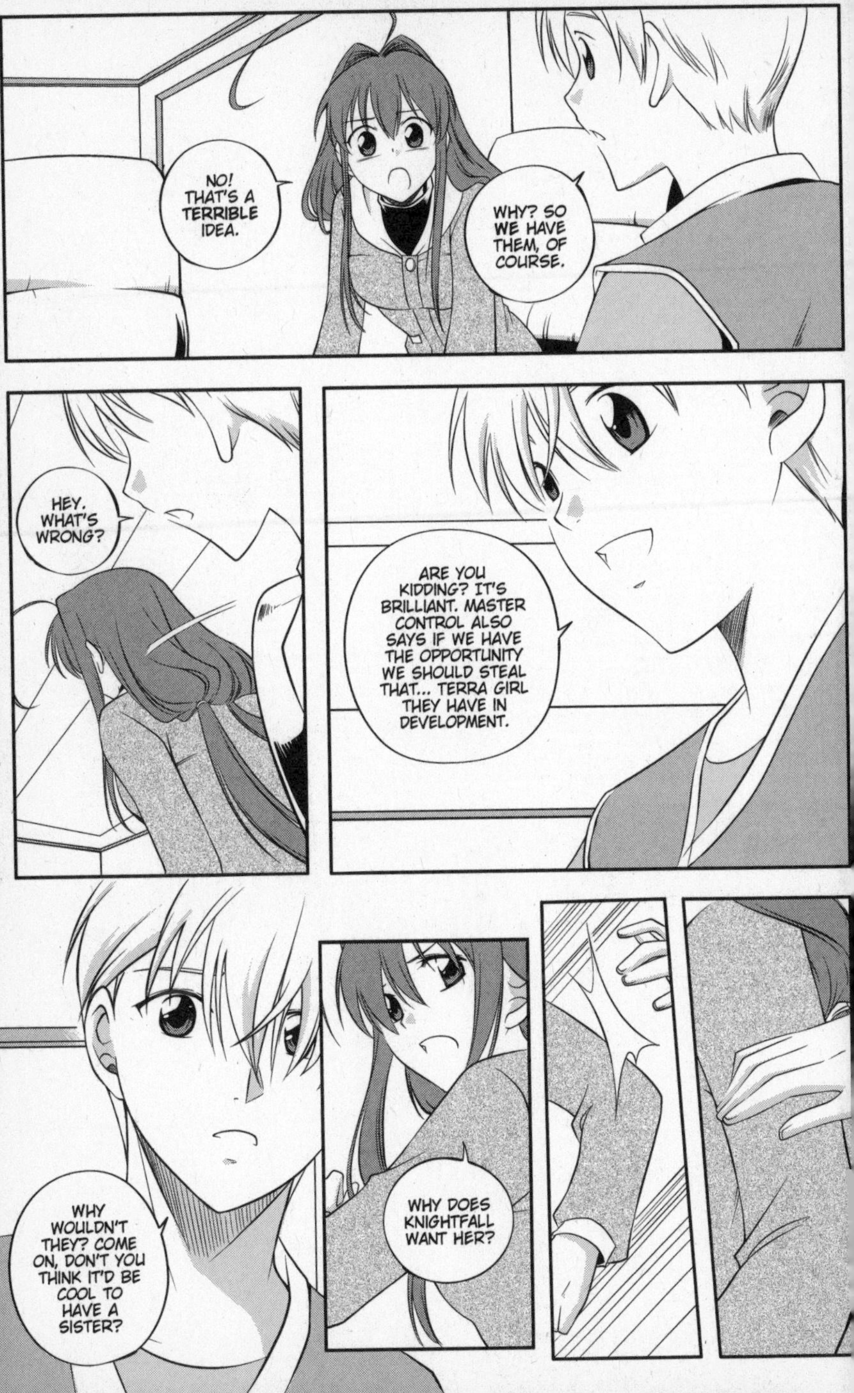
WHY? SO WE HAVE THEM, OF COURSE.
NO! THAT'S A TERRIBLE IDEA.
ARE YOU KIDDING? IT'S BRILLIANT. MASTER CONTROL ALSO SAYS IF WE HAVE THE OPPORTUNITY WE SHOULD STEAL THAT... TERRA GIRL THEY HAVE IN DEVELOPMENT.
HEY. WHAT'S WRONG?
WHY DOES KNIGHTFALL WANT HER?
WHY WOULDN'T THEY? COME ON, DON'T YOU THINK IT'D BE COOL TO HAVE A SISTER?

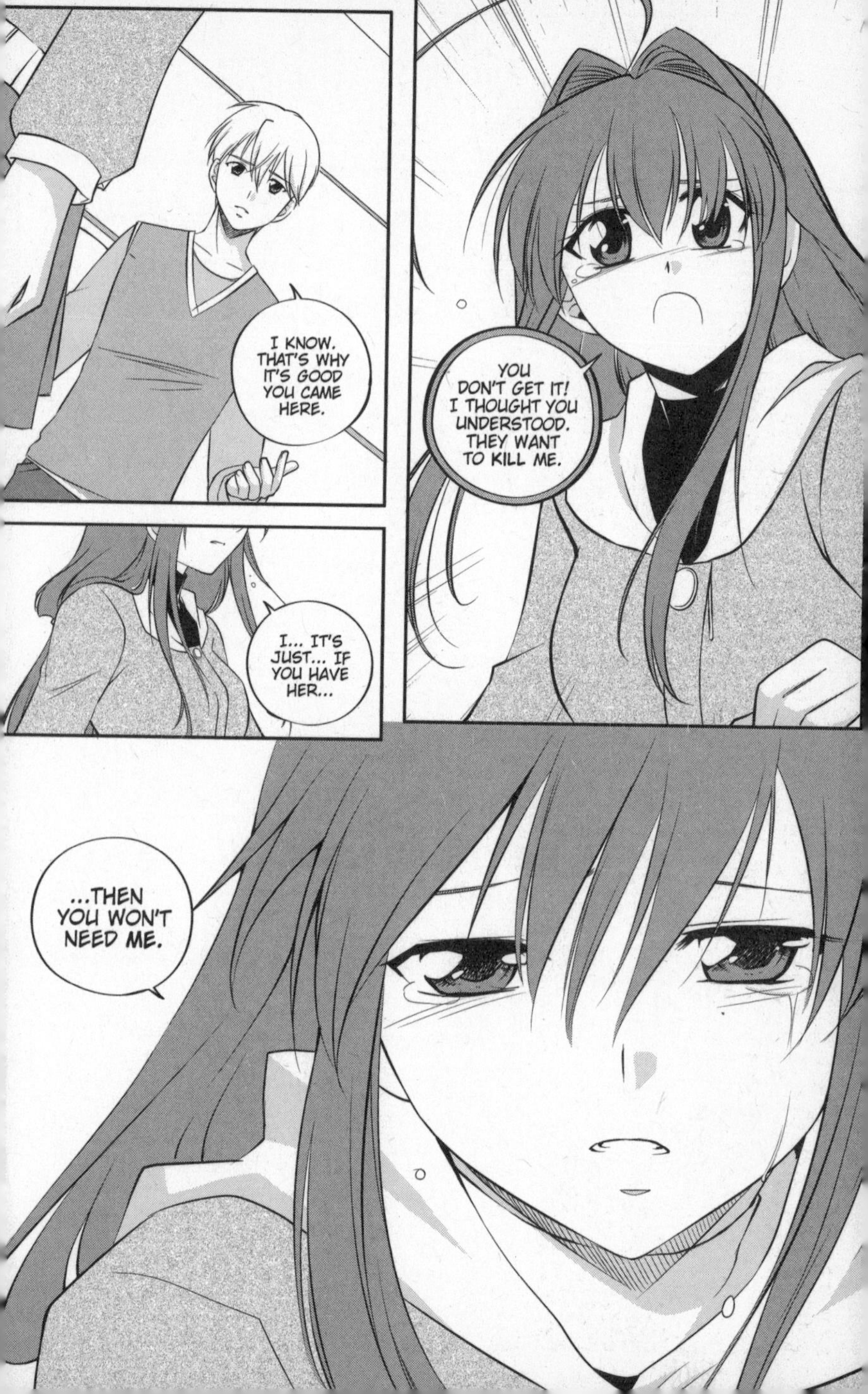
YOU DON'T GET IT! I THOUGHT YOU UNDERSTOOD. THEY WANT TO KILL ME.
I KNOW. THAT'S WHY IT'S GOOD YOU CAME HERE.
I... IT'S JUST... IF YOU HAVE HER...
...THEN YOU WON'T NEED ME.

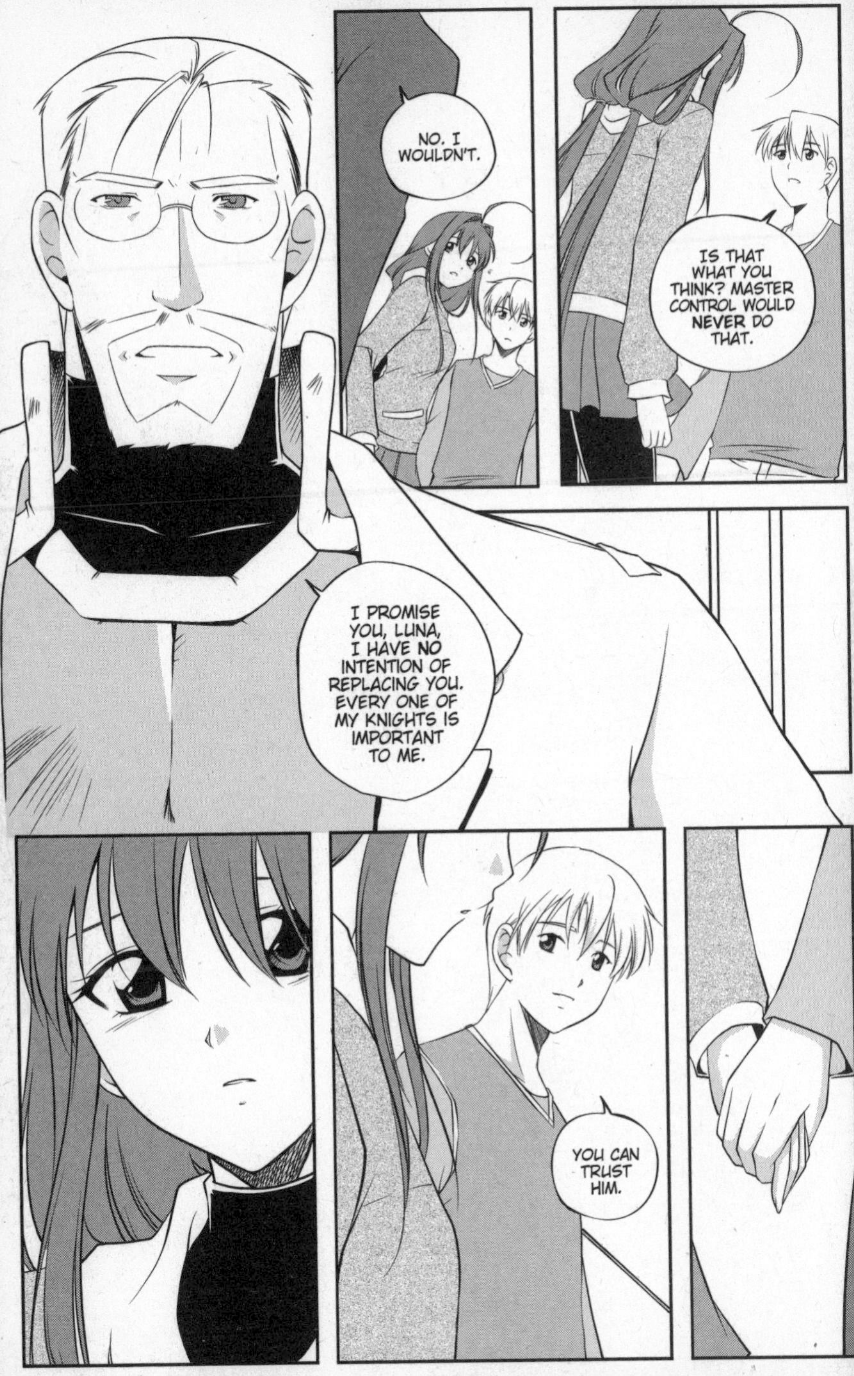
IS THAT WHAT YOU THINK? MASTER CONTROL WOULD NEVER DO THAT.
NO. I WOULDN'T.
I PROMISE YOU, LUNA, I HAVE NO INTENTION OF REPLACING YOU. EVERY ONE OF MY KNIGHTS IS IMPORTANT TO ME.
YOU CAN TRUST HIM.

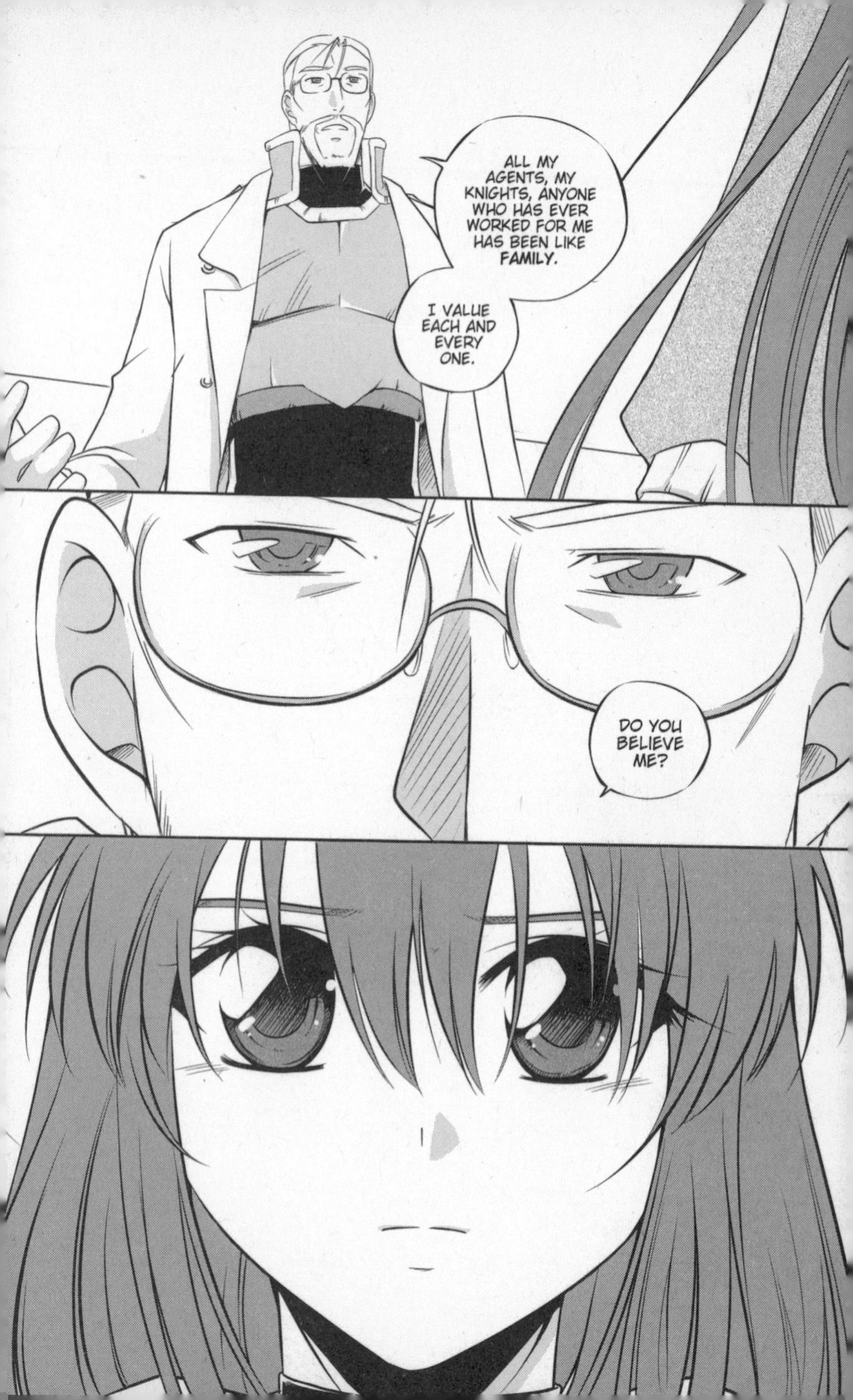
ALL MY AGENTS, MY KNIGHTS, ANYONE WHO HAS EVER WORKED FOR ME HAS BEEN LIKE FAMILY.
I VALUE EACH AND EVERY ONE.
DO YOU BELIEVE ME?

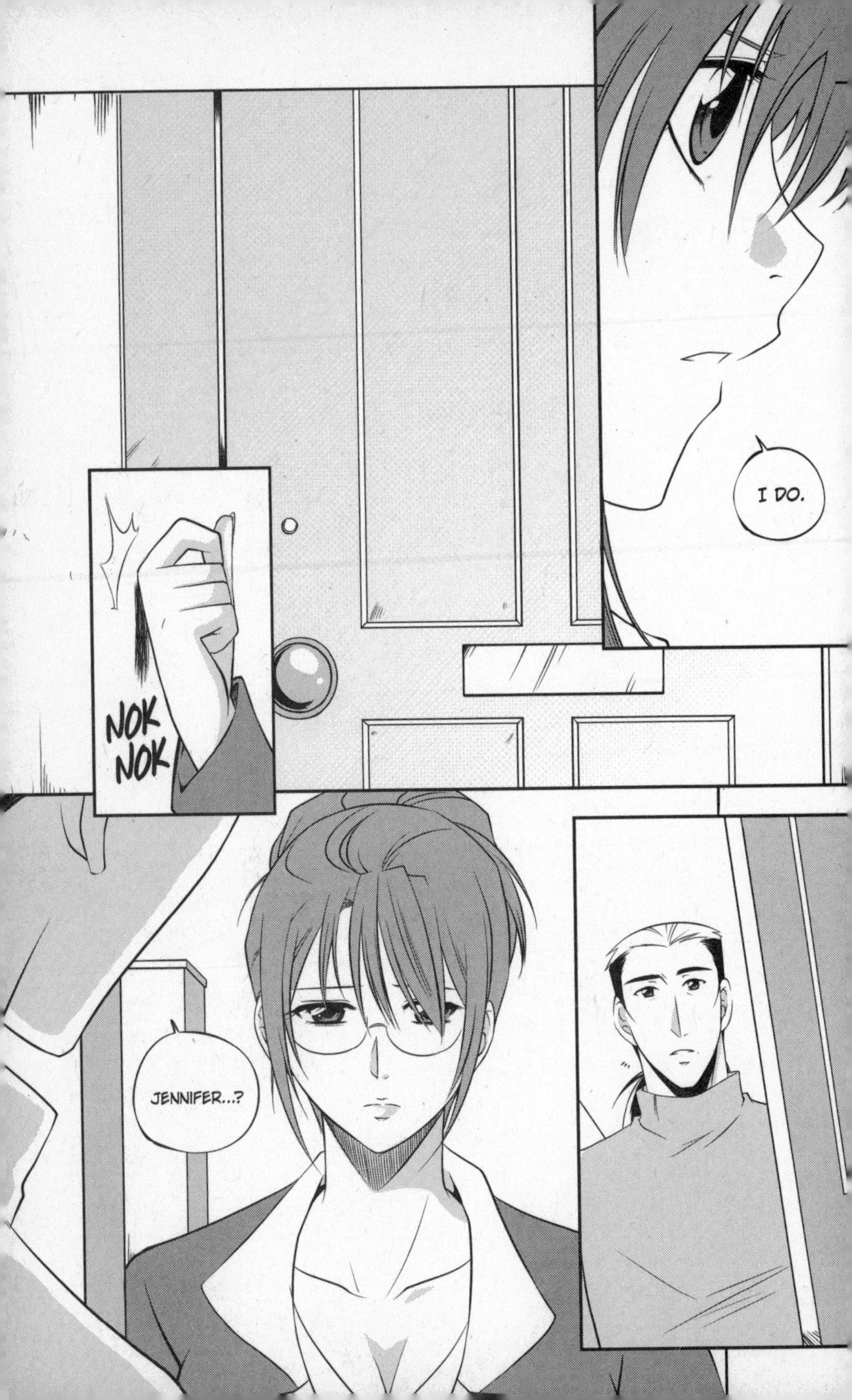
I DO.
NOK NOK
JENNIFER...?

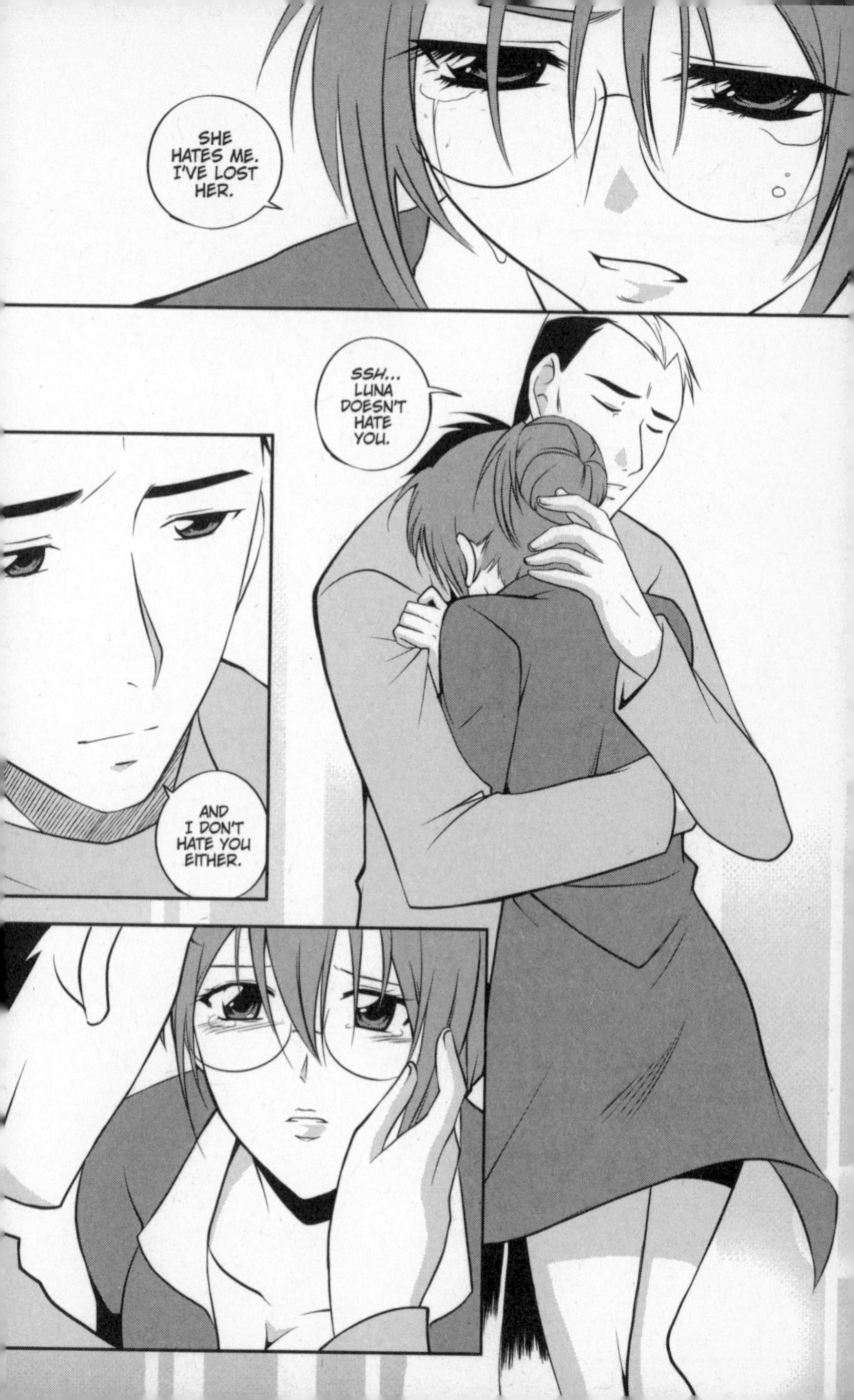
SHE HATES ME. I'VE LOST HER.
SSH... LUNA DOESN'T HATE YOU.
AND I DON'T HATE YOU EITHER.

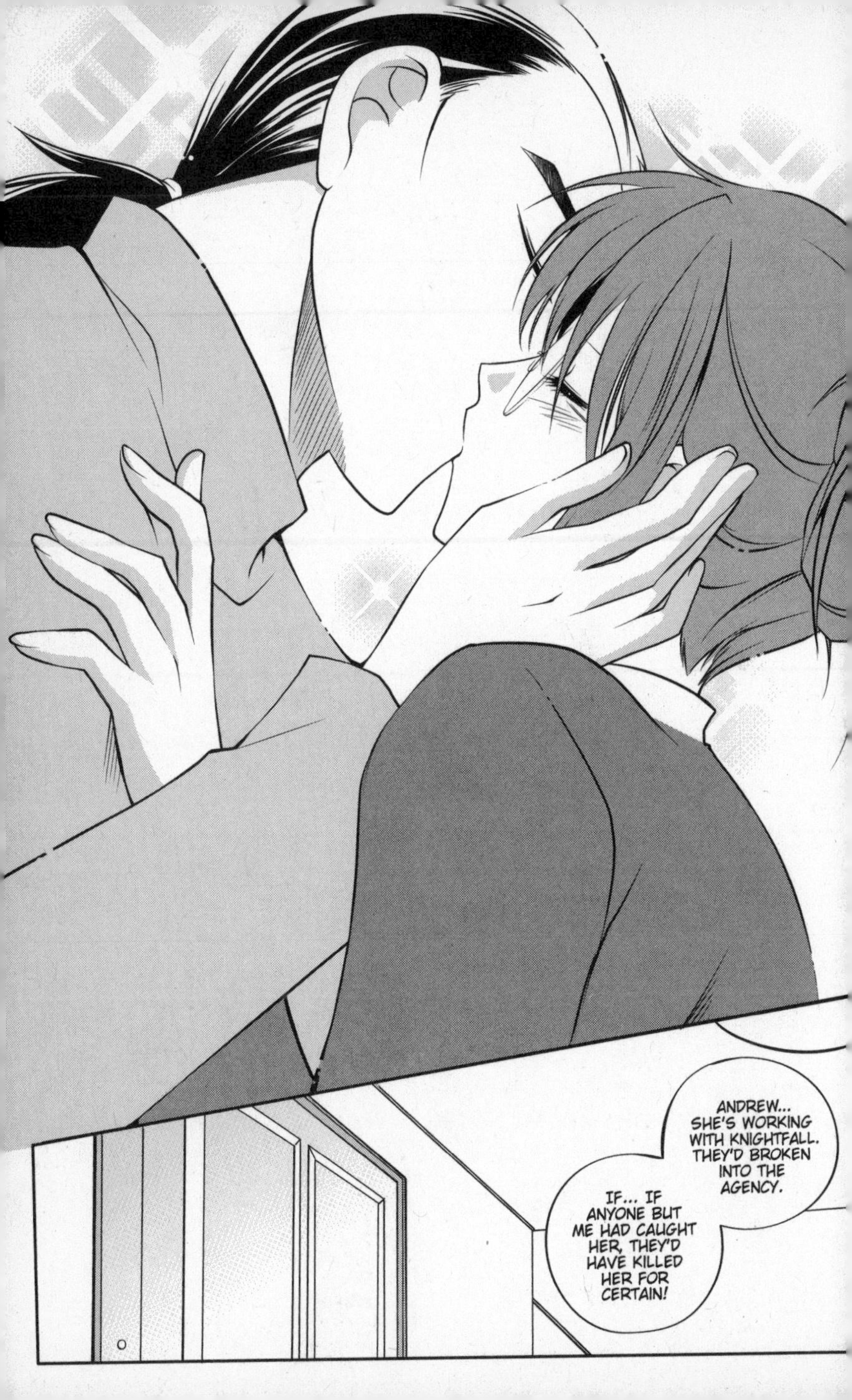
ANDREW... SHE'S WORKING WITH KNIGHTFALL. THEY'D BROKEN INTO THE AGENCY.
IF... IF ANYONE BUT ME HAD CAUGHT HER, THEY'D HAVE KILLED HER FOR CERTAIN!

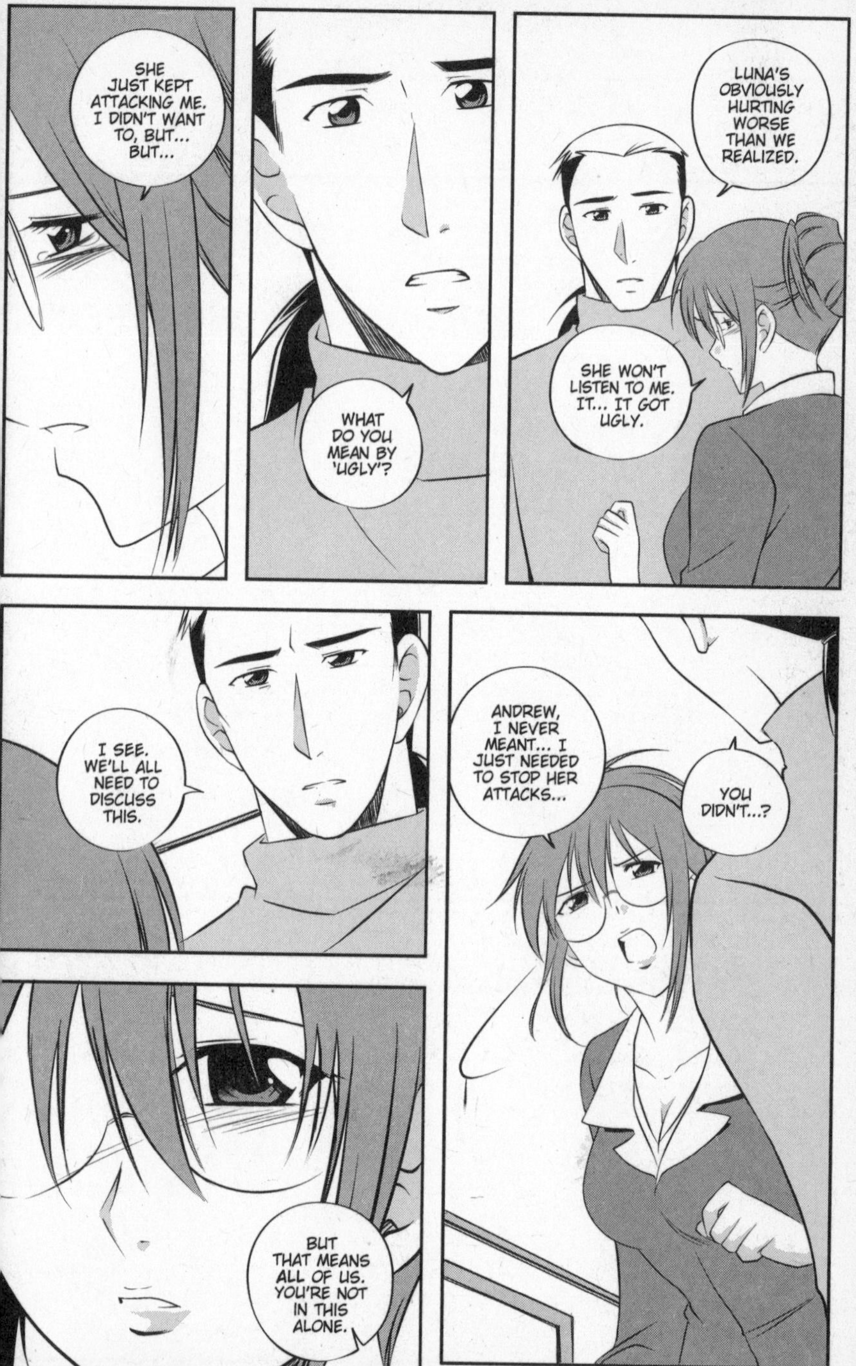
LUNA'S OBVIOUSLY HURTING WORSE THAN WE REALIZED.
SHE WON'T LISTEN TO ME. IT... IT GOT UGLY.
WHAT DO YOU MEAN BY 'UGLY'?
SHE JUST KEPT ATTACKING ME. I DIDN'T WANT TO, BUT... BUT...
YOU DIDN'T...?
ANDREW, I NEVER MEANT... I JUST NEEDED TO STOP HER ATTACKS...
I SEE. WE'LL ALL NEED TO DISCUSS THIS.
BUT THAT MEANS ALL OF US. YOU'RE NOT IN THIS ALONE.

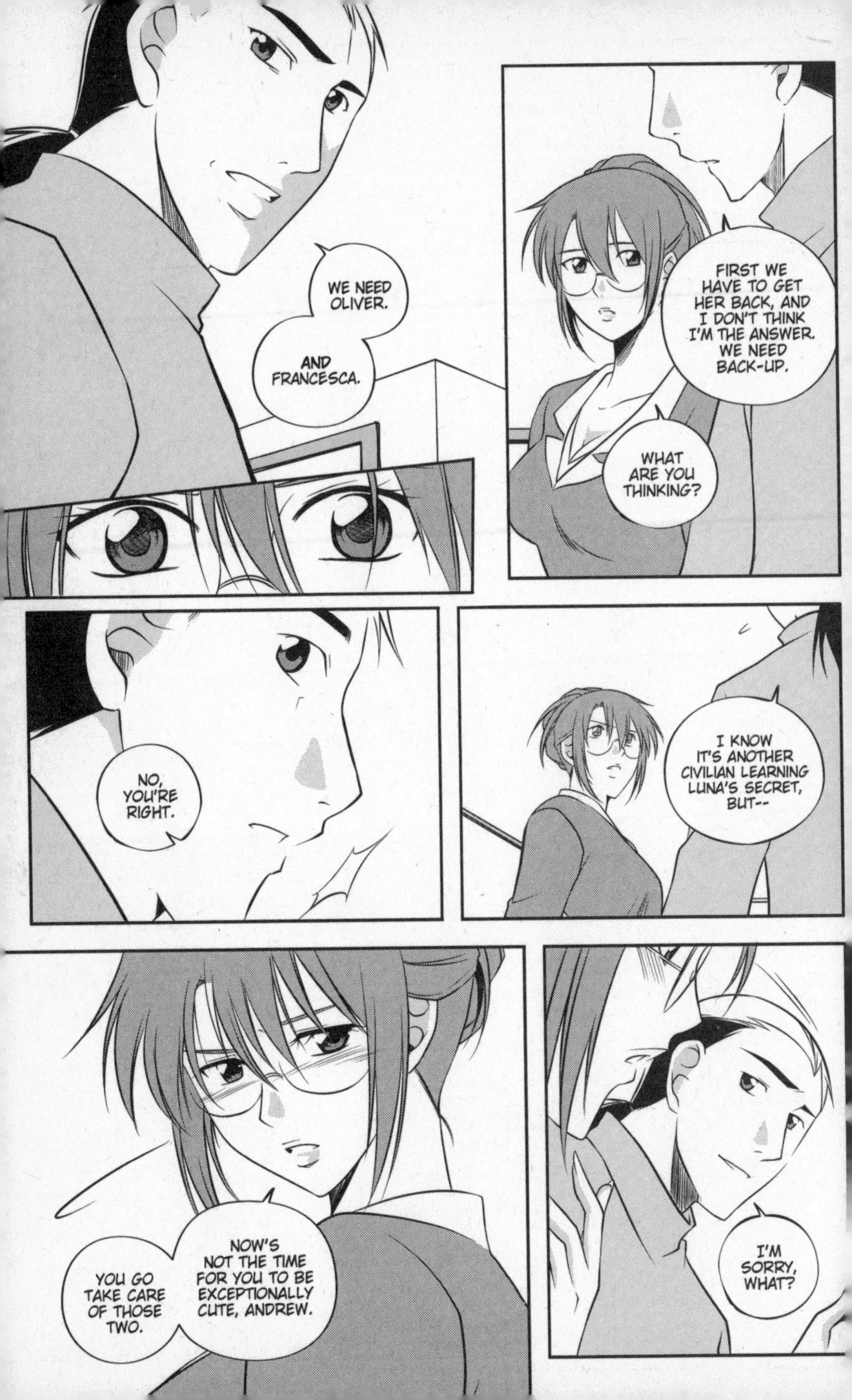
FIRST WE HAVE TO GET HER BACK, AND I DON'T THINK I'M THE ANSWER. WE NEED BACK-UP.
WHAT ARE YOU THINKING?
WE NEED OLIVER.
AND FRANCESCA.
I KNOW IT'S ANOTHER CIVILIAN LEARNING LUNA'S SECRET, BUT--
NO, YOU'RE RIGHT.
I'M SORRY, WHAT?
NOW'S NOT THE TIME FOR YOU TO BE EXCEPTIONALLY CUTE, ANDREW.
YOU GO TAKE CARE OF THOSE TWO.

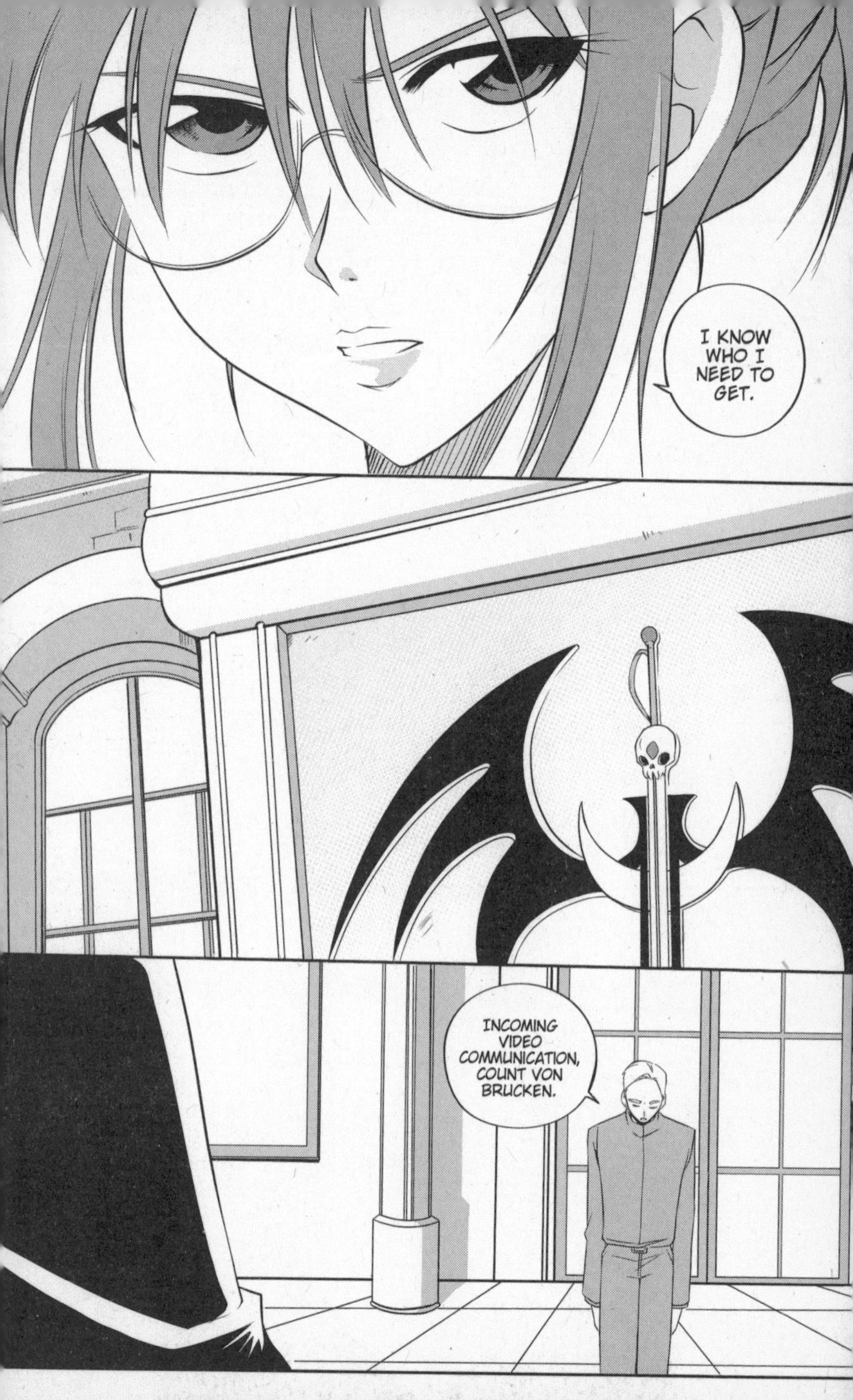
I KNOW WHO I NEED TO GET.
INCOMING VIDEO COMMUNICATION, COUNT VON BRUCKEN.

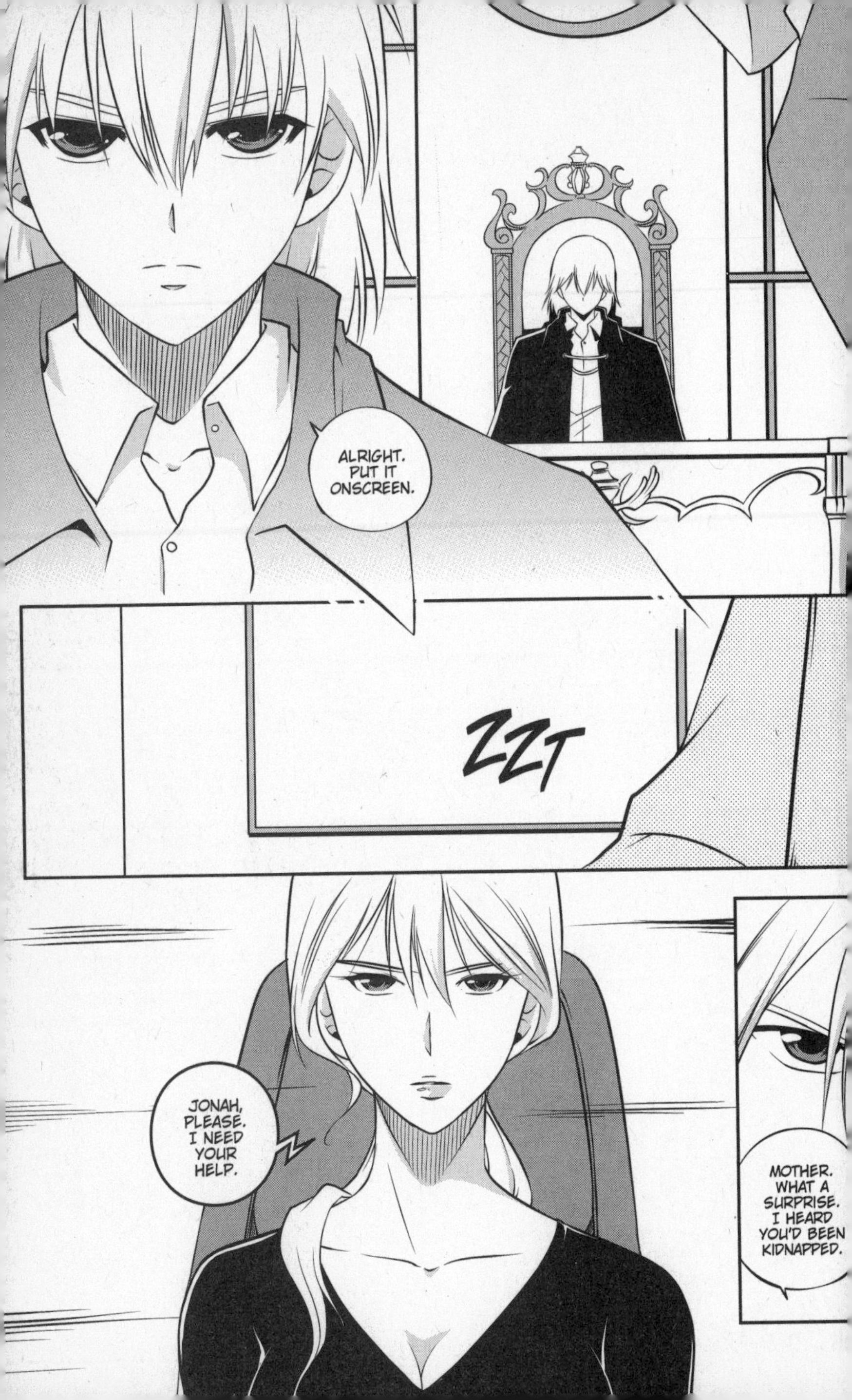
ALRIGHT. PUT IT ONSCREEN.
ZZT
MOTHER. WHAT A SURPRISE. I HEARD YOU'D BEEN KIDNAPPED.
JONAH, PLEASE. I NEED YOUR HELP.

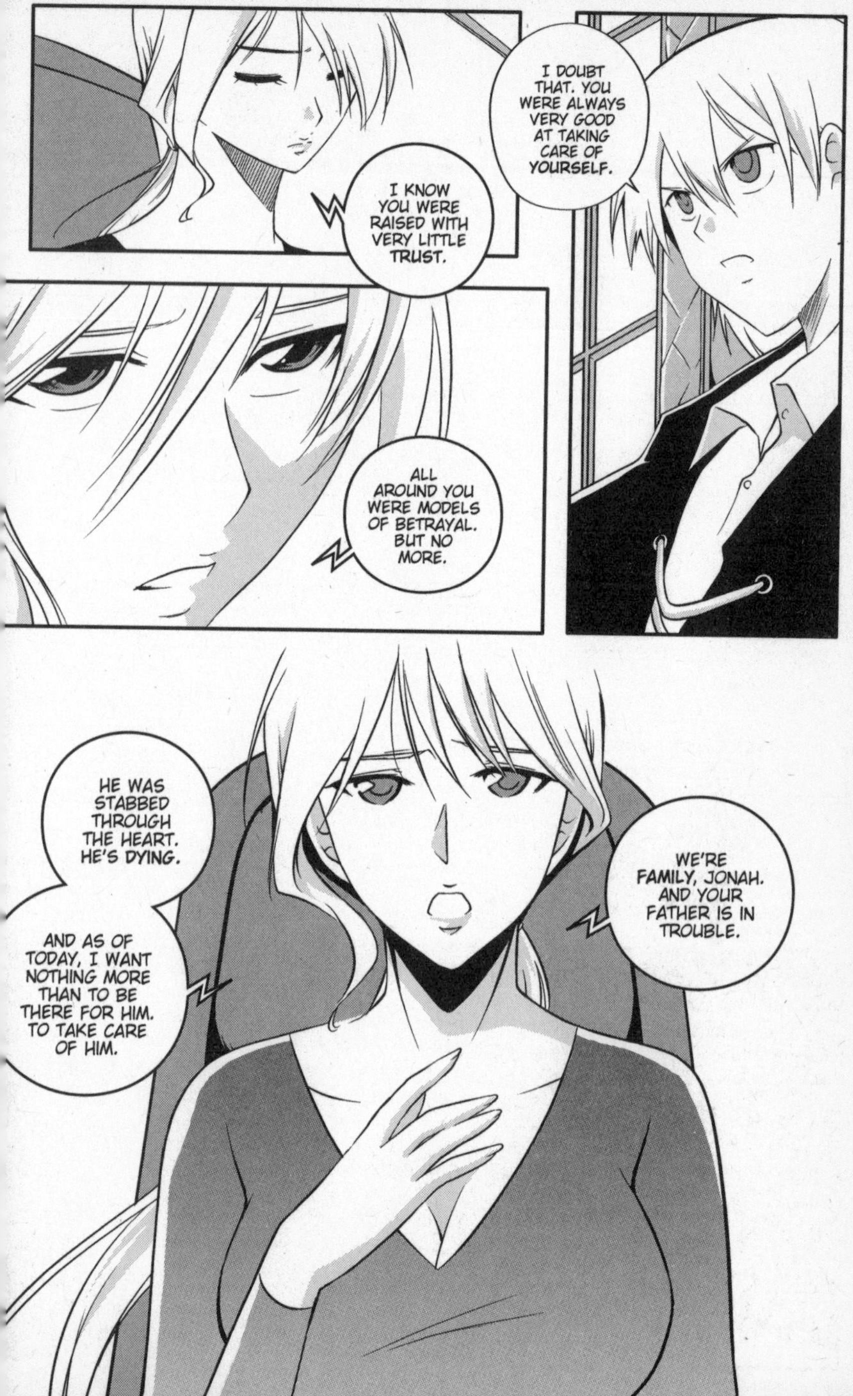
I DOUBT THAT. YOU WERE ALWAYS VERY GOOD AT TAKING CARE OF YOURSELF.
I KNOW YOU WERE RAISED WITH VERY LITTLE TRUST.
ALL AROUND YOU WERE MODELS OF BETRAYAL. BUT NO MORE.
WE'RE FAMILY, JONAH. AND YOUR FATHER IS IN TROUBLE.
HE WAS STABBED THROUGH THE HEART. HE'S DYING.
AND AS OF TODAY, I WANT NOTHING MORE THAN TO BE THERE FOR HIM. TO TAKE CARE OF HIM.

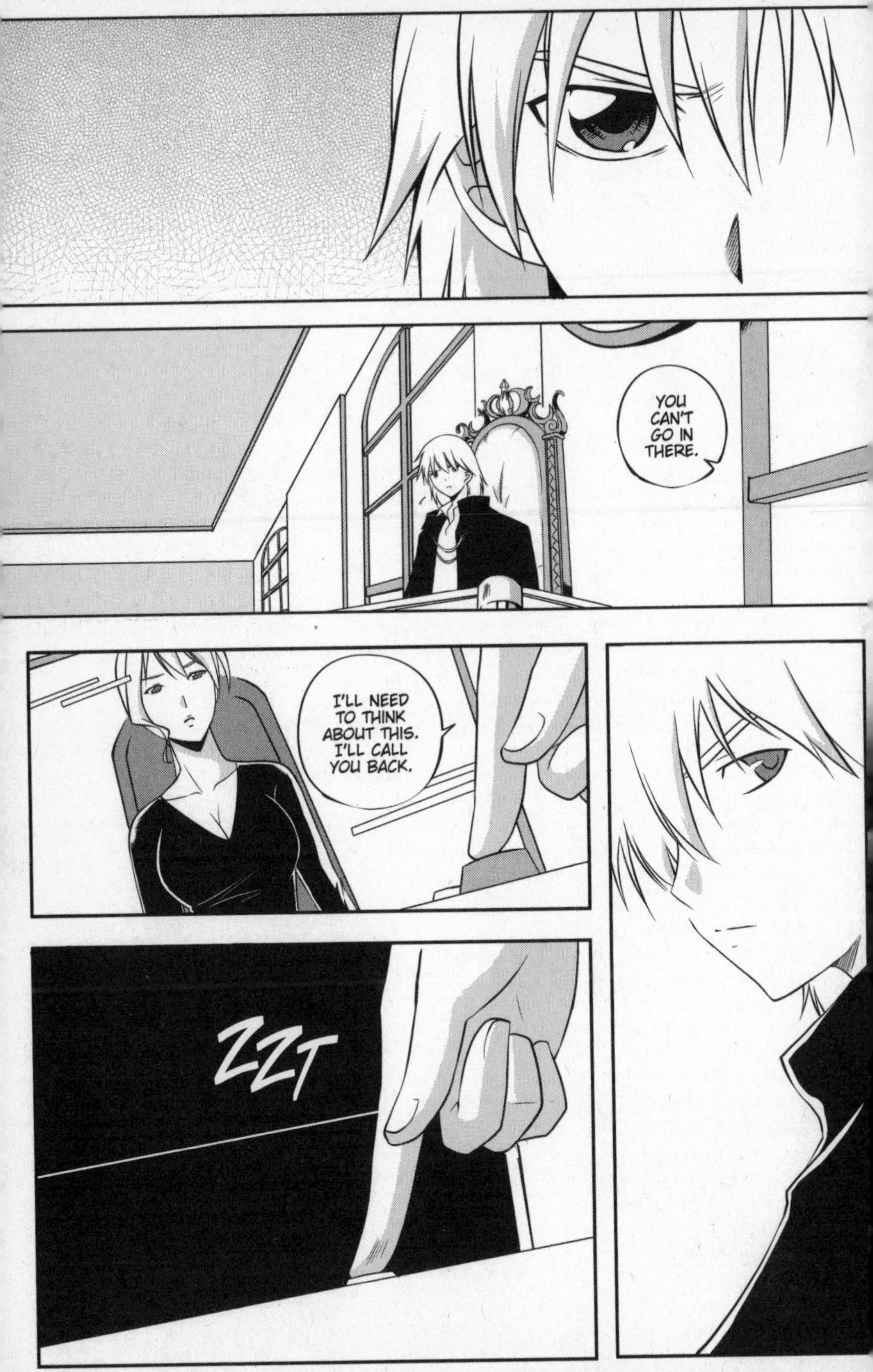
YOU CAN'T GO IN THERE.
I'LL NEED TO THINK ABOUT THIS. I'LL CALL YOU BACK.
ZZT

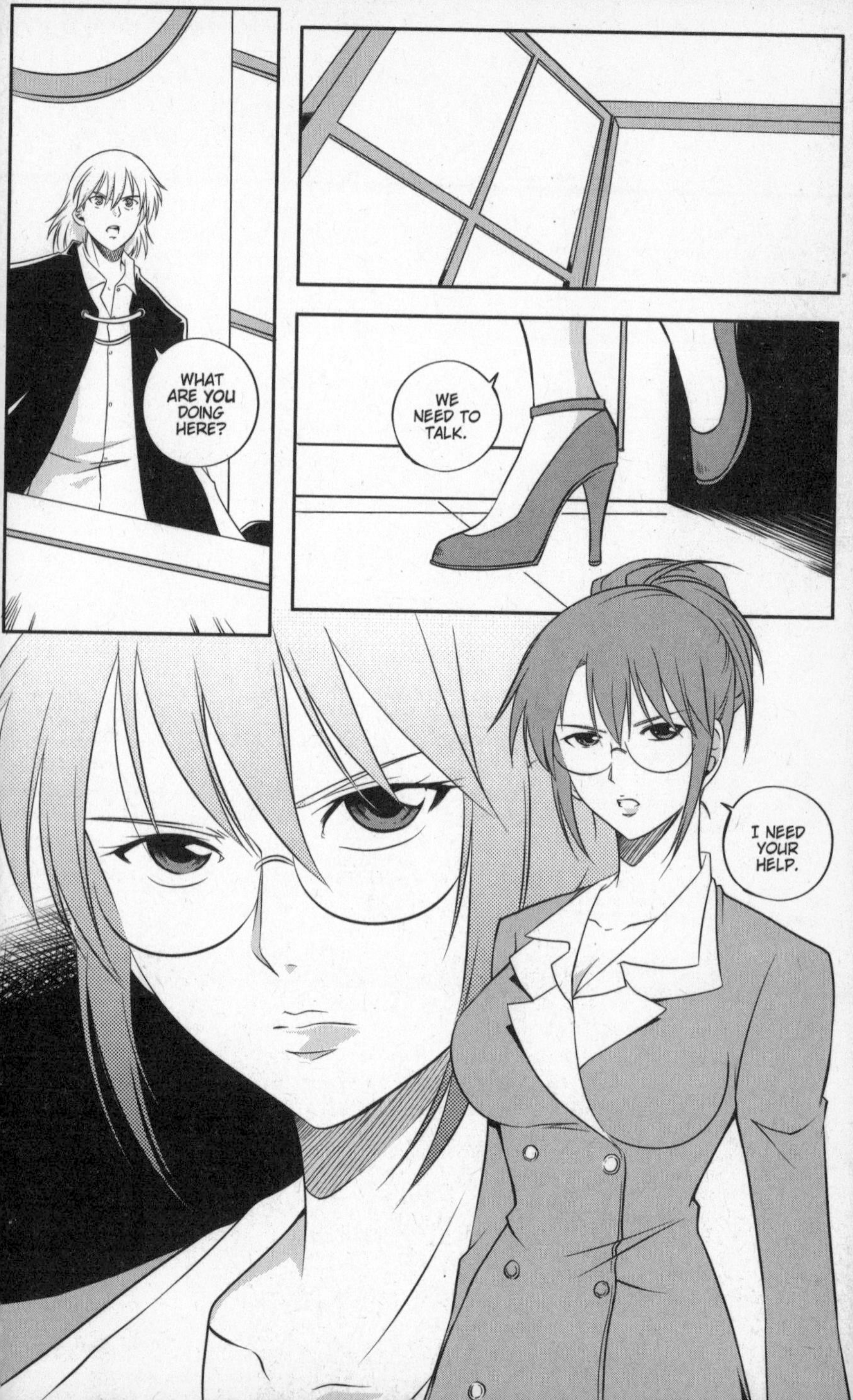
WE NEED TO TALK.
WHAT ARE YOU DOING HERE?
I NEED YOUR HELP.

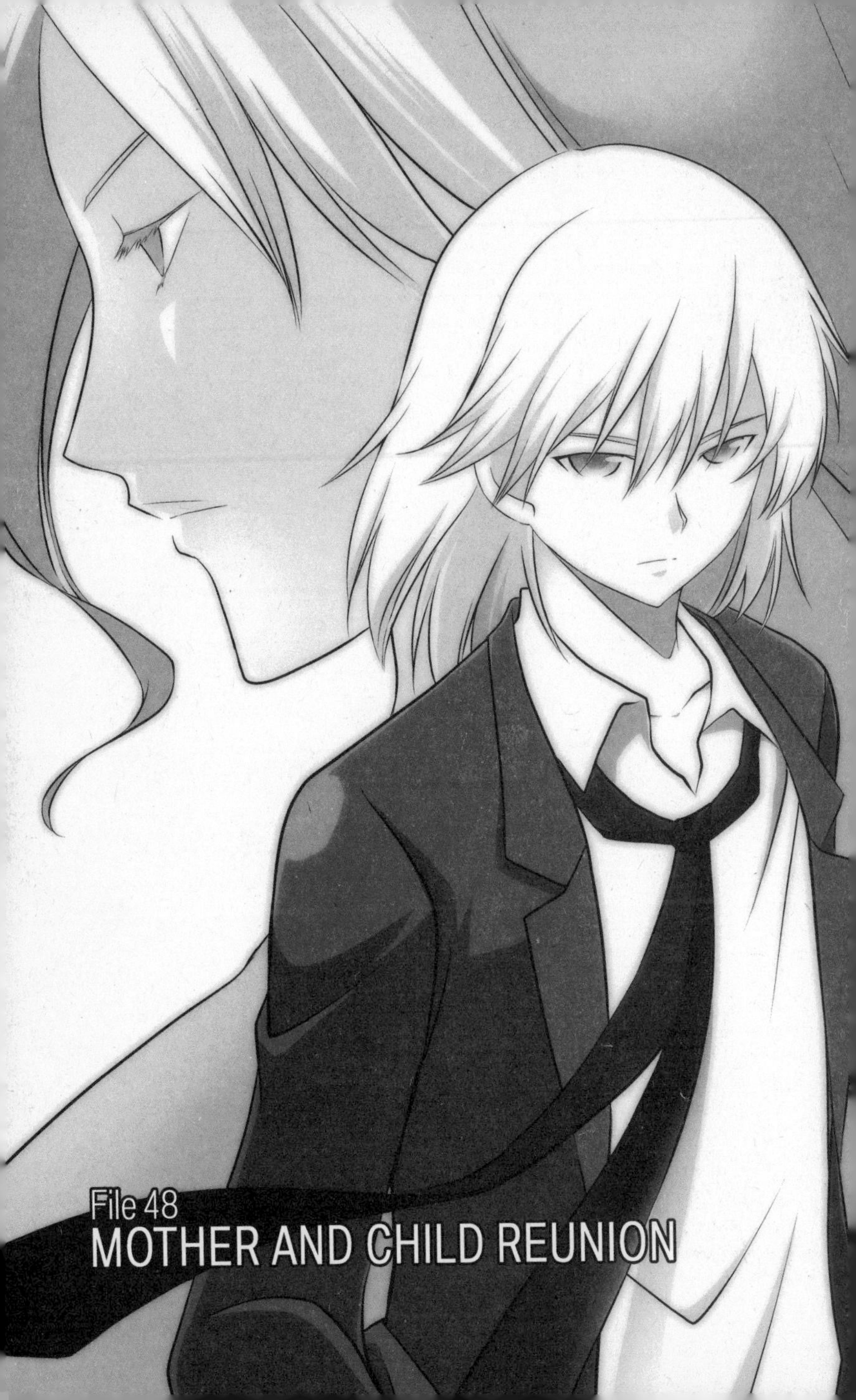

File 48

MOTHER AND CHILD REUNION

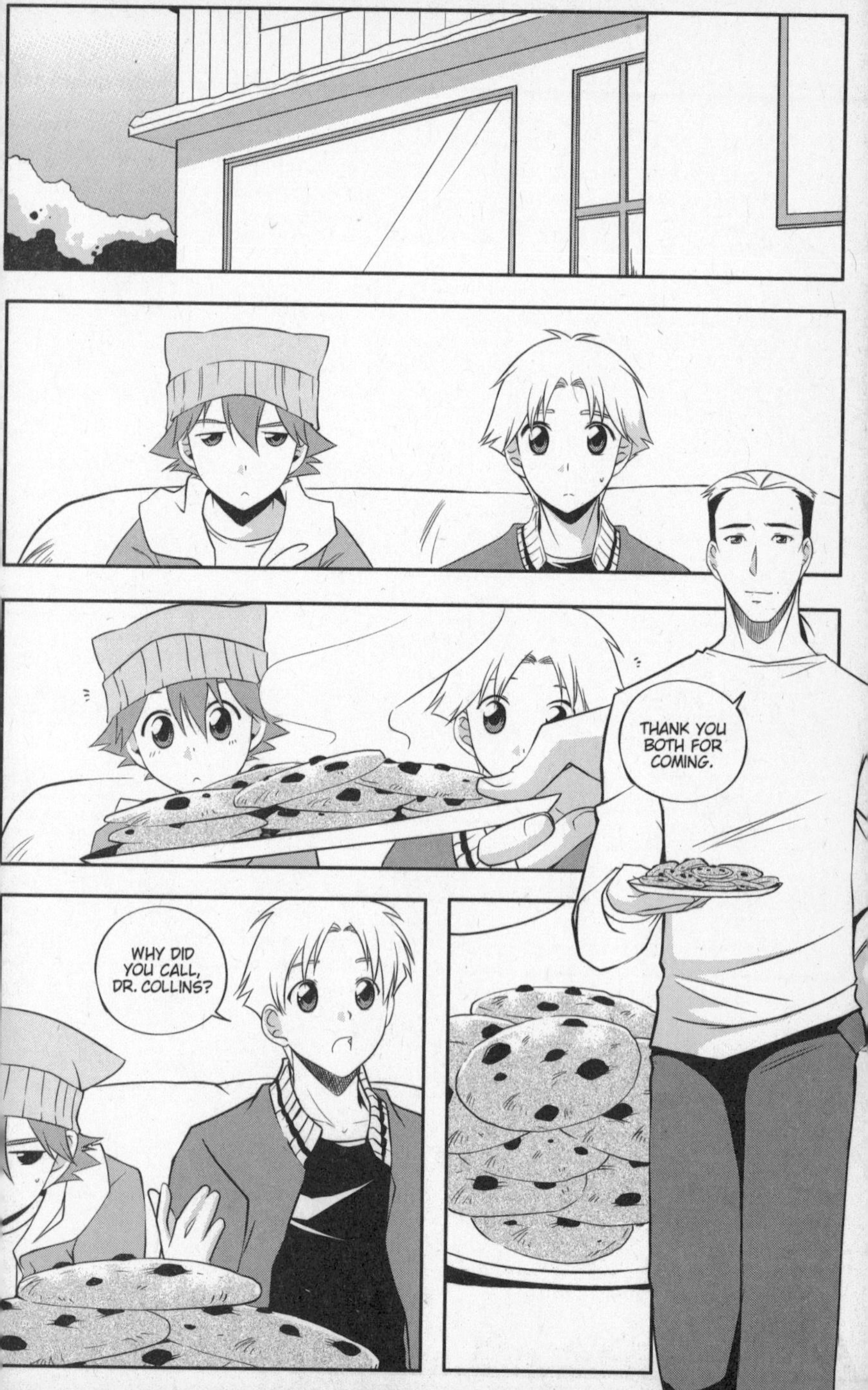
THANK YOU BOTH FOR COMING.
WHY DID YOU CALL, DR. COLLINS?

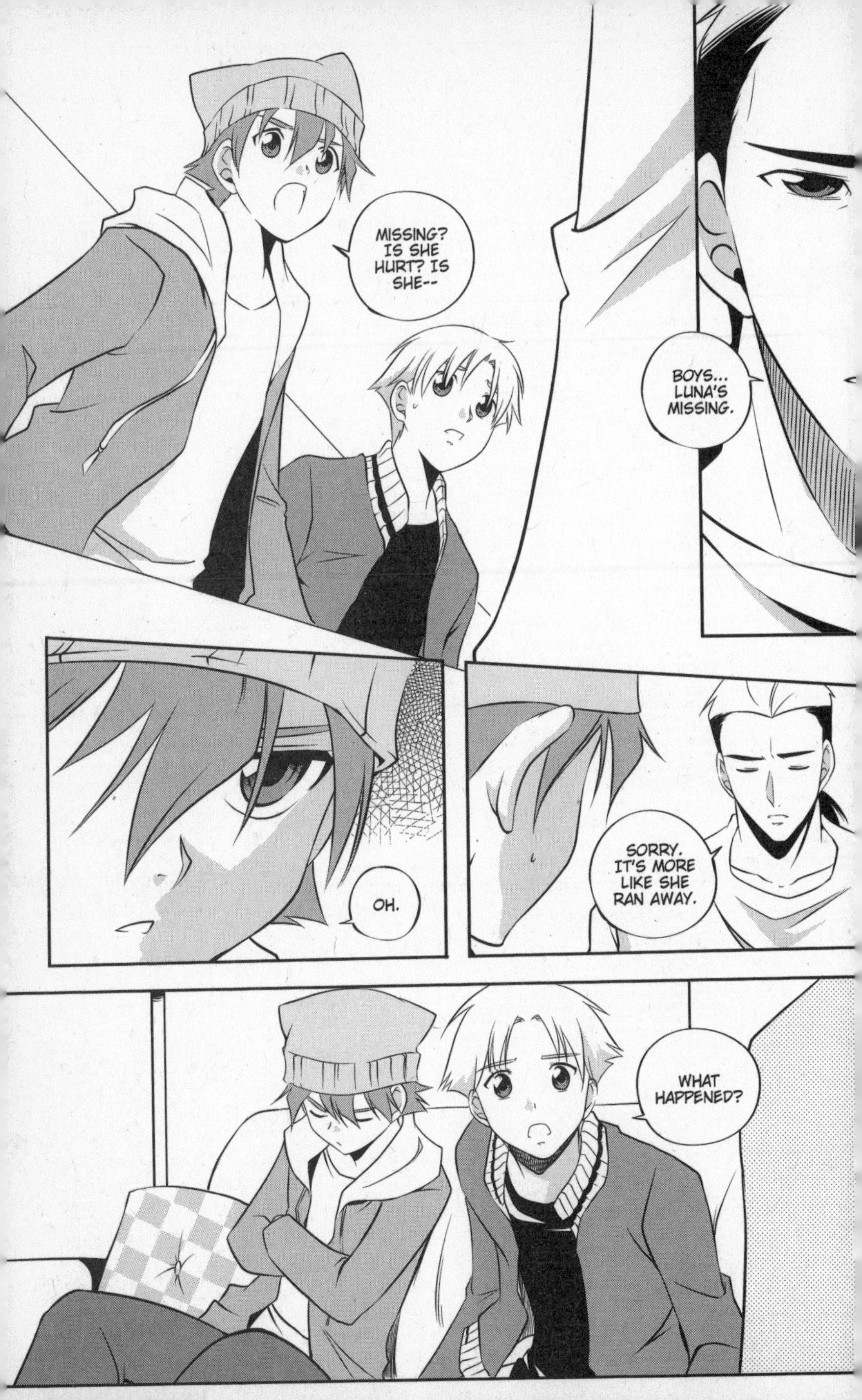
BOYS... LUNA'S MISSING.
MISSING? IS SHE HURT? IS SHE--
SORRY. IT'S MORE LIKE SHE RAN AWAY.
OH.
WHAT HAPPENED?

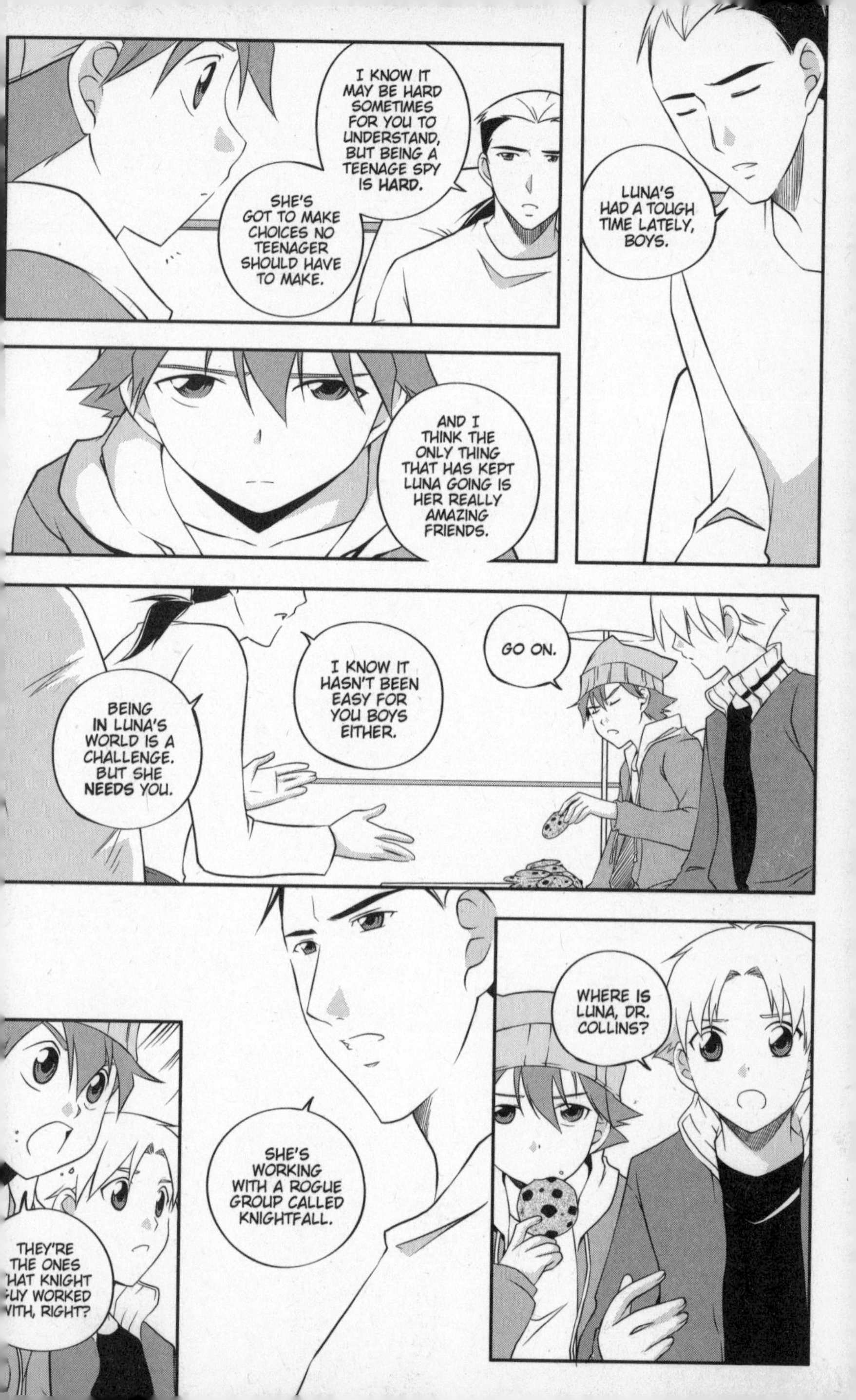
LUNA'S HAD A TOUGH TIME LATELY, BOYS.
I KNOW IT MAY BE HARD SOMETIMES FOR YOU TO UNDERSTAND, BUT BEING A TEENAGE SPY IS HARD.
SHE'S GOT TO MAKE CHOICES NO TEENAGER SHOULD HAVE TO MAKE.
AND I THINK THE ONLY THING THAT HAS KEPT LUNA GOING IS HER REALLY AMAZING FRIENDS.
GO ON.
I KNOW IT HASN'T BEEN EASY FOR YOU BOYS EITHER.
BEING IN LUNA'S WORLD IS A CHALLENGE. BUT SHE NEEDS YOU.
WHERE IS LUNA, DR. COLLINS?
SHE'S WORKING WITH A ROGUE GROUP CALLED KNIGHTFALL.
THEY'RE THE ONES HAT KNIGHT GUY WORKED WITH, RIGHT?

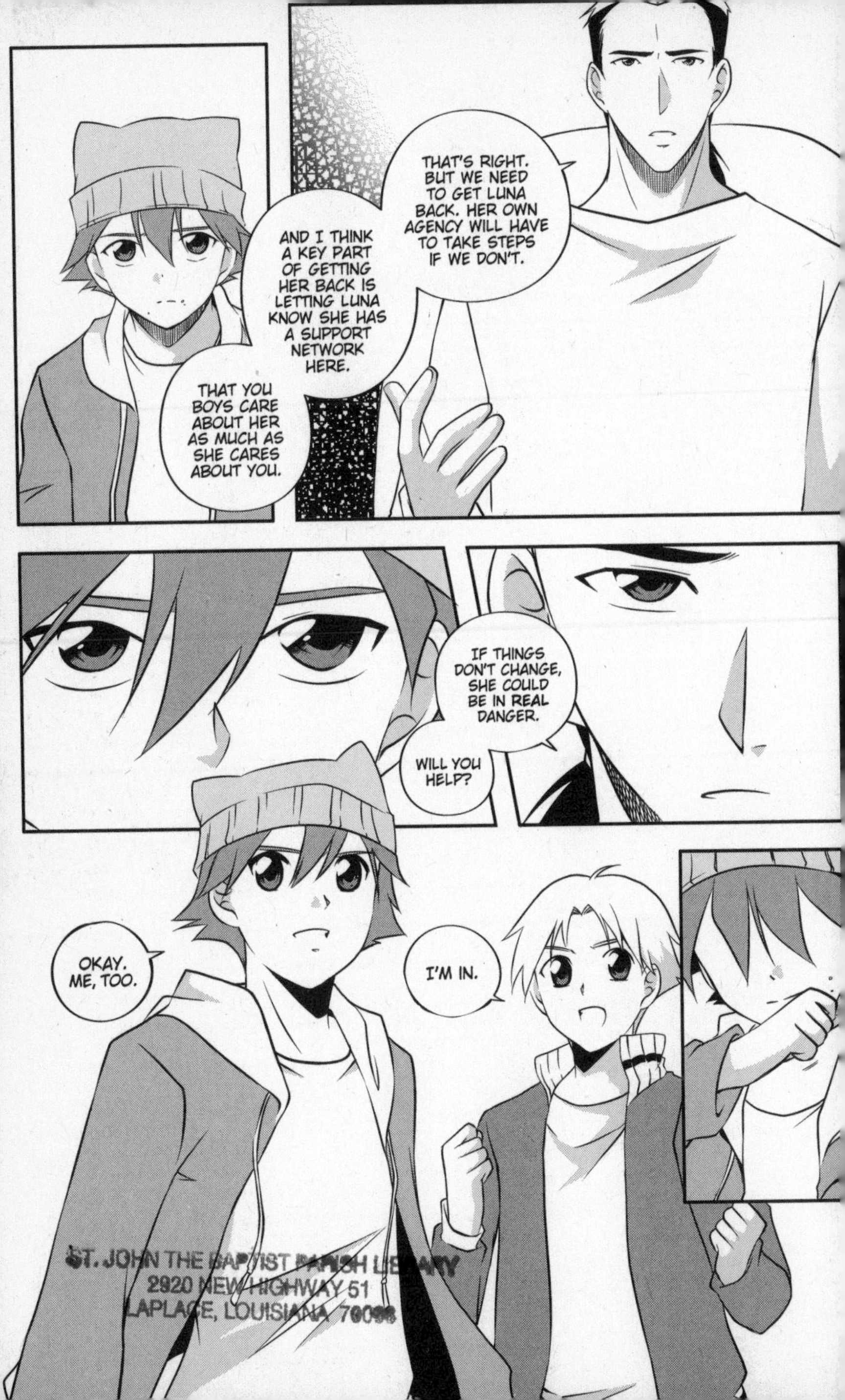
THAT'S RIGHT. BUT WE NEED TO GET LUNA BACK. HER OWN AGENCY WILL HAVE TO TAKE STEPS IF WE DON'T.
AND I THINK A KEY PART OF GETTING HER BACK IS LETTING LUNA KNOW SHE HAS A SUPPORT NETWORK HERE.
THAT YOU BOYS CARE ABOUT HER AS MUCH AS SHE CARES ABOUT YOU.
IF THINGS DON'T CHANGE, SHE COULD BE IN REAL DANGER.
WILL YOU HELP?
I'M IN.
OKAY. ME, TOO.

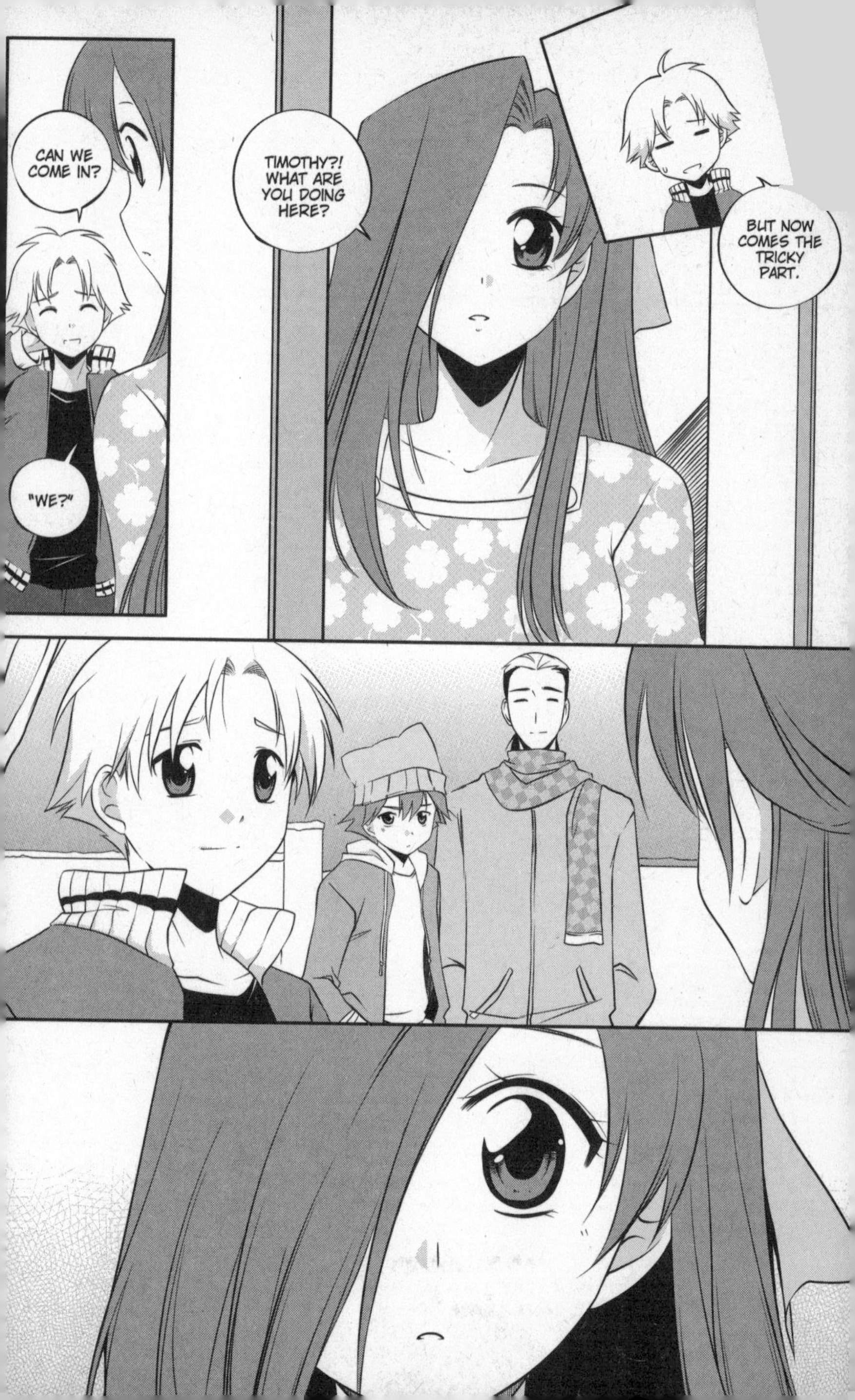
BUT NOW COMES THE TRICKY PART.
TIMOTHY?! WHAT ARE YOU DOING HERE?
CAN WE COME IN?
"WE?"

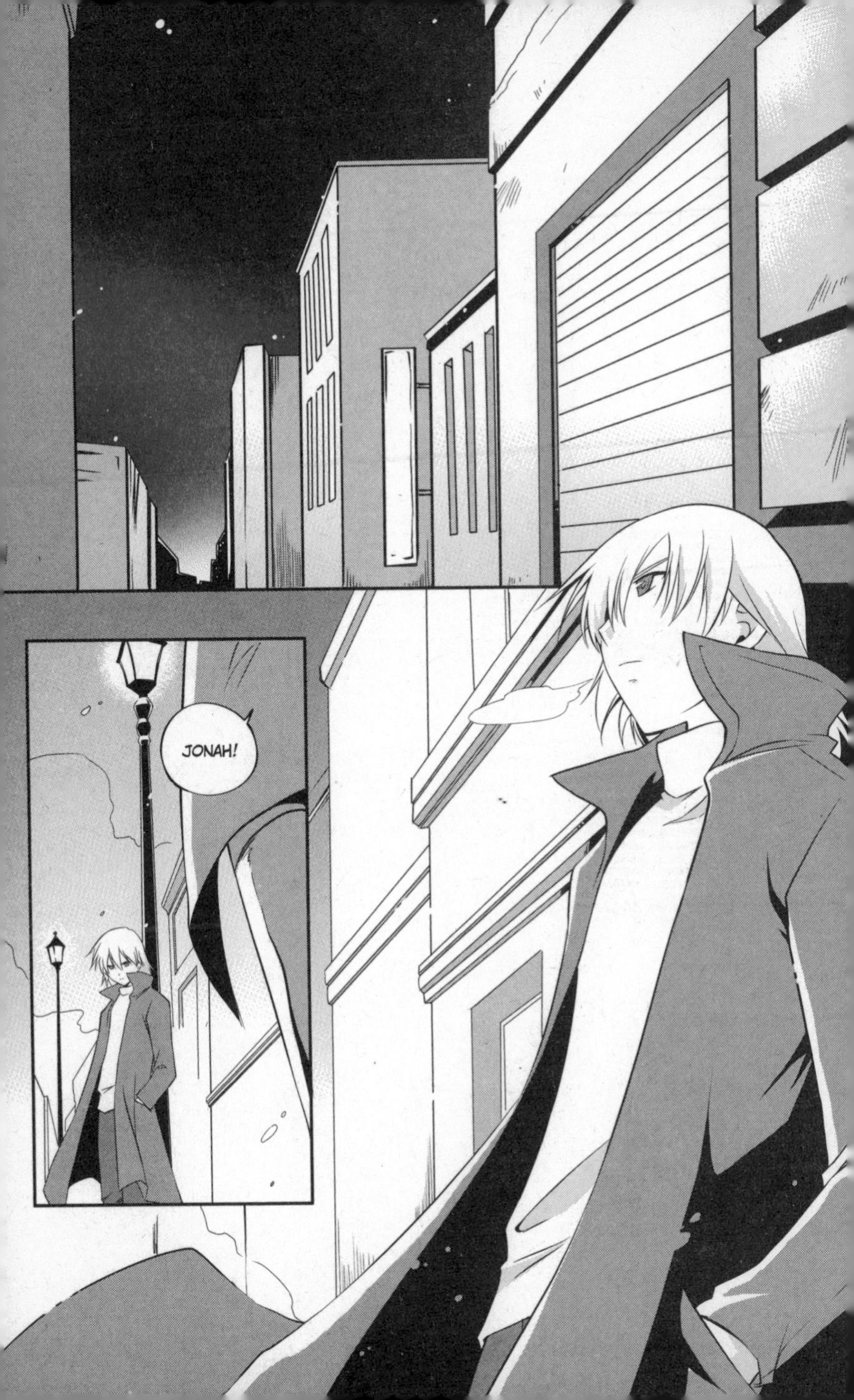
JONAH!

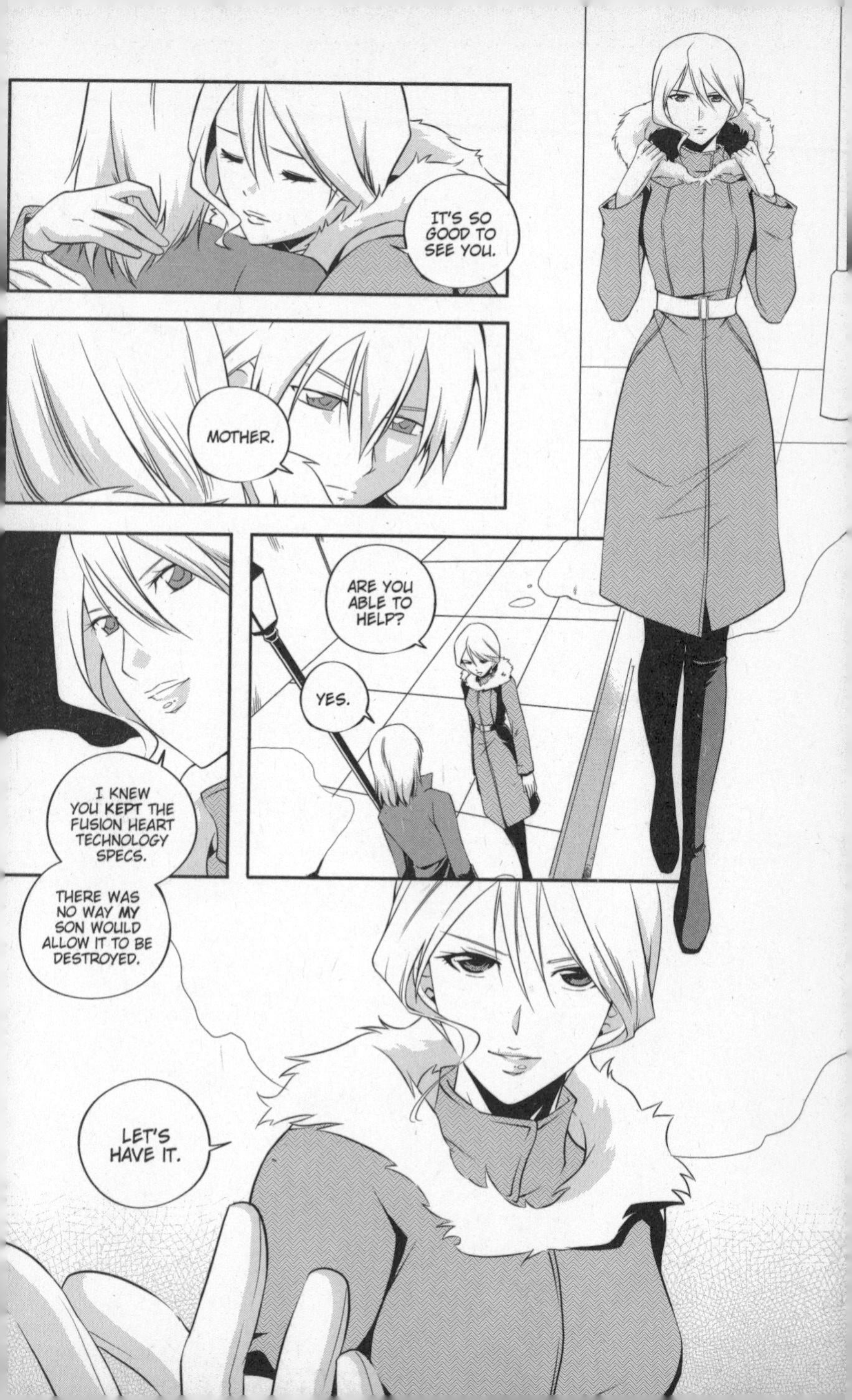
IT'S SO GOOD TO SEE YOU.
MOTHER.
ARE YOU ABLE TO HELP?
YES.
I KNEW YOU KEPT THE FUSION HEART TECHNOLOGY SPECS.
THERE WAS NO WAY MY SON WOULD ALLOW IT TO BE DESTROYED.
LET'S HAVE IT.

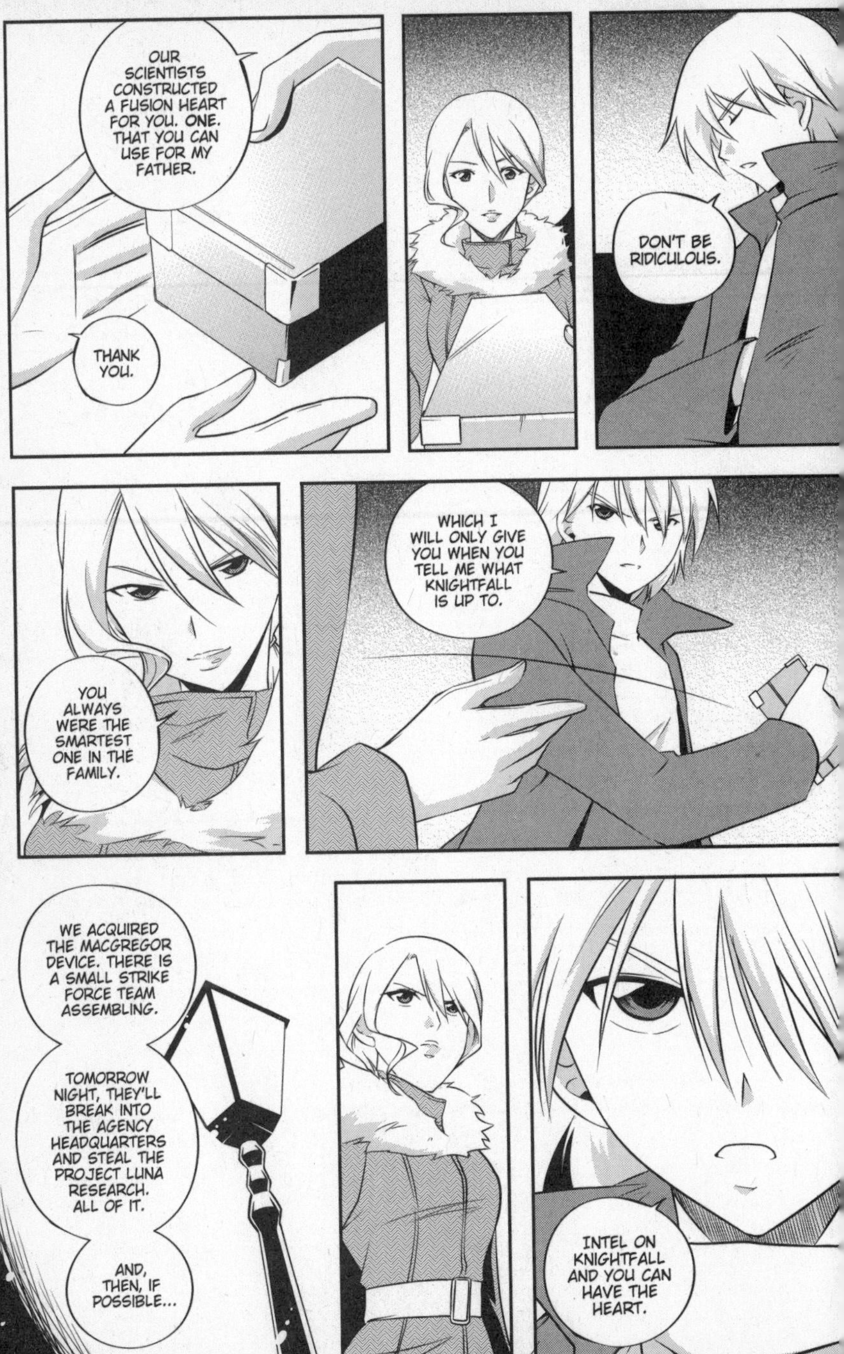
DON'T BE RIDICULOUS.
OUR SCIENTISTS CONSTRUCTED A FUSION HEART FOR YOU. ONE. THAT YOU CAN USE FOR MY FATHER.
THANK YOU.
WHICH I WILL ONLY GIVE YOU WHEN YOU TELL ME WHAT KNIGHTFALL IS UP TO.
YOU ALWAYS WERE THE SMARTEST ONE IN THE FAMILY.
INTEL ON KNIGHTFALL AND YOU CAN HAVE THE HEART.
WE ACQUIRED THE MACGREGOR DEVICE. THERE IS A SMALL STRIKE FORCE TEAM ASSEMBLING.
TOMORROW NIGHT, THEY'LL BREAK INTO THE AGENCY HEADQUARTERS AND STEAL THE PROJECT LUNA RESEARCH. ALL OF IT.
AND, THEN, IF POSSIBLE...

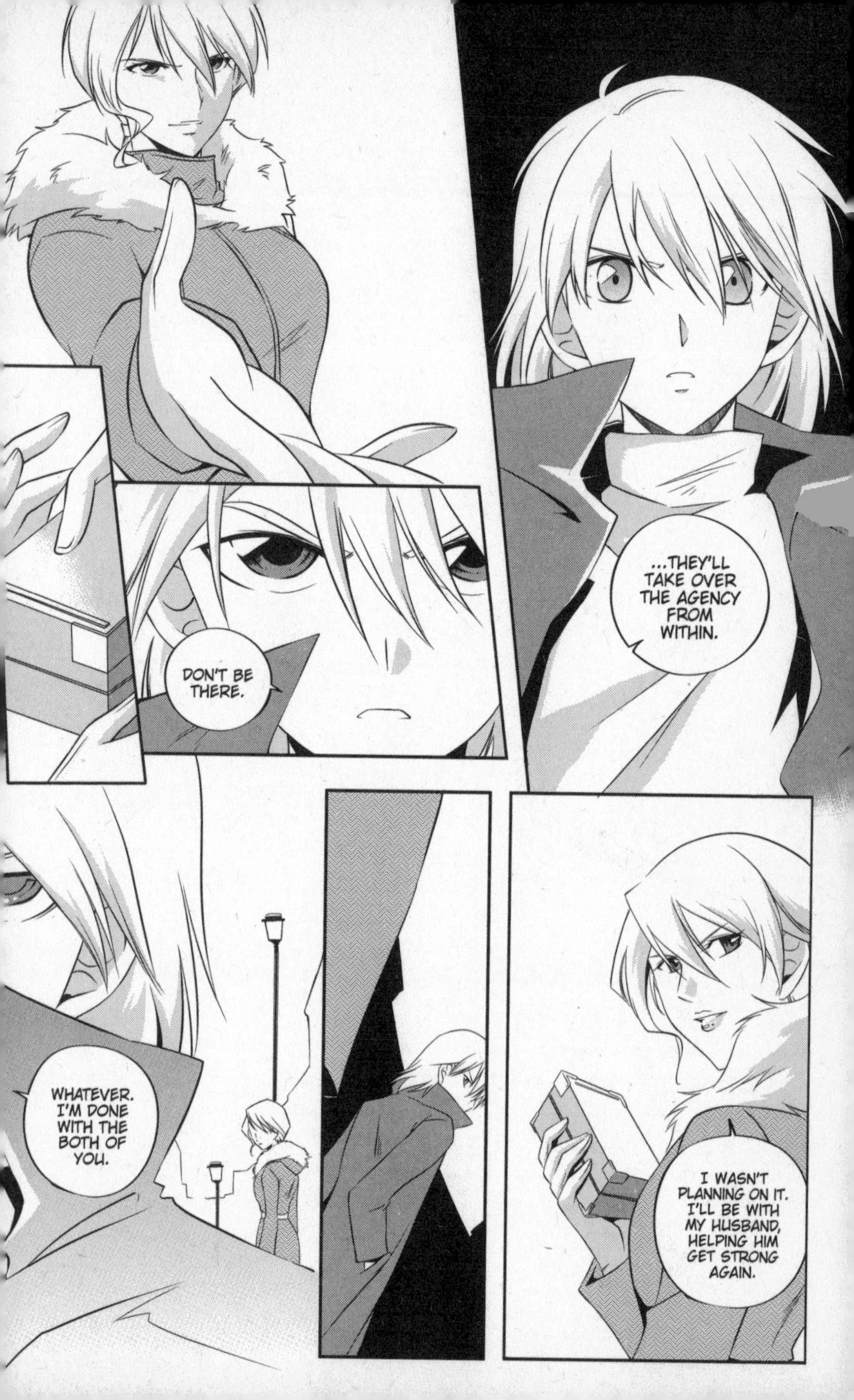
...THEY'LL TAKE OVER THE AGENCY FROM WITHIN.
DON'T BE THERE.
I WASN'T PLANNING ON IT. I'LL BE WITH MY HUSBAND, HELPING HIM GET STRONG AGAIN.
WHATEVER. I'M DONE WITH THE BOTH OF YOU.

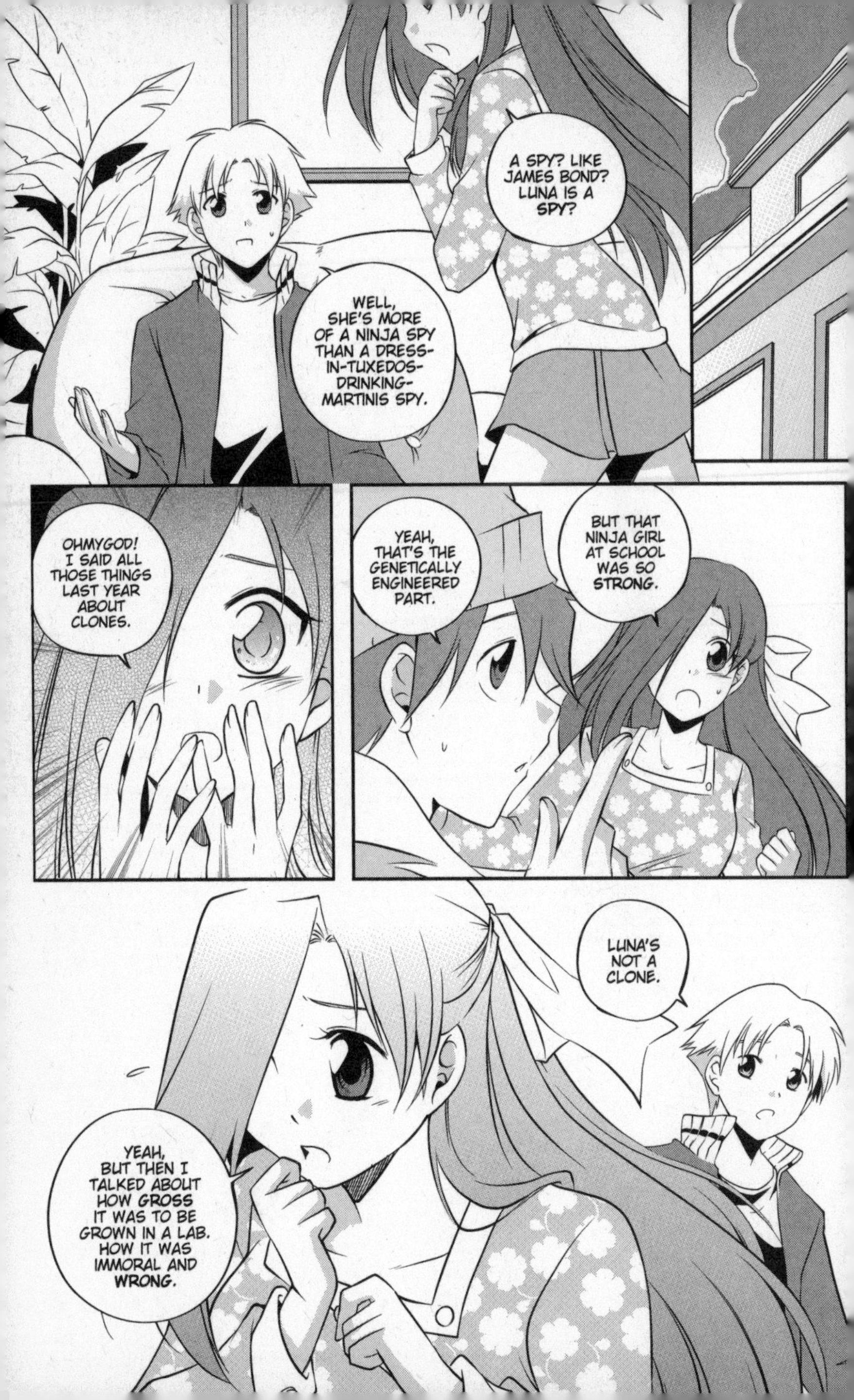
A SPY? LIKE JAMES BOND? LUNA IS A SPY?
WELL, SHE'S MORE OF A NINJA SPY THAN A DRESS-IN-TUXEDOS-DRINKING-MARTINIS SPY.
BUT THAT NINJA GIRL AT SCHOOL WAS SO STRONG.
YEAH, THAT'S THE GENETICALLY ENGINEERED PART.
OHMYGOD! I SAID ALL THOSE THINGS LAST YEAR ABOUT CLONES.
LUNA'S NOT A CLONE.
YEAH, BUT THEN I TALKED ABOUT HOW GROSS IT WAS TO BE GROWN IN A LAB. HOW IT WAS IMMORAL AND WRONG.

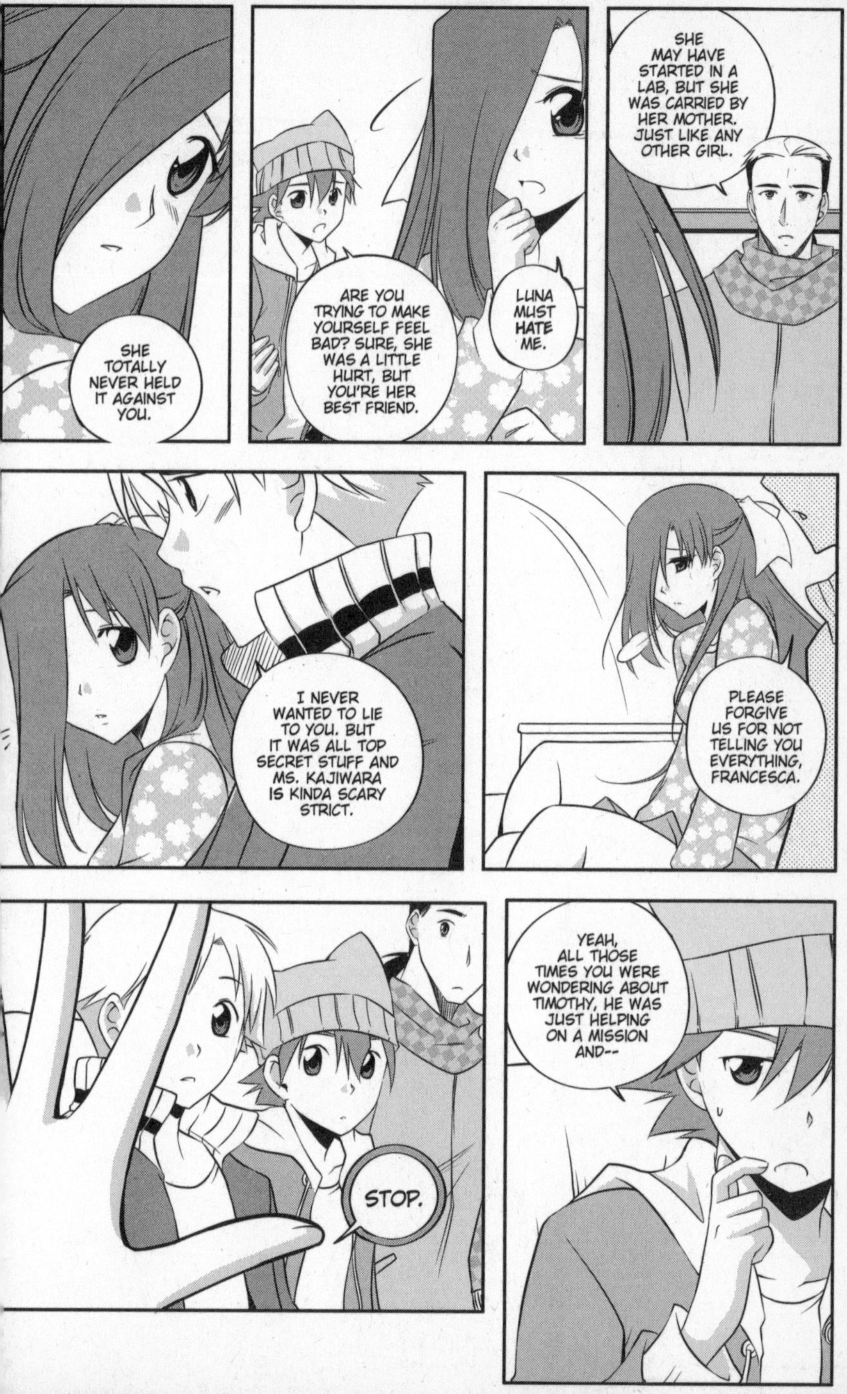
SHE MAY HAVE STARTED IN A LAB, BUT SHE WAS CARRIED BY HER MOTHER. JUST LIKE ANY OTHER GIRL.
LUNA MUST HATE ME.
ARE YOU TRYING TO MAKE YOURSELF FEEL BAD? SURE, SHE WAS A LITTLE HURT, BUT YOU'RE HER BEST FRIEND.
SHE TOTALLY NEVER HELD IT AGAINST YOU.
PLEASE FORGIVE US FOR NOT TELLING YOU EVERYTHING, FRANCESCA.
I NEVER WANTED TO LIE TO YOU. BUT IT WAS ALL TOP SECRET STUFF AND MS. KAJIWARA IS KINDA SCARY STRICT.
YEAH, ALL THOSE TIMES YOU WERE WONDERING ABOUT TIMOTHY, HE WAS JUST HELPING ON A MISSION AND--
STOP.

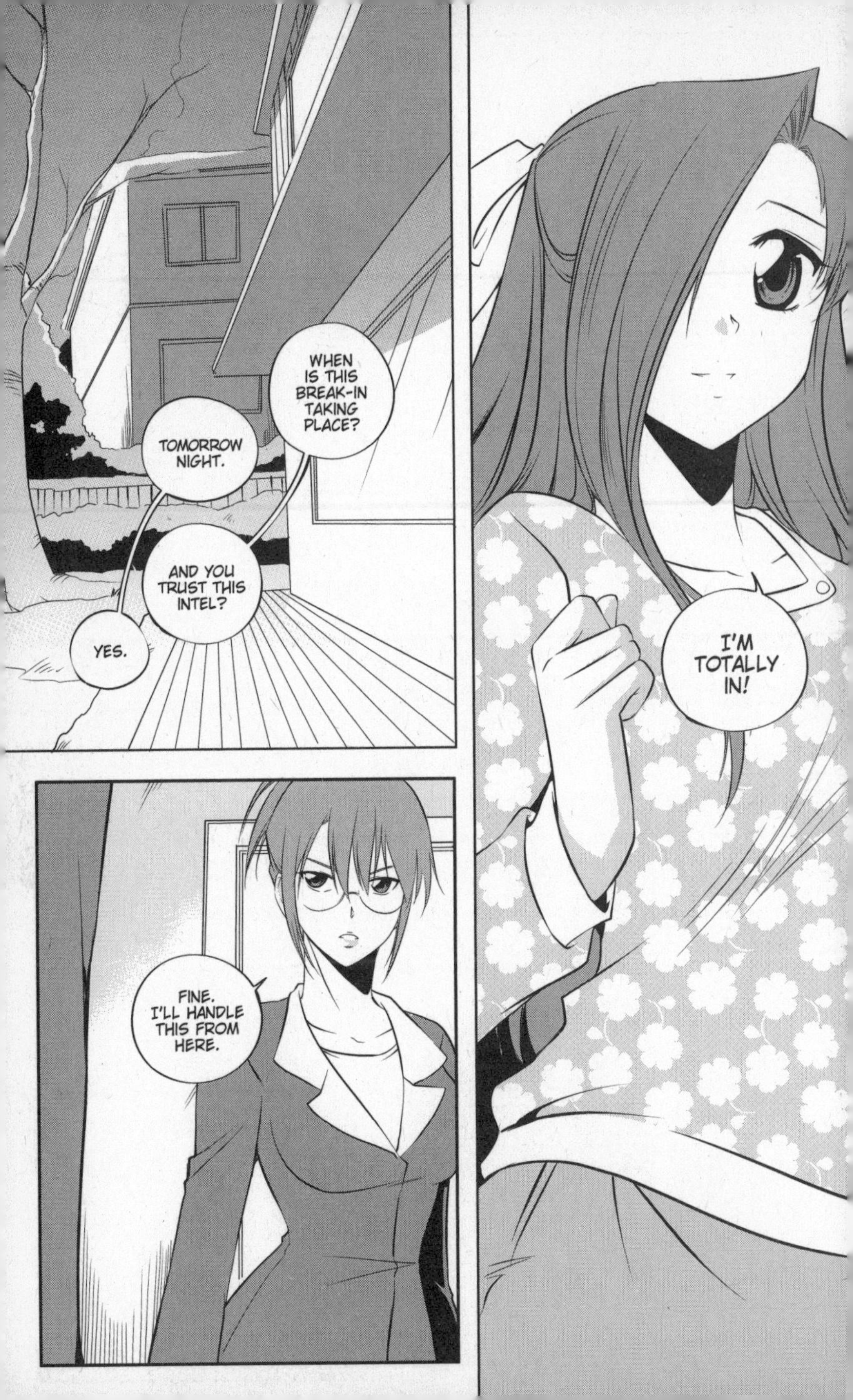
I'M TOTALLY IN!
WHEN IS THIS BREAK-IN TAKING PLACE?
TOMORROW NIGHT.
AND YOU TRUST THIS INTEL?
YES.
FINE. I'LL HANDLE THIS FROM HERE.

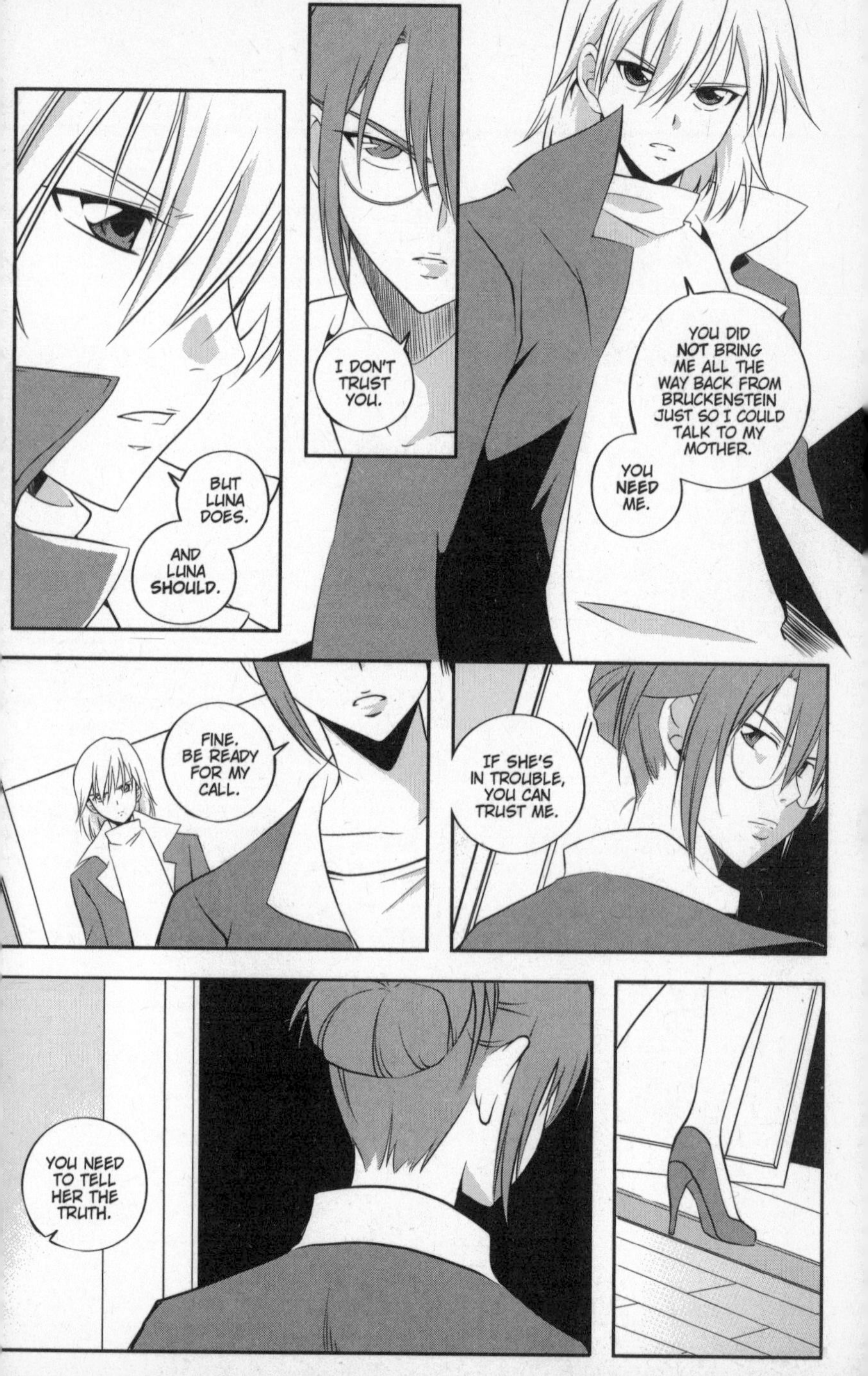
YOU DID NOT BRING ME ALL THE WAY BACK FROM BRUCKENSTEIN JUST SO I COULD TALK TO MY MOTHER.
YOU NEED ME.
I DON'T TRUST YOU.
BUT LUNA DOES.
AND LUNA SHOULD.
IF SHE'S IN TROUBLE, YOU CAN TRUST ME.
FINE. BE READY FOR MY CALL.
YOU NEED TO TELL HER THE TRUTH.

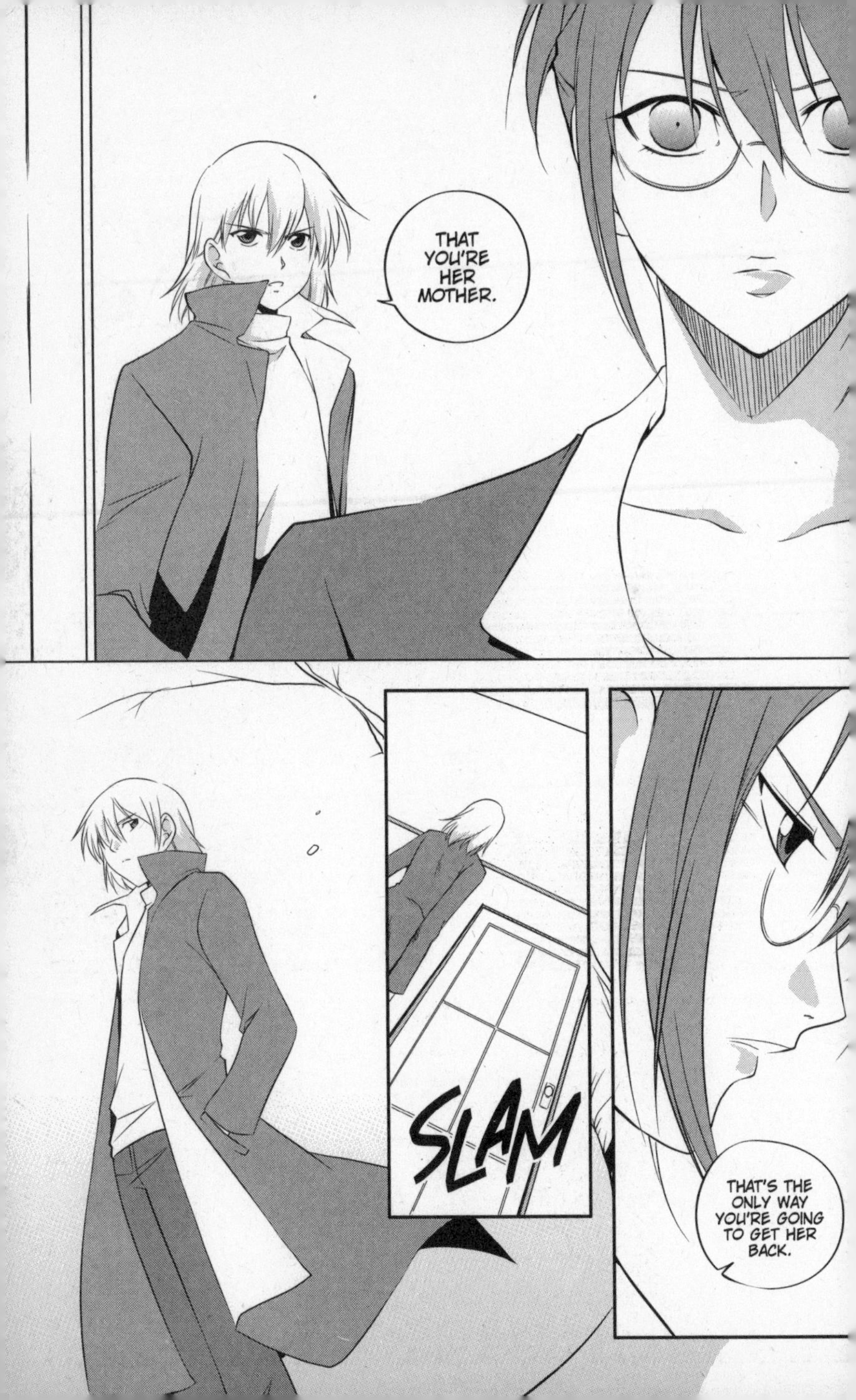
THAT YOU'RE HER MOTHER.
THAT'S THE ONLY WAY YOU'RE GOING TO GET HER BACK.
SLAM

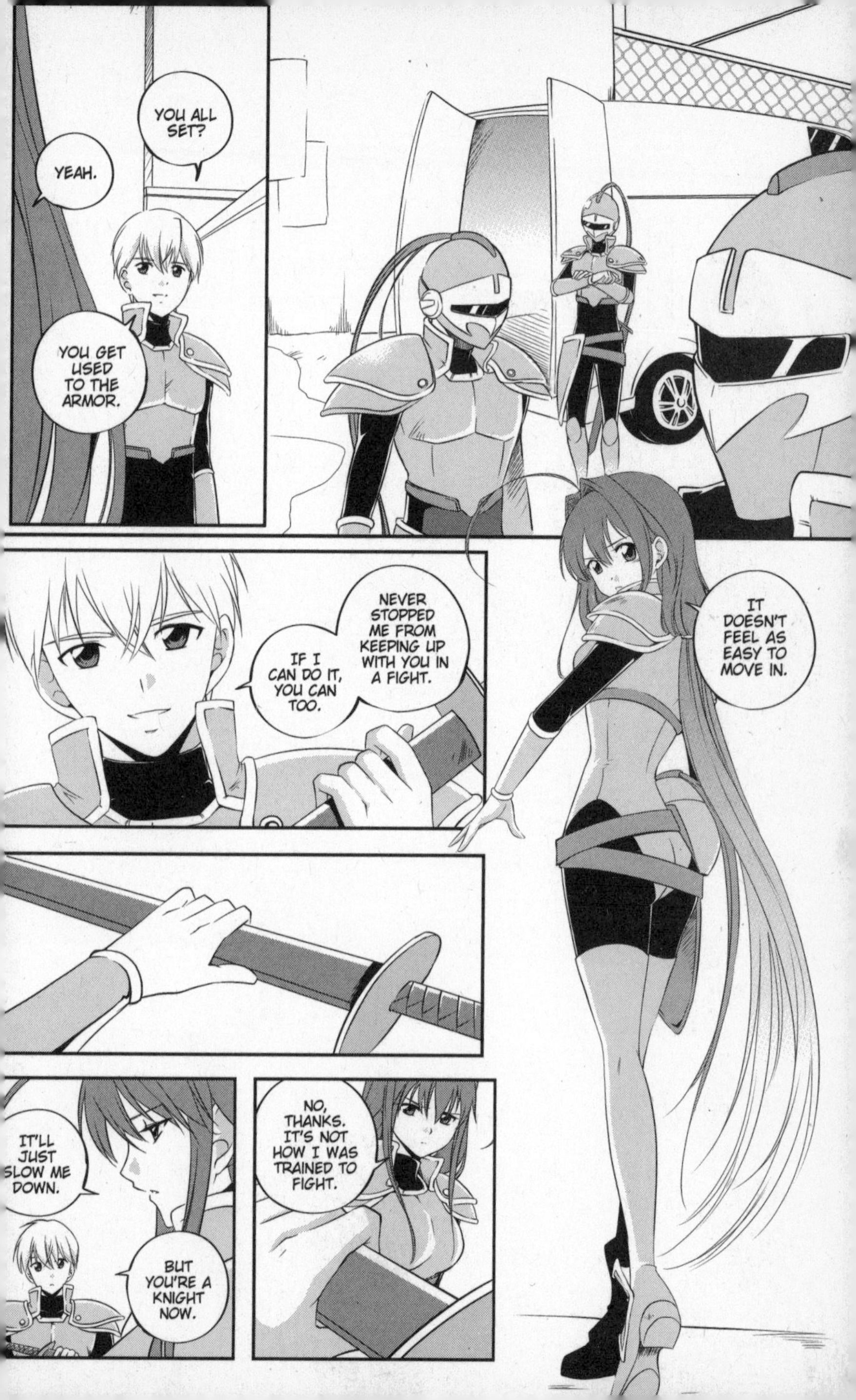
YOU ALL SET?
YEAH.
YOU GET USED TO THE ARMOR.
IT DOESN'T FEEL AS EASY TO MOVE IN.
NEVER STOPPED ME FROM KEEPING UP WITH YOU IN A FIGHT.
IF I CAN DO IT, YOU CAN TOO.
NO, THANKS. IT'S NOT HOW I WAS TRAINED TO FIGHT.
IT'LL JUST SLOW ME DOWN.
BUT YOU'RE A KNIGHT NOW.

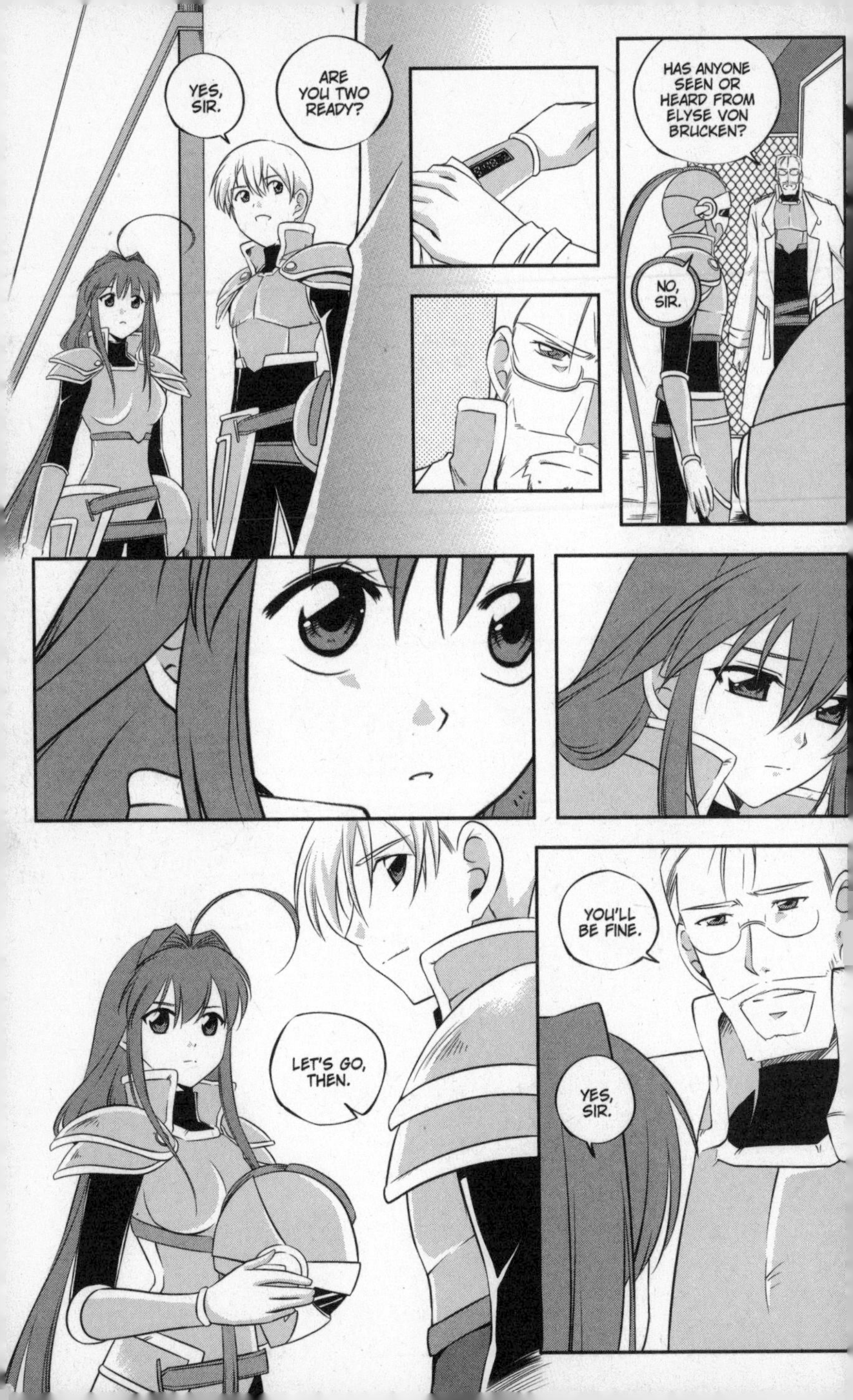
HAS ANYONE SEEN OR HEARD FROM ELYSE VON BRUCKEN?
NO, SIR.
ARE YOU TWO READY?
YES, SIR.
YOU'LL BE FINE.
YES, SIR.
LET'S GO, THEN.

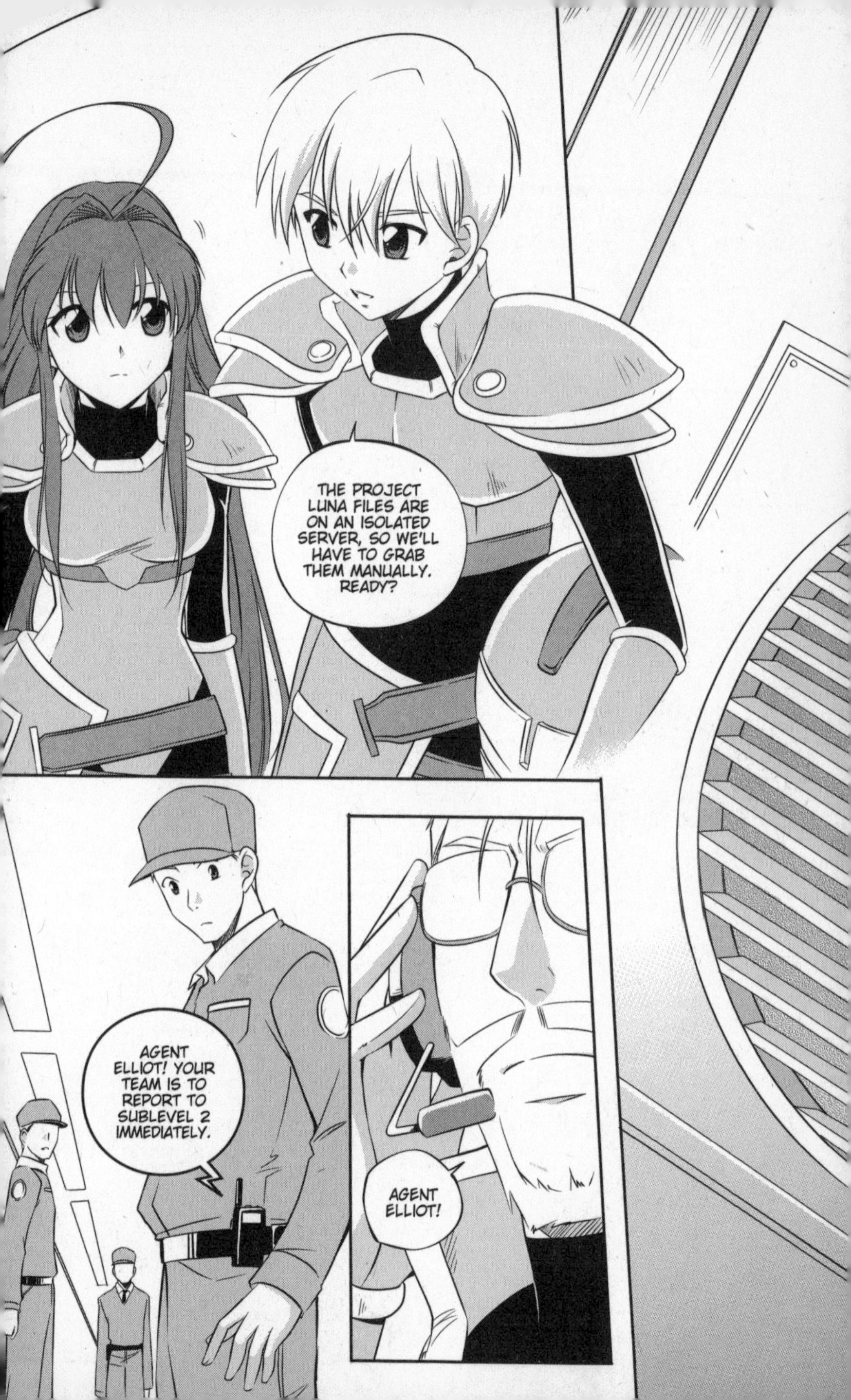
THE PROJECT LUNA FILES ARE ON AN ISOLATED SERVER, SO WE'LL HAVE TO GRAB THEM MANUALLY. READY?
AGENT ELLIOT!
AGENT ELLIOT! YOUR TEAM IS TO REPORT TO SUBLEVEL 2 IMMEDIATELY.

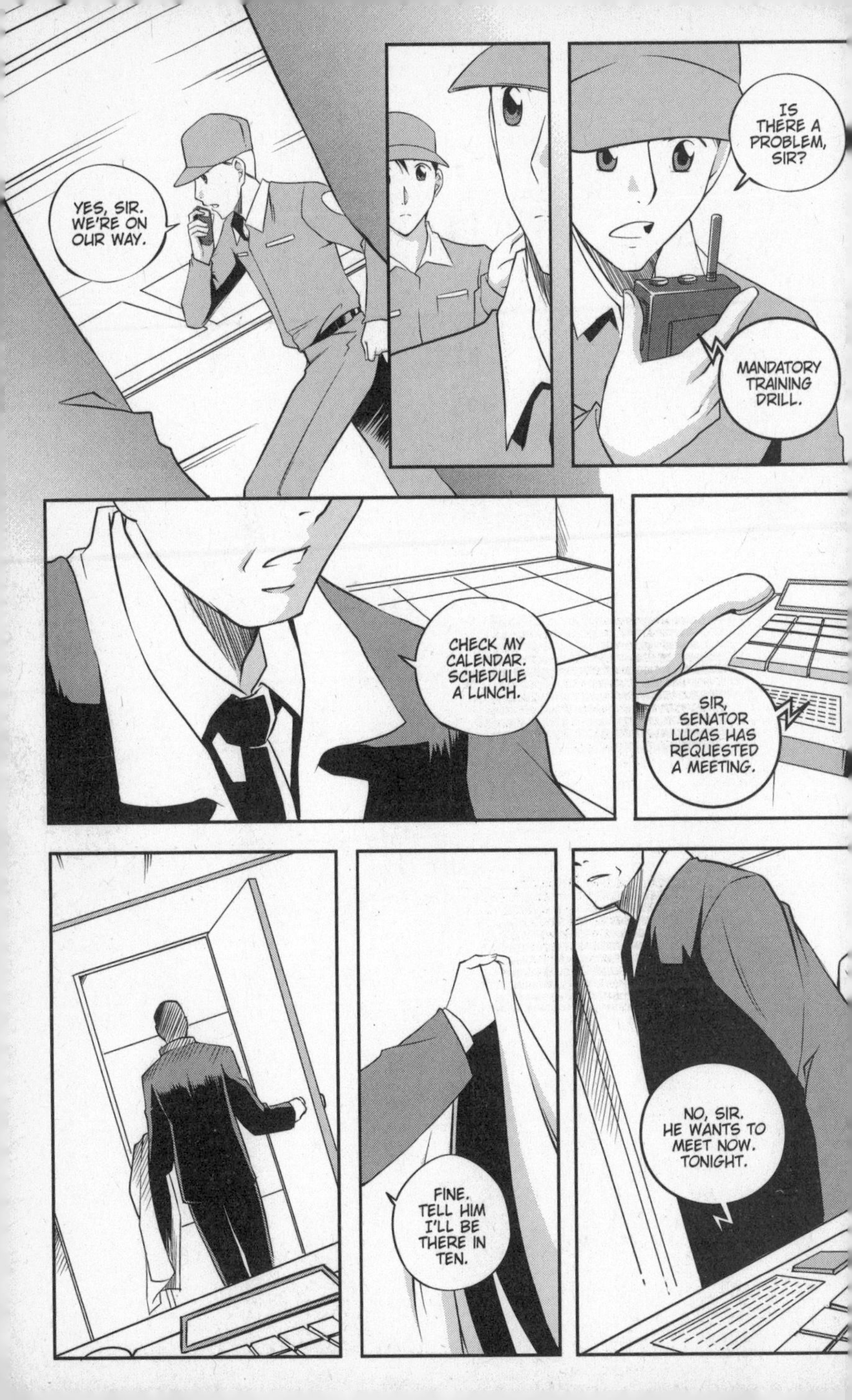
IS THERE A PROBLEM, SIR?
MANDATORY TRAINING DRILL.
YES, SIR. WE'RE ON OUR WAY.
SIR, SENATOR LUCAS HAS REQUESTED A MEETING.
CHECK MY CALENDAR. SCHEDULE A LUNCH.
NO, SIR. HE WANTS TO MEET NOW. TONIGHT.
FINE. TELL HIM I'LL BE THERE IN TEN.

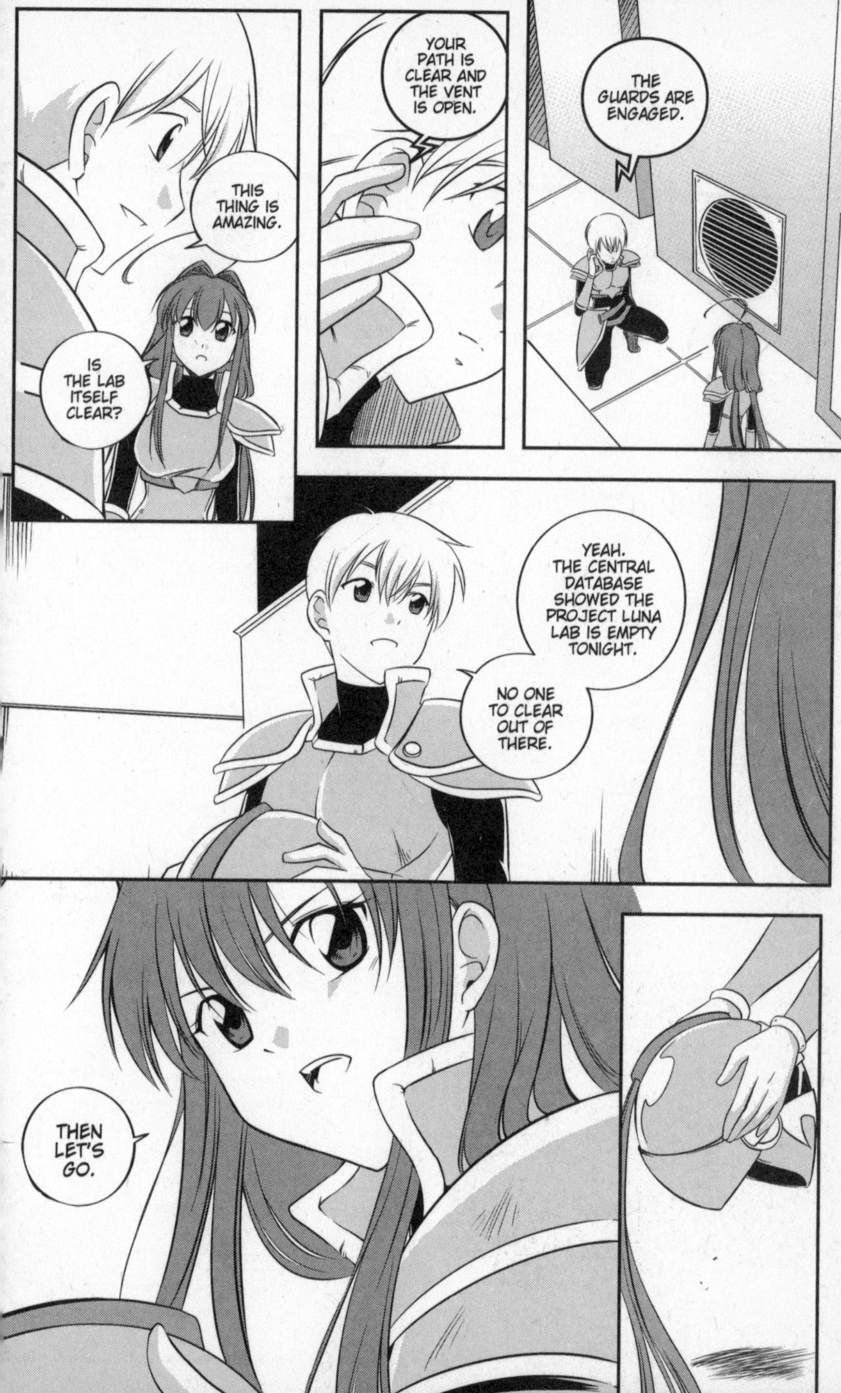
THE GUARDS ARE ENGAGED.
YOUR PATH IS CLEAR AND THE VENT IS OPEN.
THIS THING IS AMAZING.
IS THE LAB ITSELF CLEAR?
YEAH. THE CENTRAL DATABASE SHOWED THE PROJECT LUNA LAB IS EMPTY TONIGHT.
NO ONE TO CLEAR OUT OF THERE.
THEN LET'S GO.

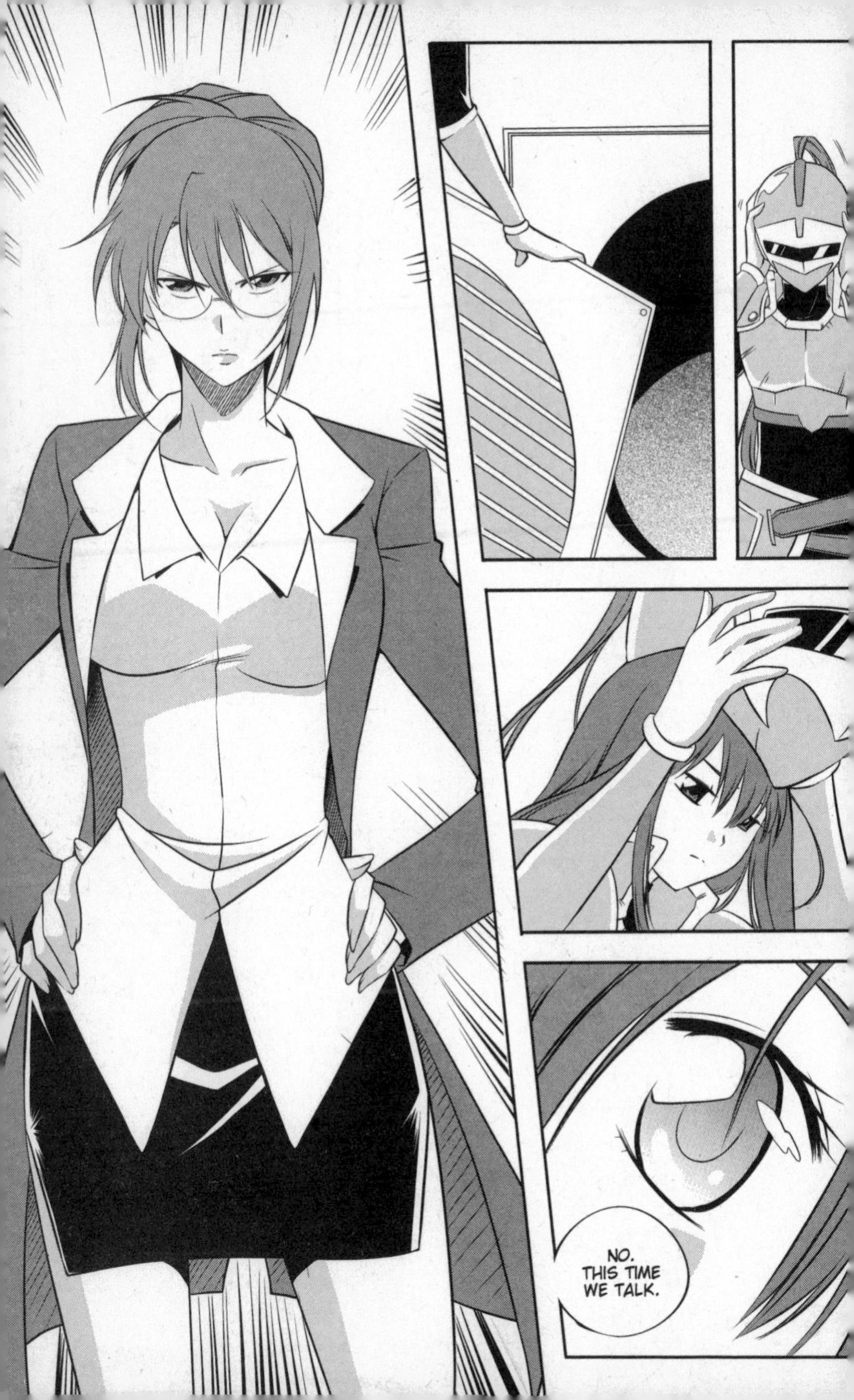
NO. THIS TIME WE TALK.

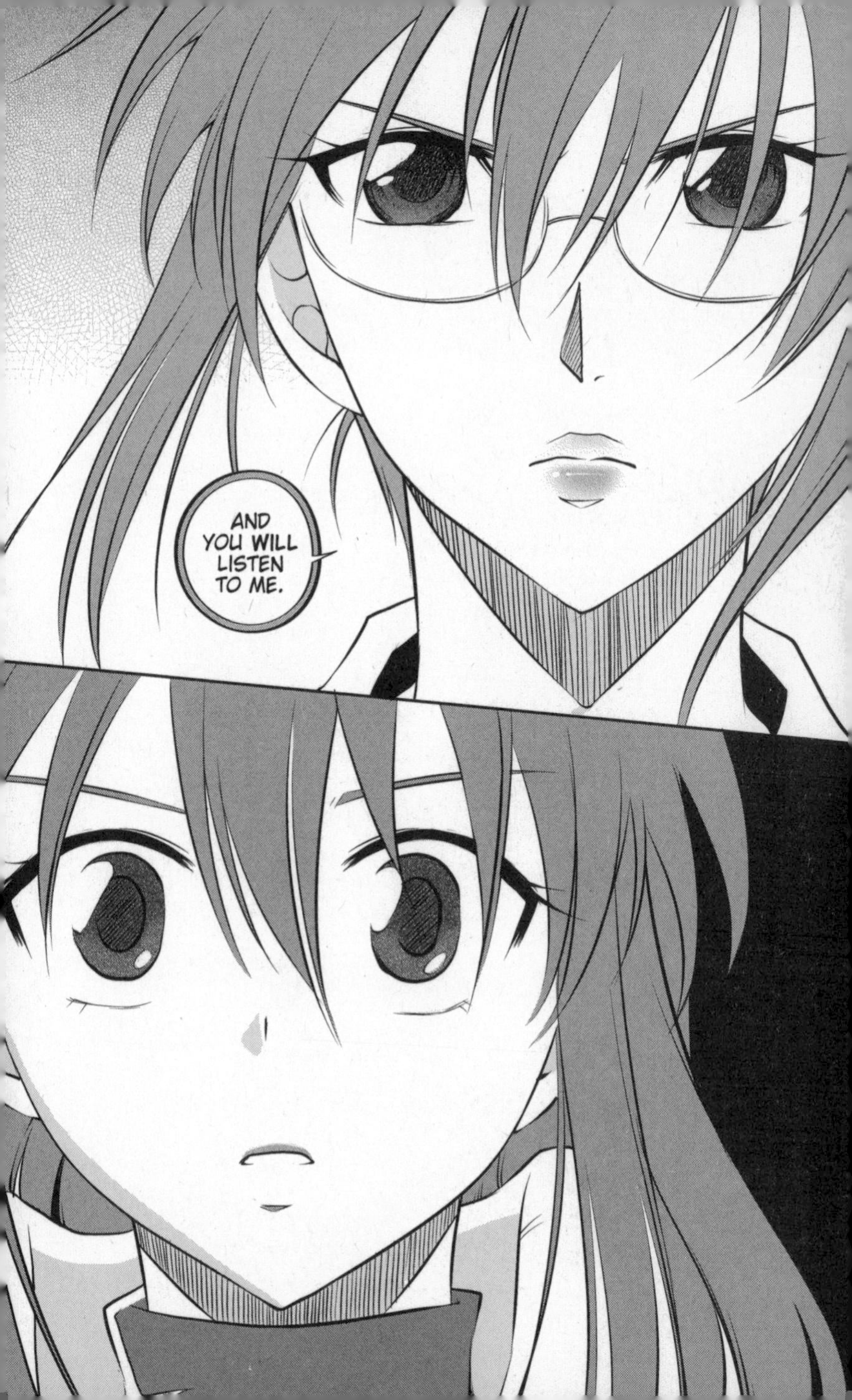
AND YOU WILL LISTEN TO ME.

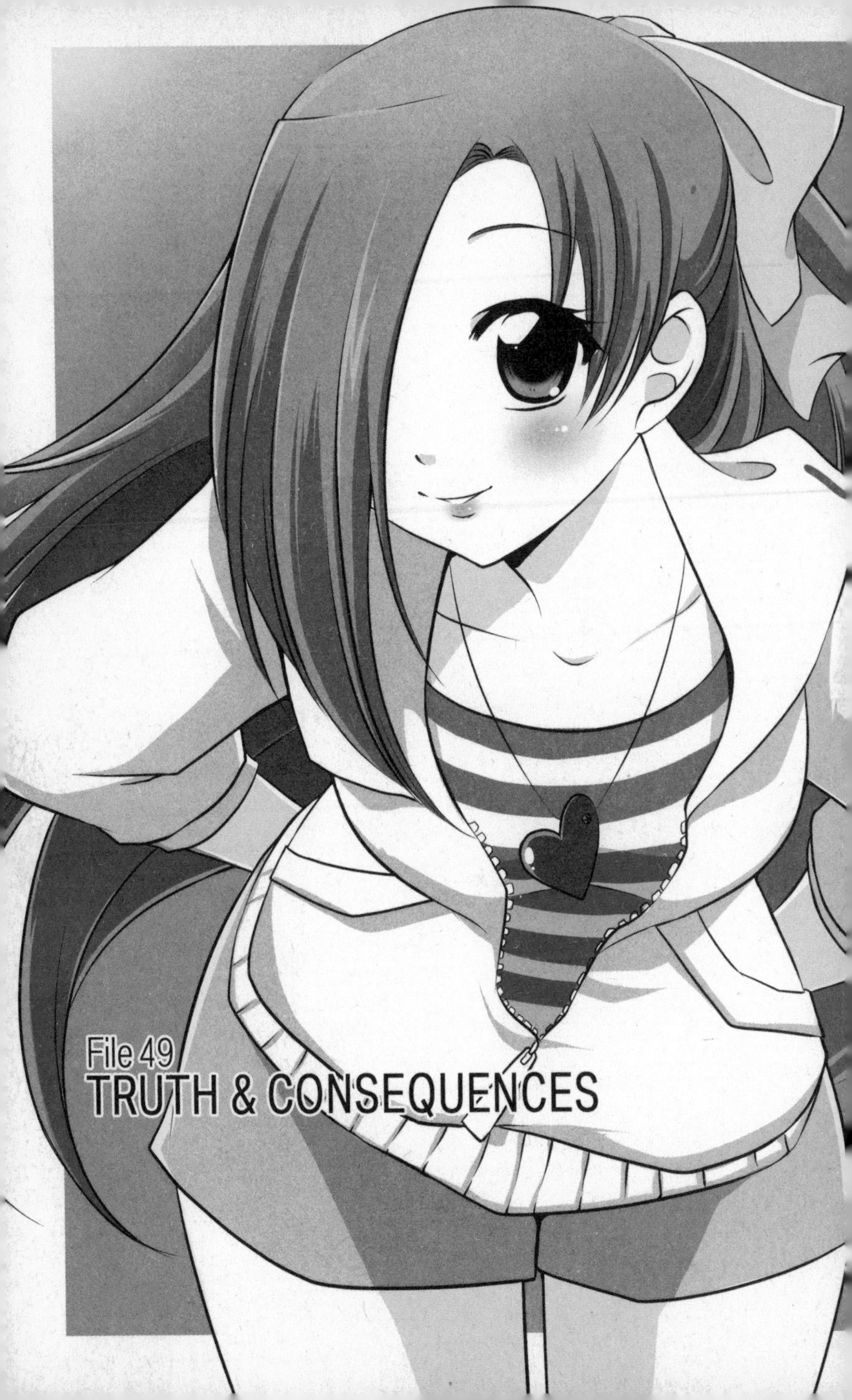
File 49
TRUTH & CONSEQUENCES

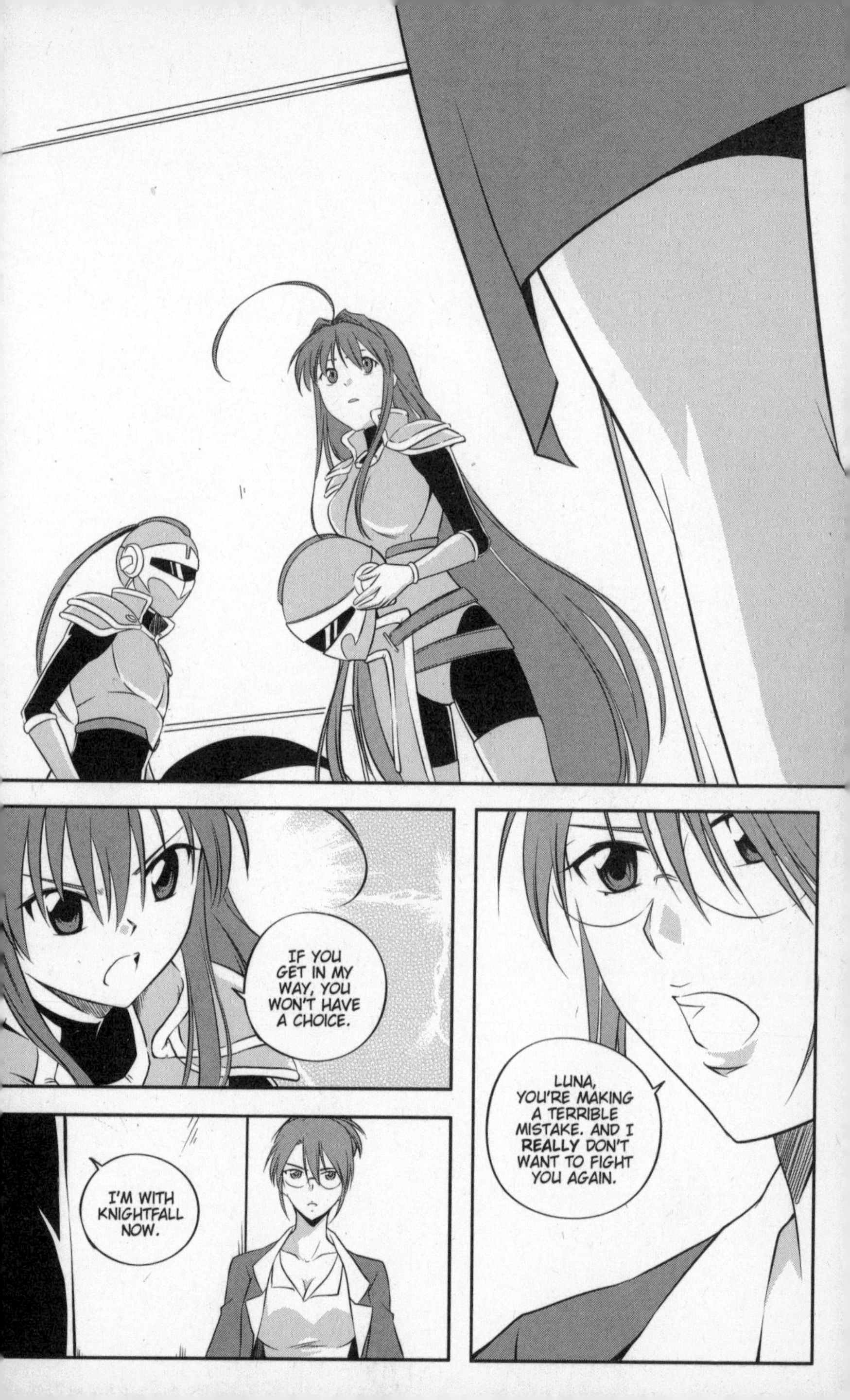
LUNA, YOU'RE MAKING A TERRIBLE MISTAKE. AND I REALLY DON'T WANT TO FIGHT YOU AGAIN.
IF YOU GET IN MY WAY, YOU WON'T HAVE A CHOICE.
I'M WITH KNIGHTFALL NOW.

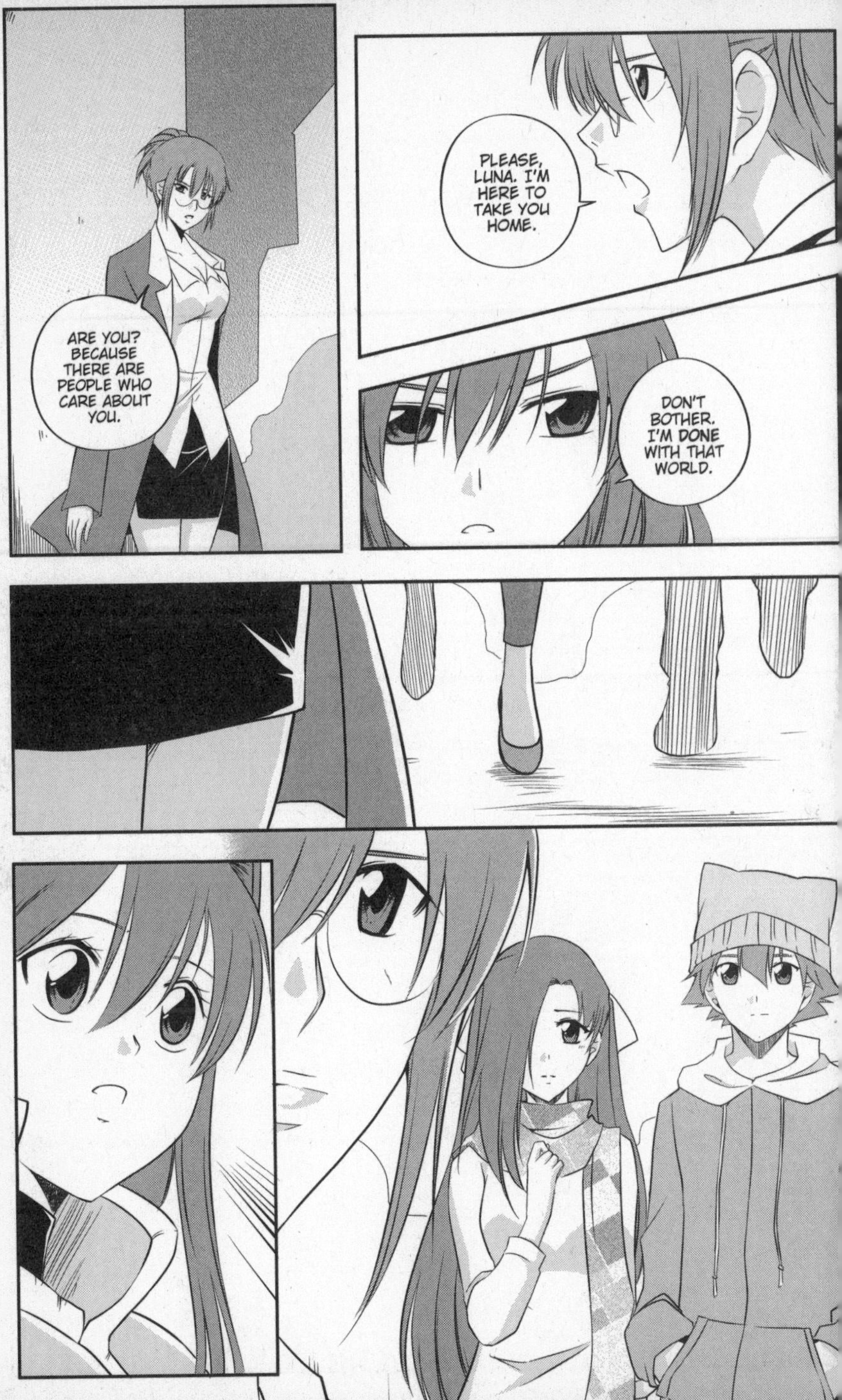
PLEASE, LUNA. I'M HERE TO TAKE YOU HOME.
DON'T BOTHER. I'M DONE WITH THAT WORLD.
ARE YOU? BECAUSE THERE ARE PEOPLE WHO CARE ABOUT YOU.

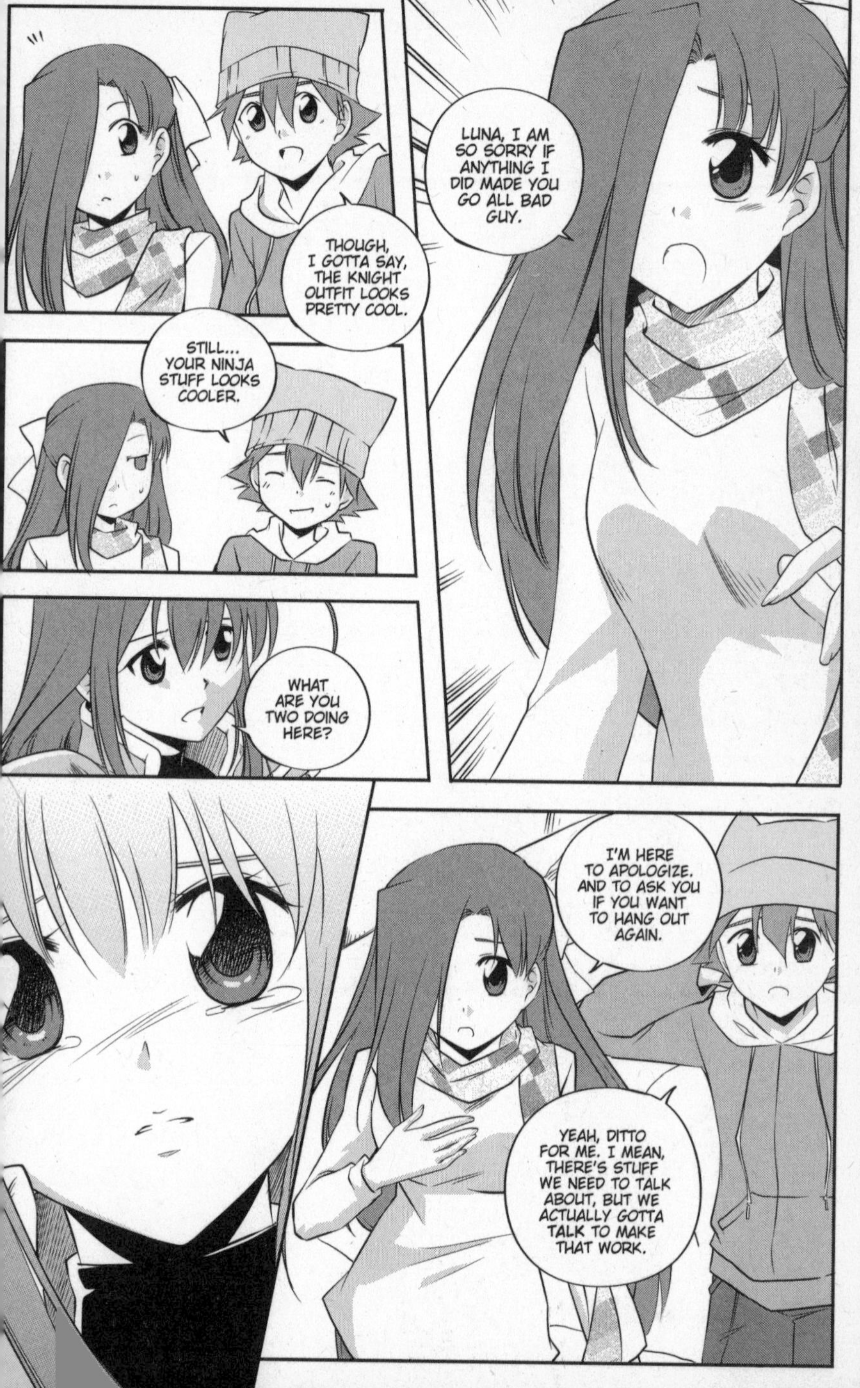
LUNA, I AM SO SORRY IF ANYTHING I DID MADE YOU GO ALL BAD GUY.
THOUGH, I GOTTA SAY, THE KNIGHT OUTFIT LOOKS PRETTY COOL.
STILL... YOUR NINJA STUFF LOOKS COOLER.
WHAT ARE YOU TWO DOING HERE?
I'M HERE TO APOLOGIZE. AND TO ASK YOU IF YOU WANT TO HANG OUT AGAIN.
YEAH, DITTO FOR ME. I MEAN, THERE'S STUFF WE NEED TO TALK ABOUT, BUT WE ACTUALLY GOTTA TALK TO MAKE THAT WORK.

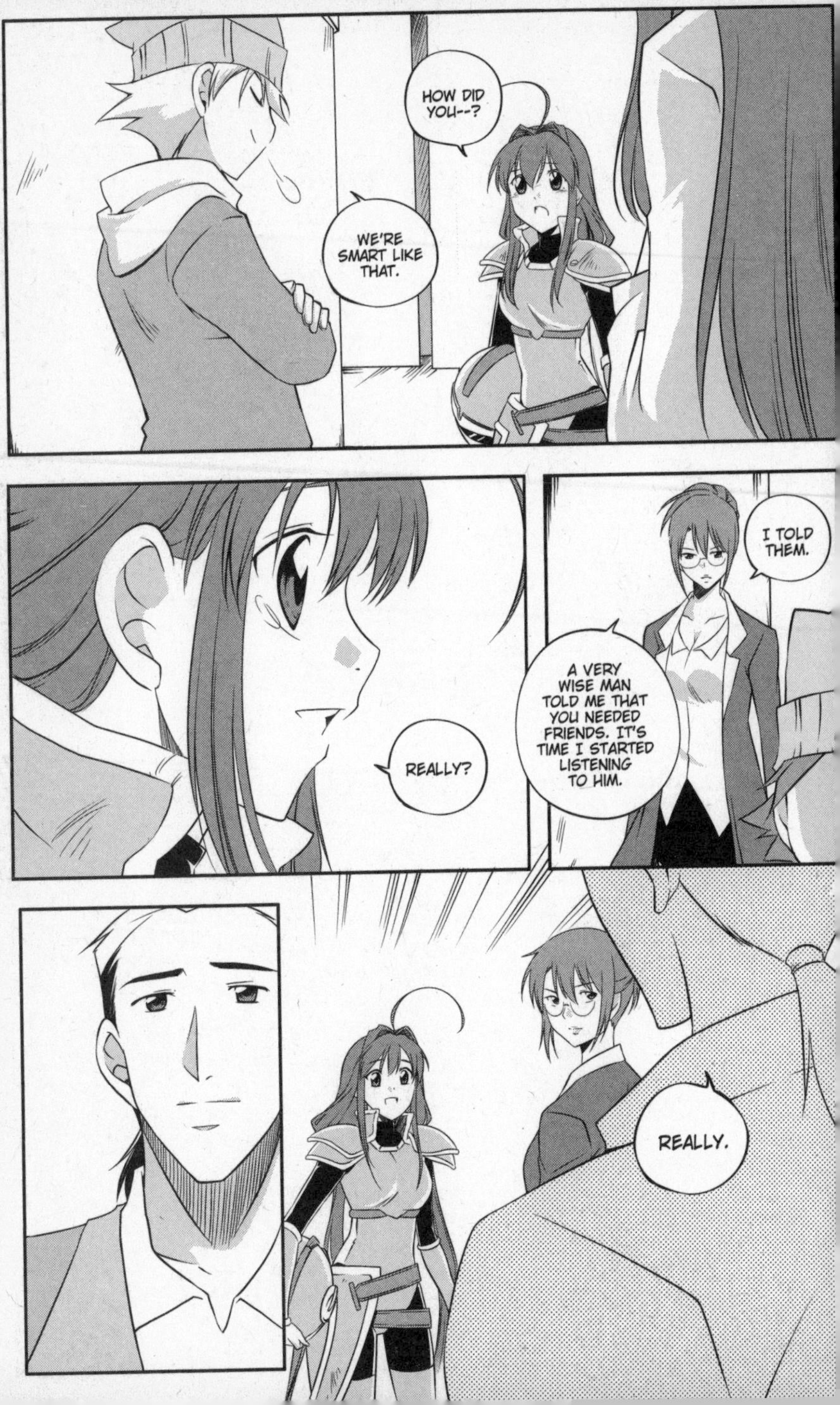
HOW DID YOU--?
WE'RE SMART LIKE THAT.
I TOLD THEM.
A VERY WISE MAN TOLD ME THAT YOU NEEDED FRIENDS. IT'S TIME I STARTED LISTENING TO HIM.
REALLY?
REALLY.

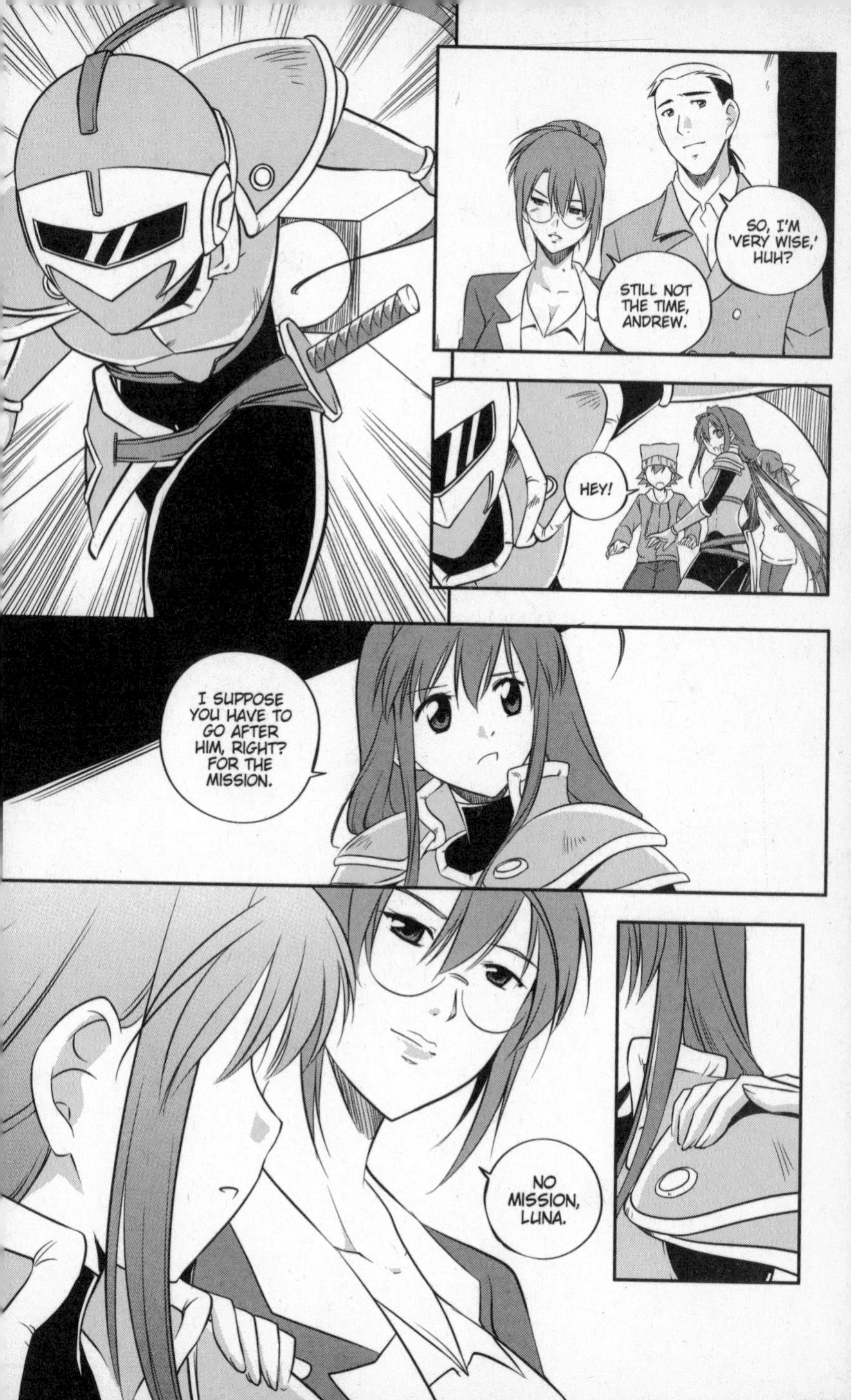
SO, I'M 'VERY WISE,' HUH?
STILL NOT THE TIME, ANDREW.
HEY!
I SUPPOSE YOU HAVE TO GO AFTER HIM, RIGHT? FOR THE MISSION.
NO MISSION, LUNA.

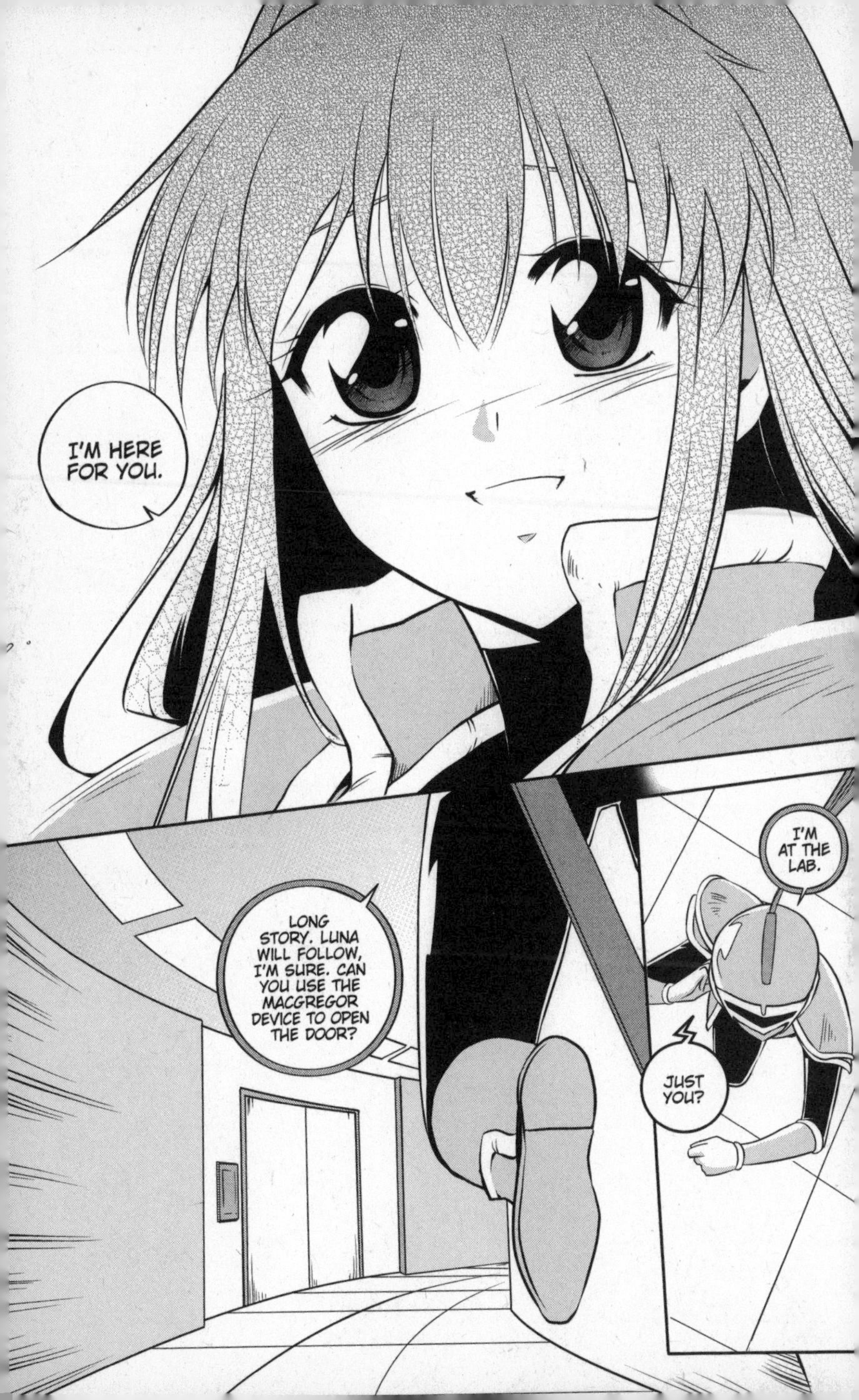
I'M HERE FOR YOU.
I'M AT THE LAB.
JUST YOU?
LONG STORY. LUNA WILL FOLLOW, I'M SURE. CAN YOU USE THE MACGREGOR DEVICE TO OPEN THE DOOR?

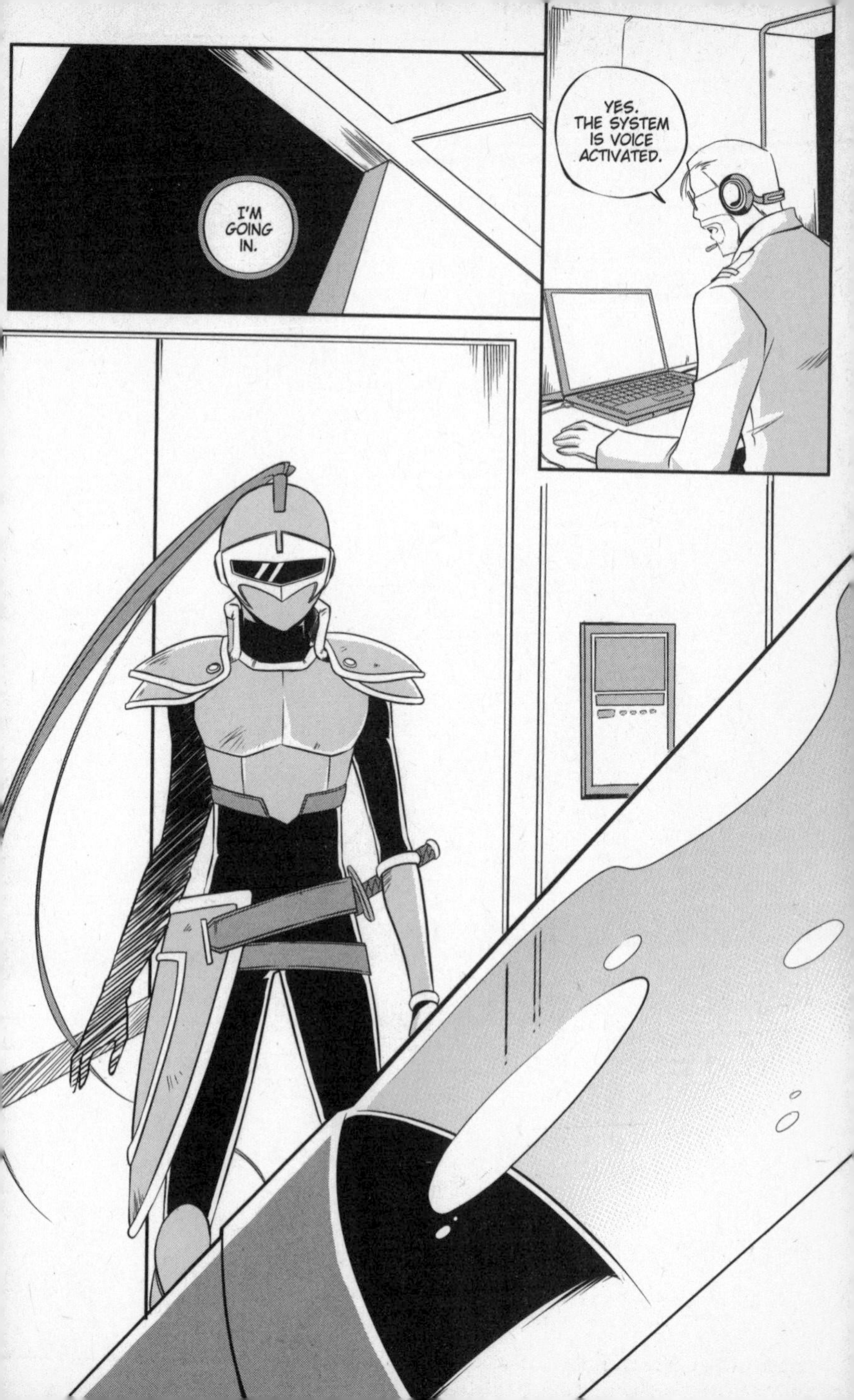
YES. THE SYSTEM IS VOICE ACTIVATED.
I'M GOING IN.

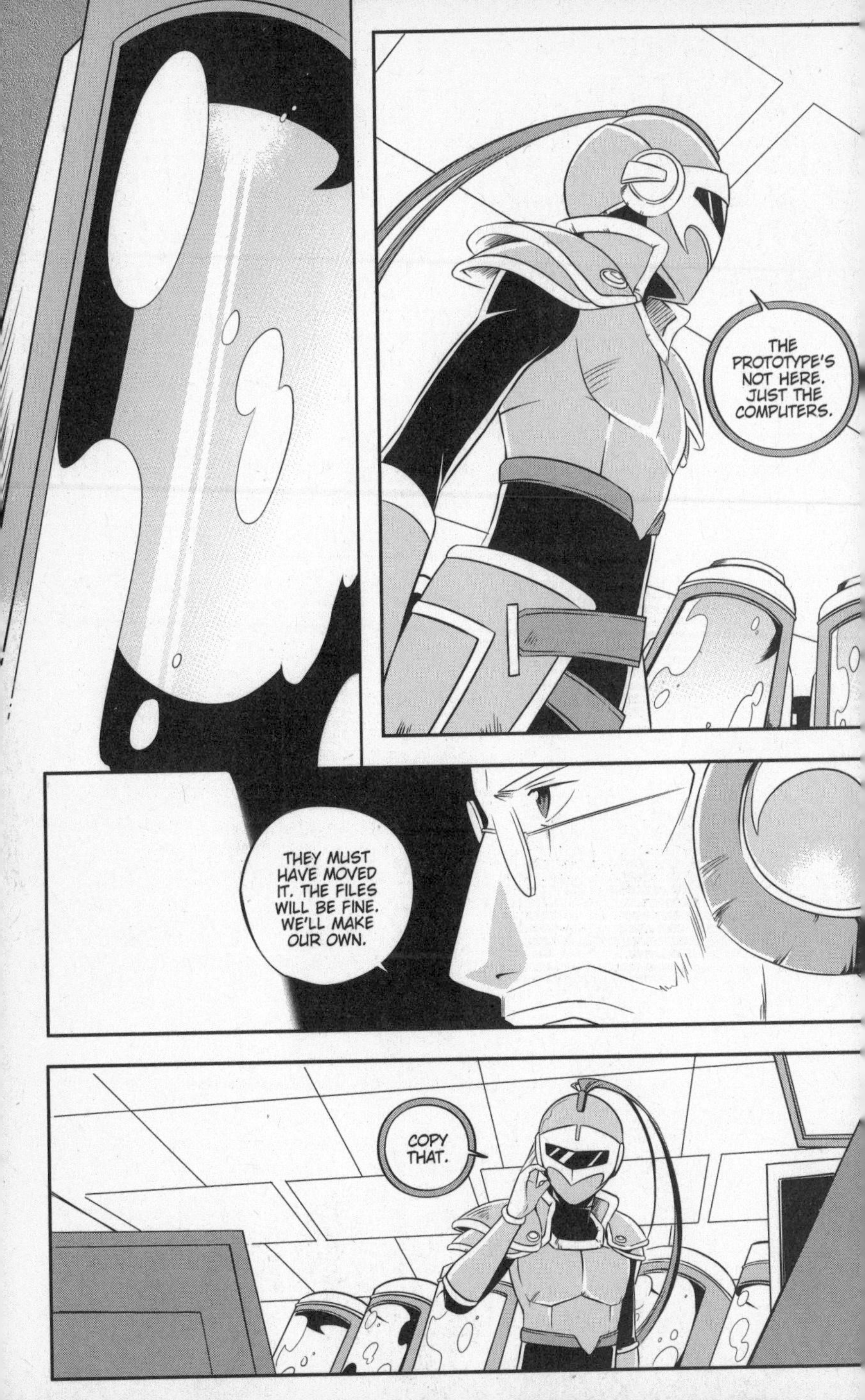
THE PROTOTYPE'S NOT HERE. JUST THE COMPUTERS.
THEY MUST HAVE MOVED IT. THE FILES WILL BE FINE. WE'LL MAKE OUR OWN.
COPY THAT.

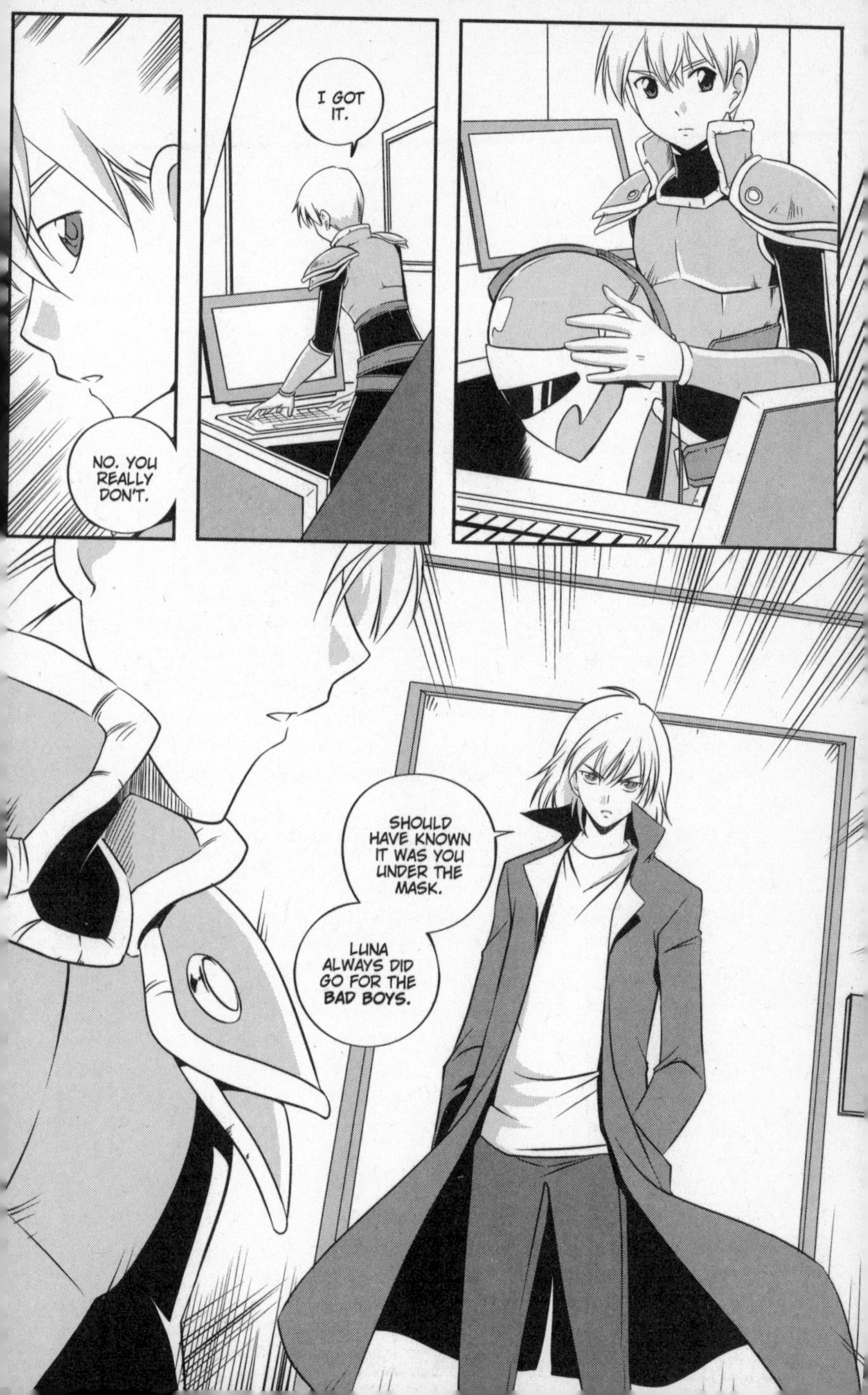
I GOT IT.
NO. YOU REALLY DON'T.
SHOULD HAVE KNOWN IT WAS YOU UNDER THE MASK.
LUNA ALWAYS DID GO FOR THE BAD BOYS.

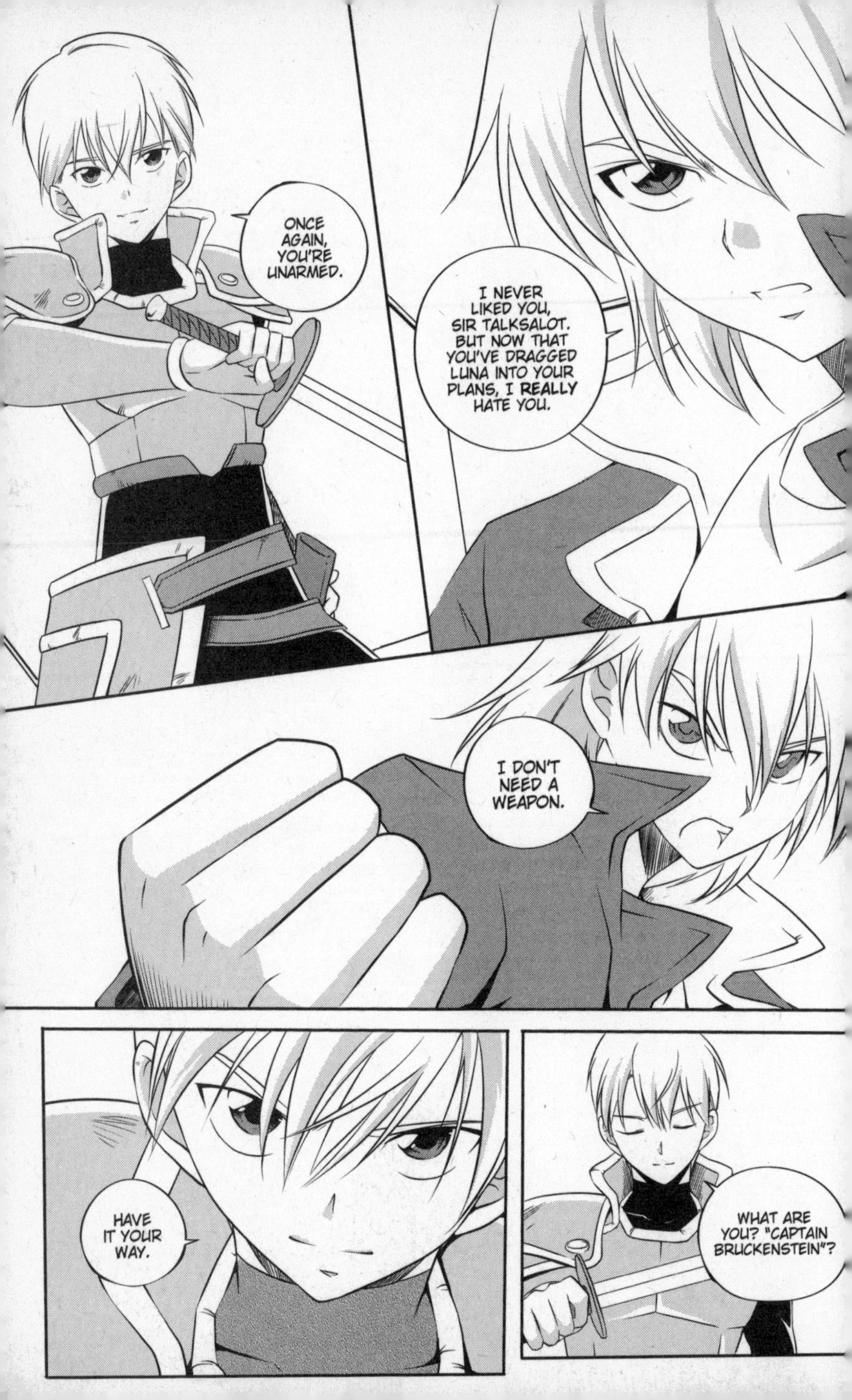
I NEVER LIKED YOU, SIR TALKSALOT. BUT NOW THAT YOU'VE DRAGGED LUNA INTO YOUR PLANS, I **REALLY** HATE YOU.
ONCE AGAIN, YOU'RE UNARMED.
I DON'T NEED A WEAPON.
WHAT ARE YOU? "CAPTAIN BRUCKENSTEIN"?
HAVE IT YOUR WAY.

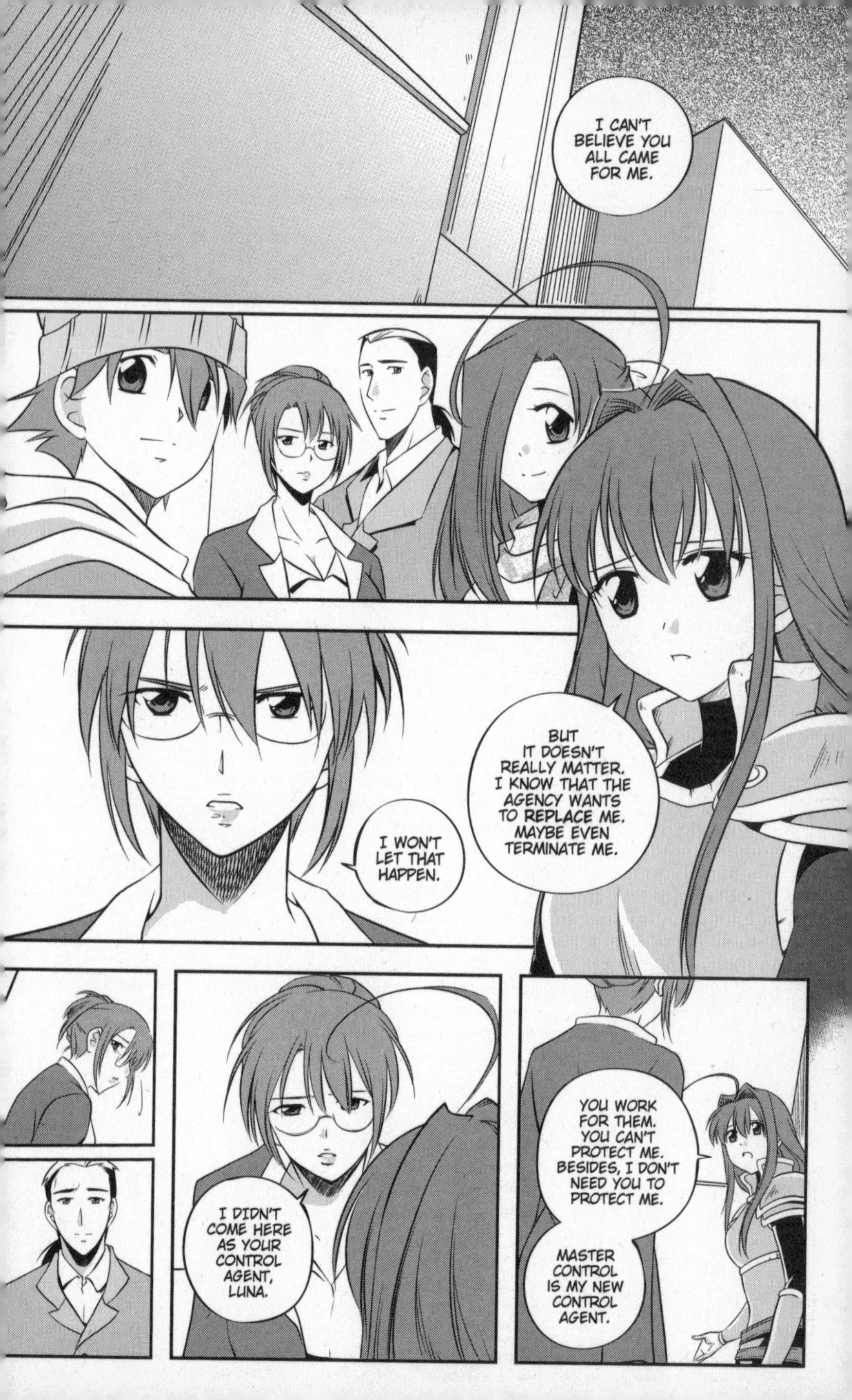
I CAN'T BELIEVE YOU ALL CAME FOR ME.
BUT IT DOESN'T REALLY MATTER. I KNOW THAT THE AGENCY WANTS TO REPLACE ME. MAYBE EVEN TERMINATE ME.
I WON'T LET THAT HAPPEN.
YOU WORK FOR THEM. YOU CAN'T PROTECT ME. BESIDES, I DON'T NEED YOU TO PROTECT ME.
MASTER CONTROL IS MY NEW CONTROL AGENT.
I DIDN'T COME HERE AS YOUR CONTROL AGENT, LUNA.

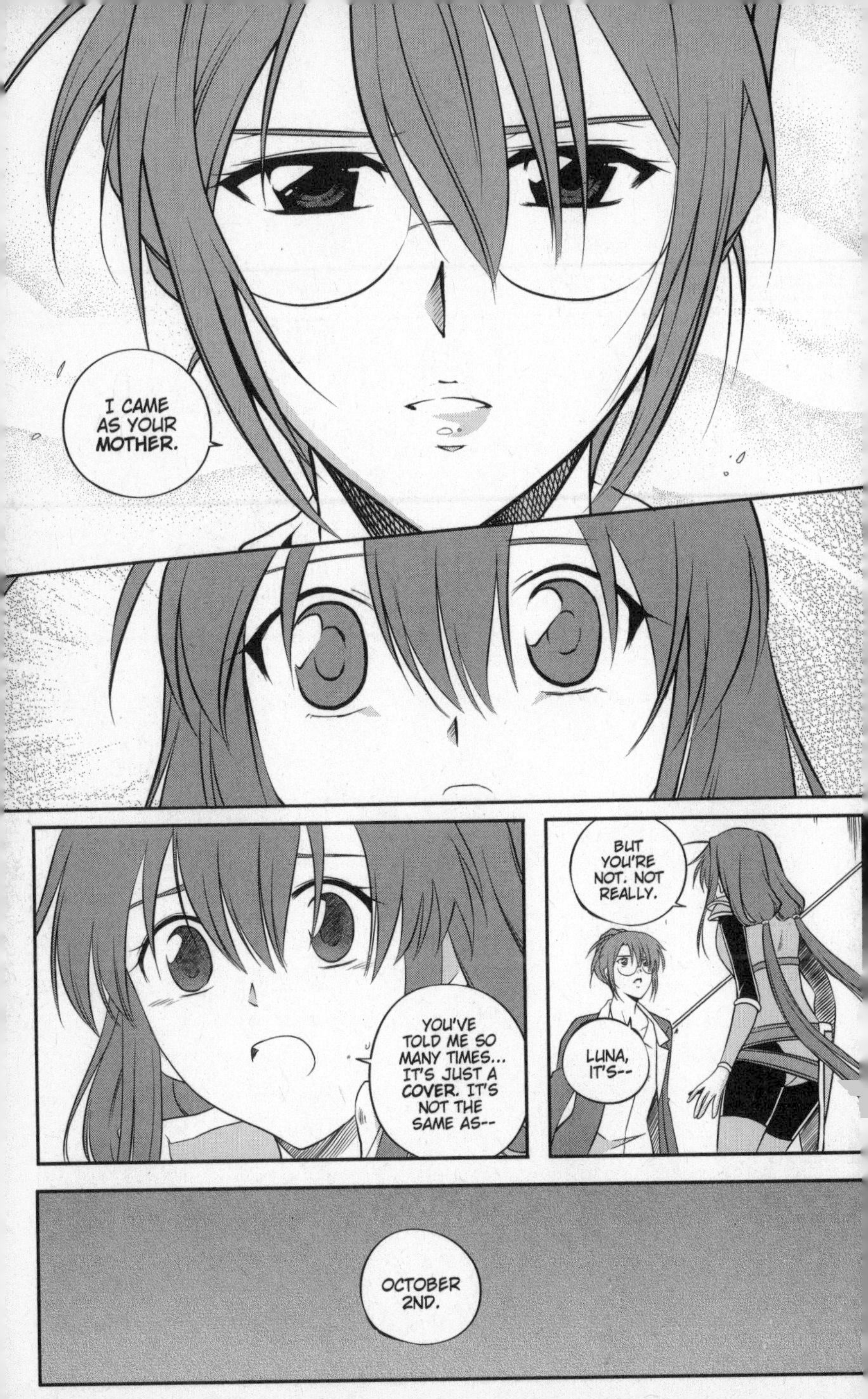
I CAME AS YOUR MOTHER.
BUT YOU'RE NOT. NOT REALLY.
LUNA, IT'S--
YOU'VE TOLD ME SO MANY TIMES... IT'S JUST A COVER. IT'S NOT THE SAME AS--
OCTOBER 2ND.

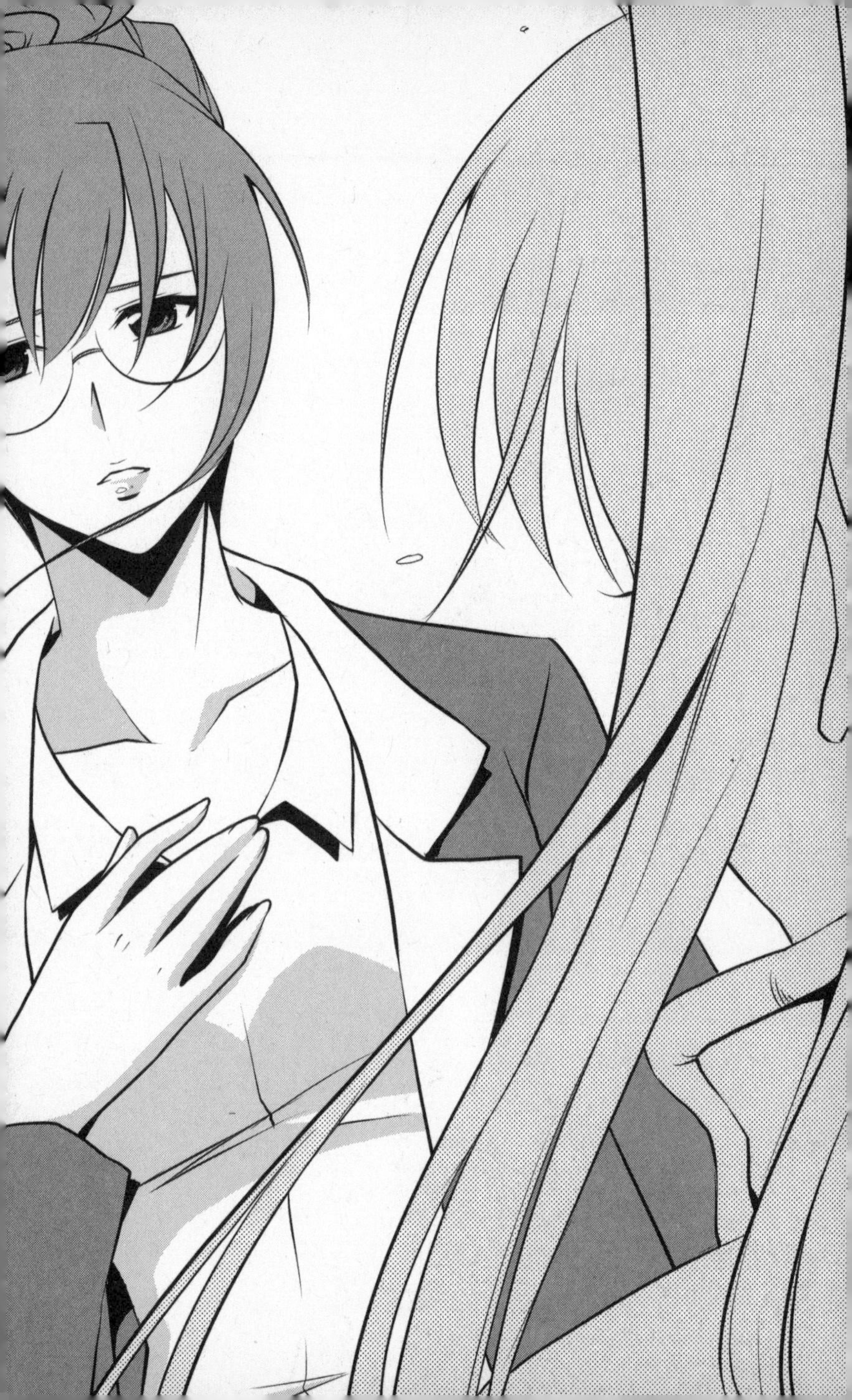

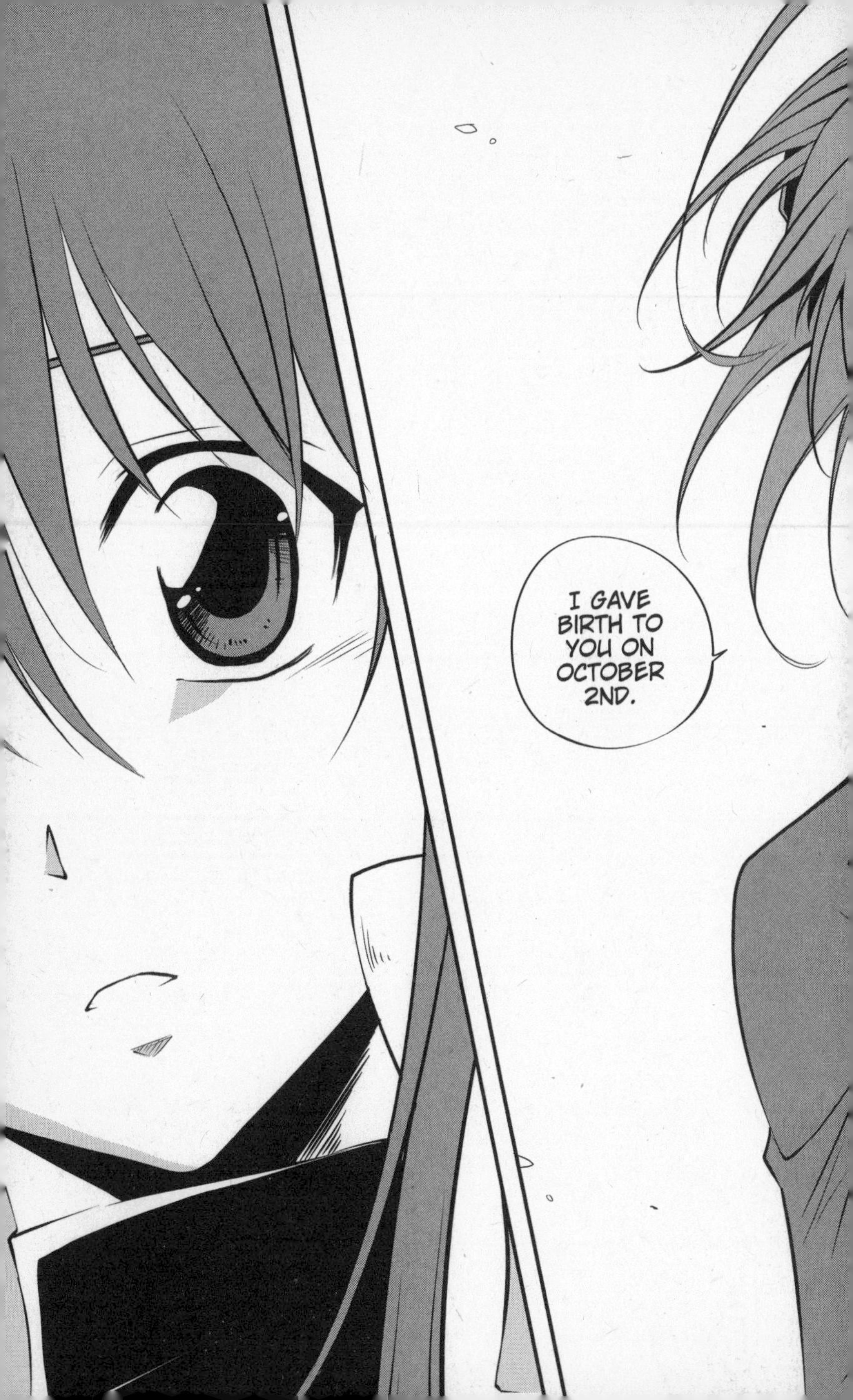
I GAVE BIRTH TO YOU ON OCTOBER 2ND.

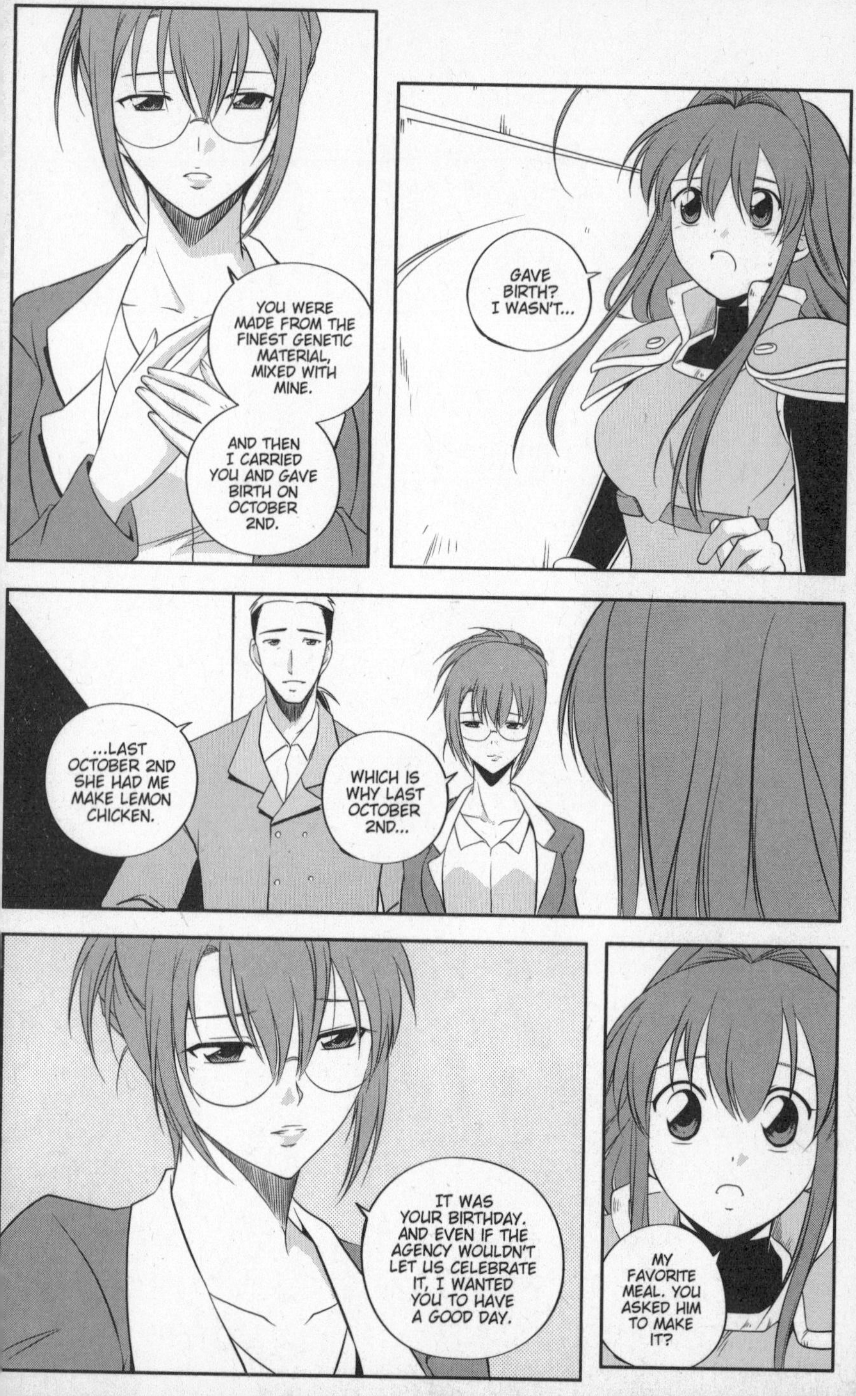
GAVE BIRTH? I WASN'T...
YOU WERE MADE FROM THE FINEST GENETIC MATERIAL, MIXED WITH MINE.
AND THEN I CARRIED YOU AND GAVE BIRTH ON OCTOBER 2ND.
WHICH IS WHY LAST OCTOBER 2ND...
...LAST OCTOBER 2ND SHE HAD ME MAKE LEMON CHICKEN.
MY FAVORITE MEAL. YOU ASKED HIM TO MAKE IT?
IT WAS YOUR BIRTHDAY. AND EVEN IF THE AGENCY WOULDN'T LET US CELEBRATE IT, I WANTED YOU TO HAVE A GOOD DAY.

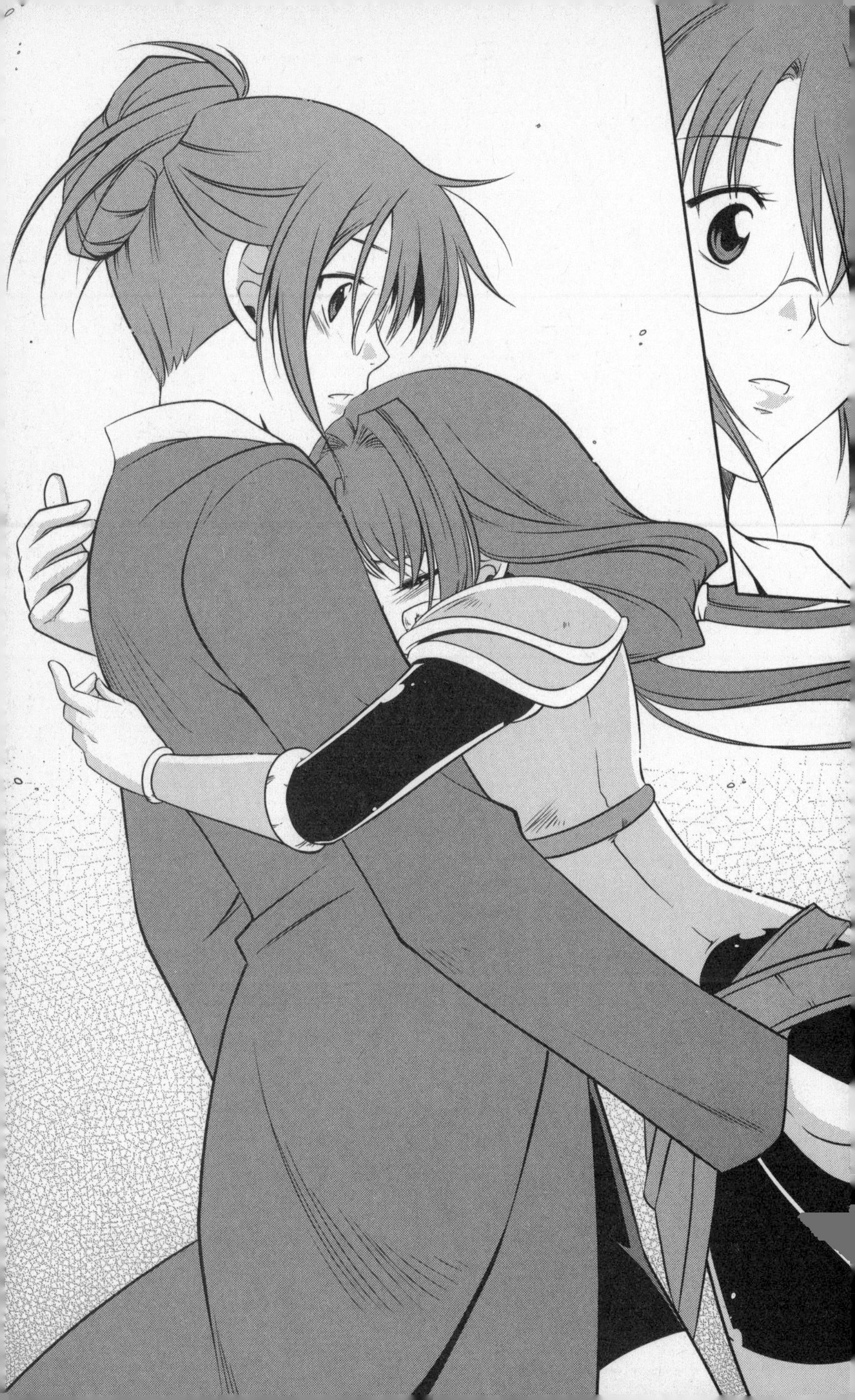

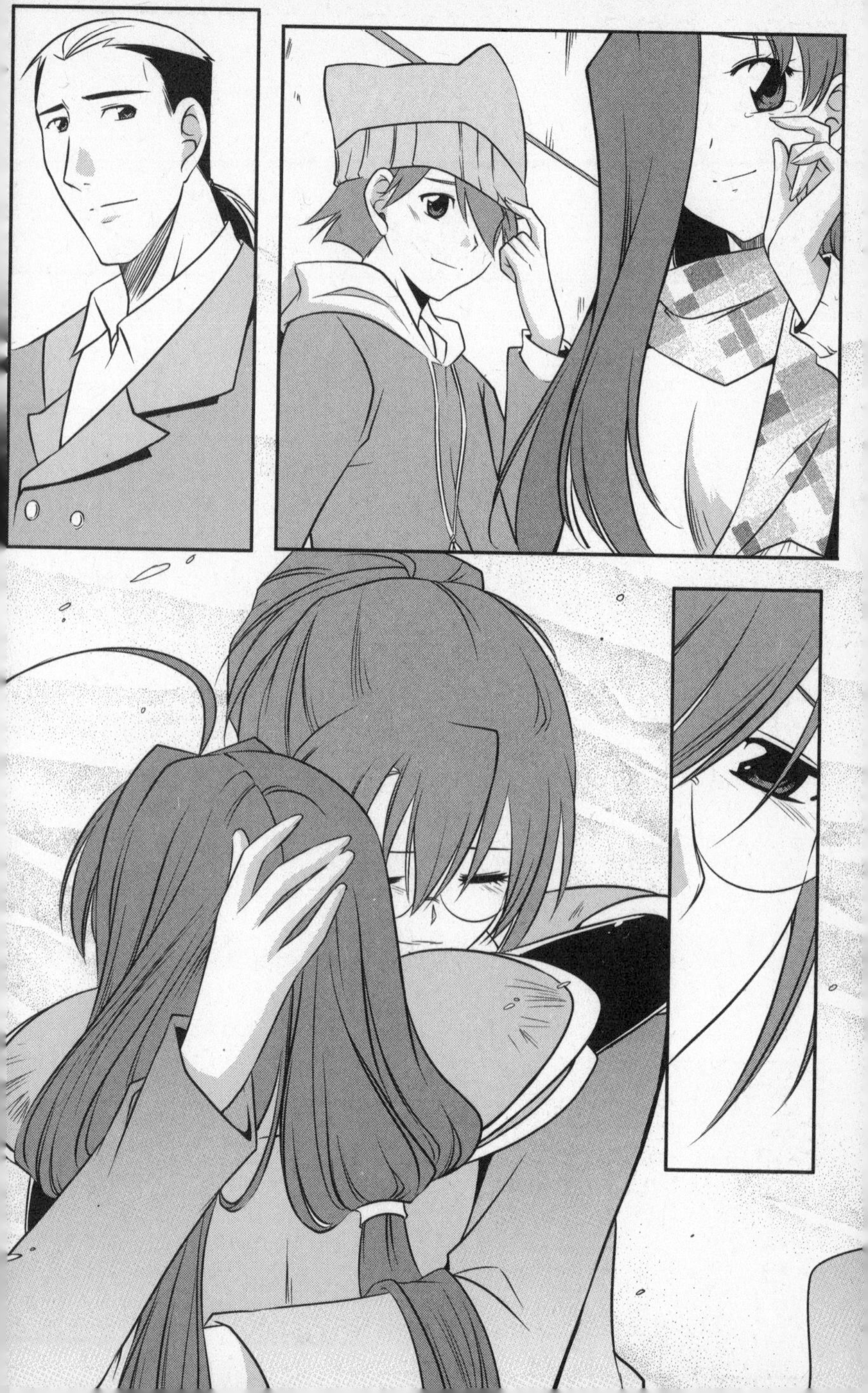

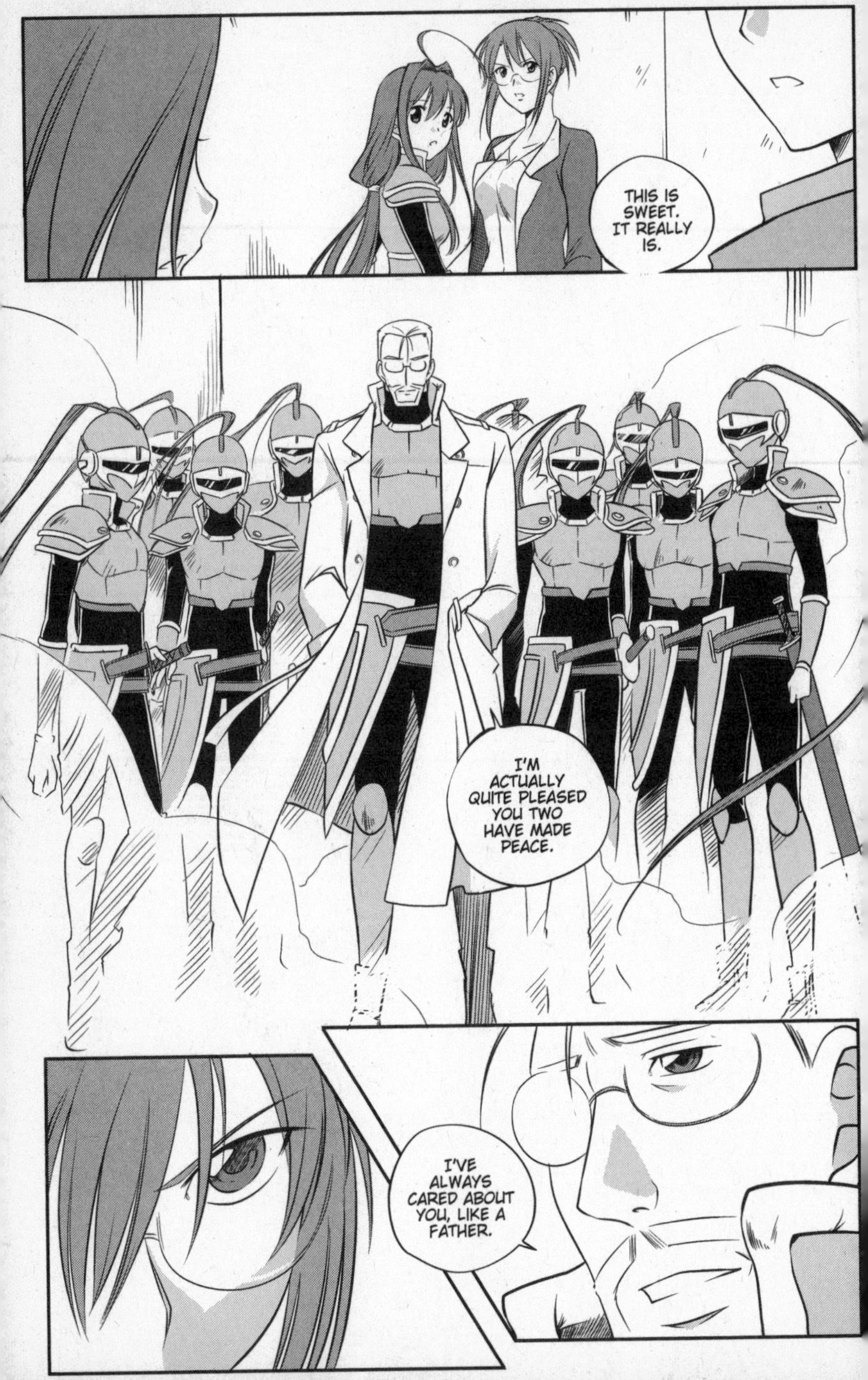
THIS IS SWEET. IT REALLY IS.
I'M ACTUALLY QUITE PLEASED YOU TWO HAVE MADE PEACE.
I'VE ALWAYS CARED ABOUT YOU, LIKE A FATHER.

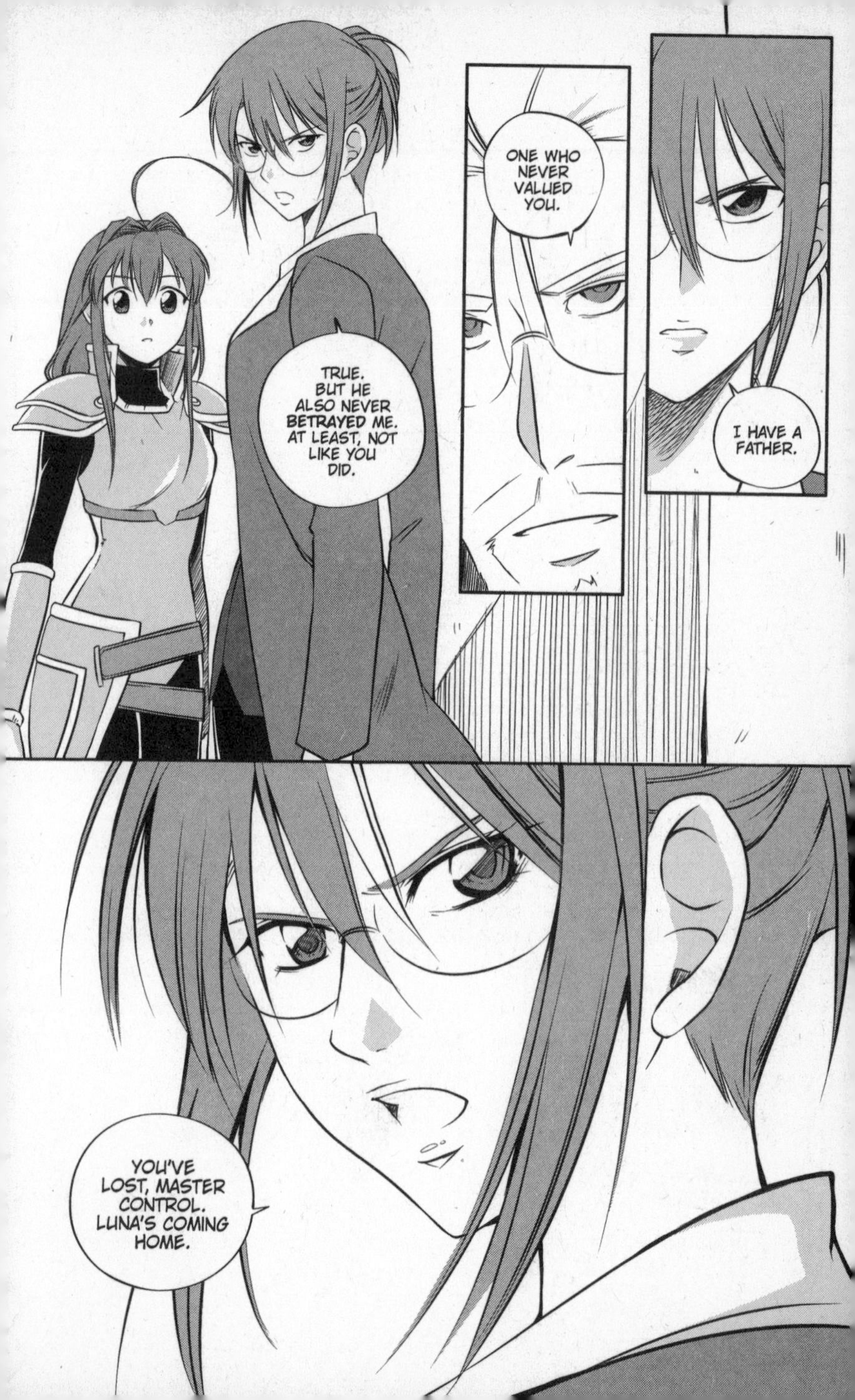
I HAVE A FATHER.
ONE WHO NEVER VALUED YOU.
TRUE. BUT HE ALSO NEVER BETRAYED ME. AT LEAST, NOT LIKE YOU DID.
YOU'VE LOST, MASTER CONTROL. LUNA'S COMING HOME.

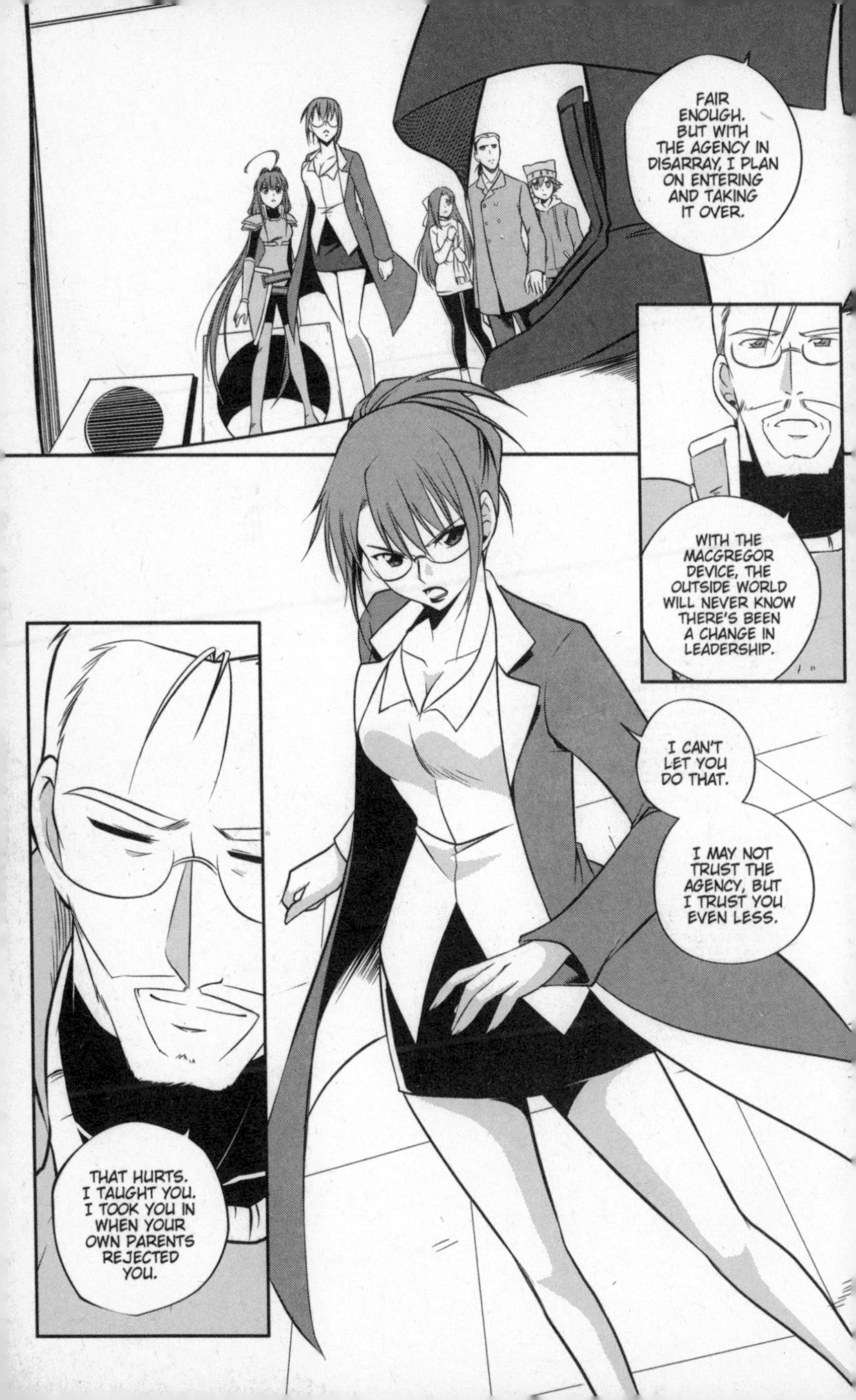
FAIR ENOUGH. BUT WITH THE AGENCY IN DISARRAY, I PLAN ON ENTERING AND TAKING IT OVER.
WITH THE MACGREGOR DEVICE, THE OUTSIDE WORLD WILL NEVER KNOW THERE'S BEEN A CHANGE IN LEADERSHIP.
I CAN'T LET YOU DO THAT.
I MAY NOT TRUST THE AGENCY, BUT I TRUST YOU EVEN LESS.
THAT HURTS. I TAUGHT YOU. I TOOK YOU IN WHEN YOUR OWN PARENTS REJECTED YOU.

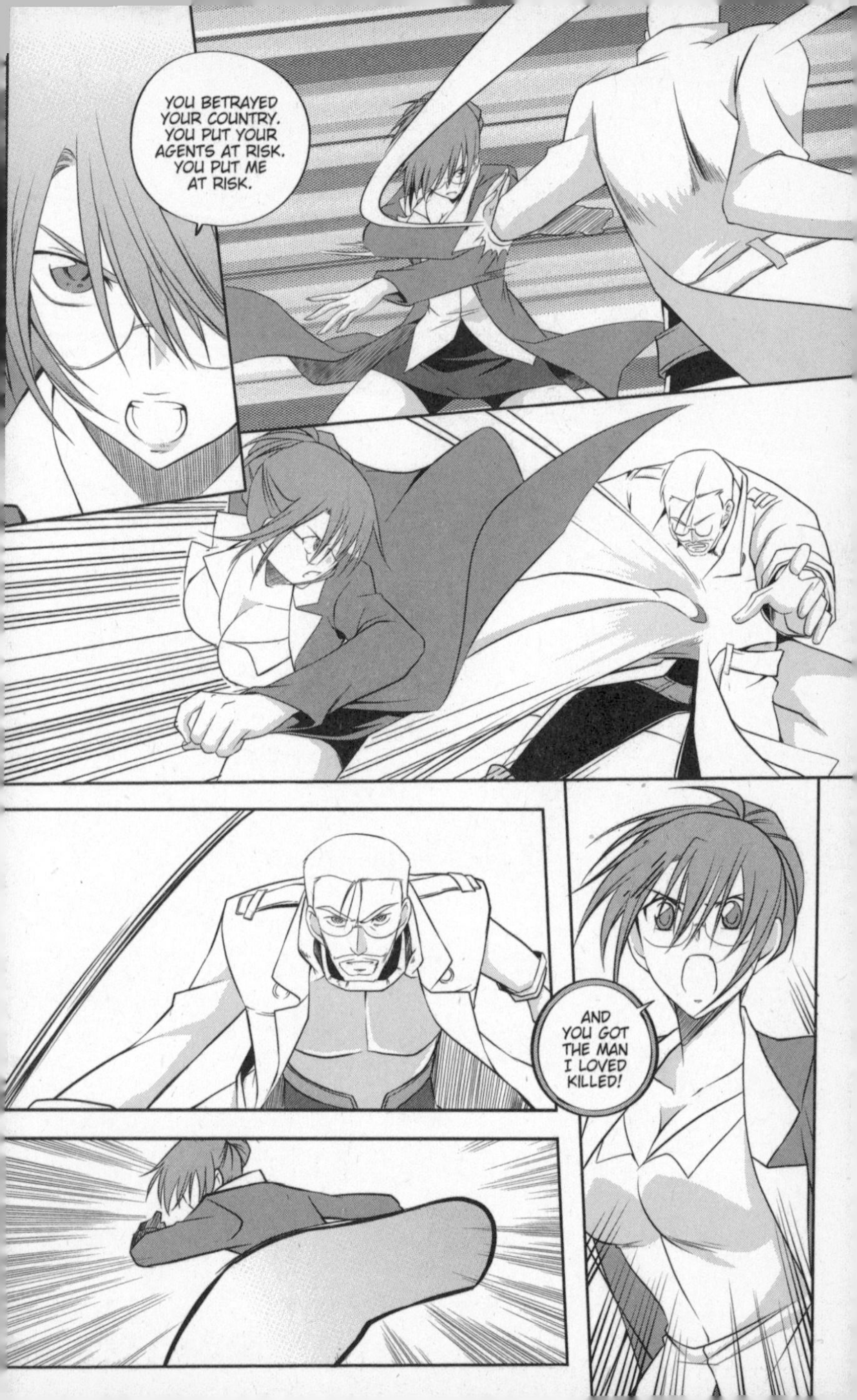
YOU BETRAYED YOUR COUNTRY. YOU PUT YOUR AGENTS AT RISK. YOU PUT ME AT RISK.
AND YOU GOT THE MAN I LOVED KILLED!

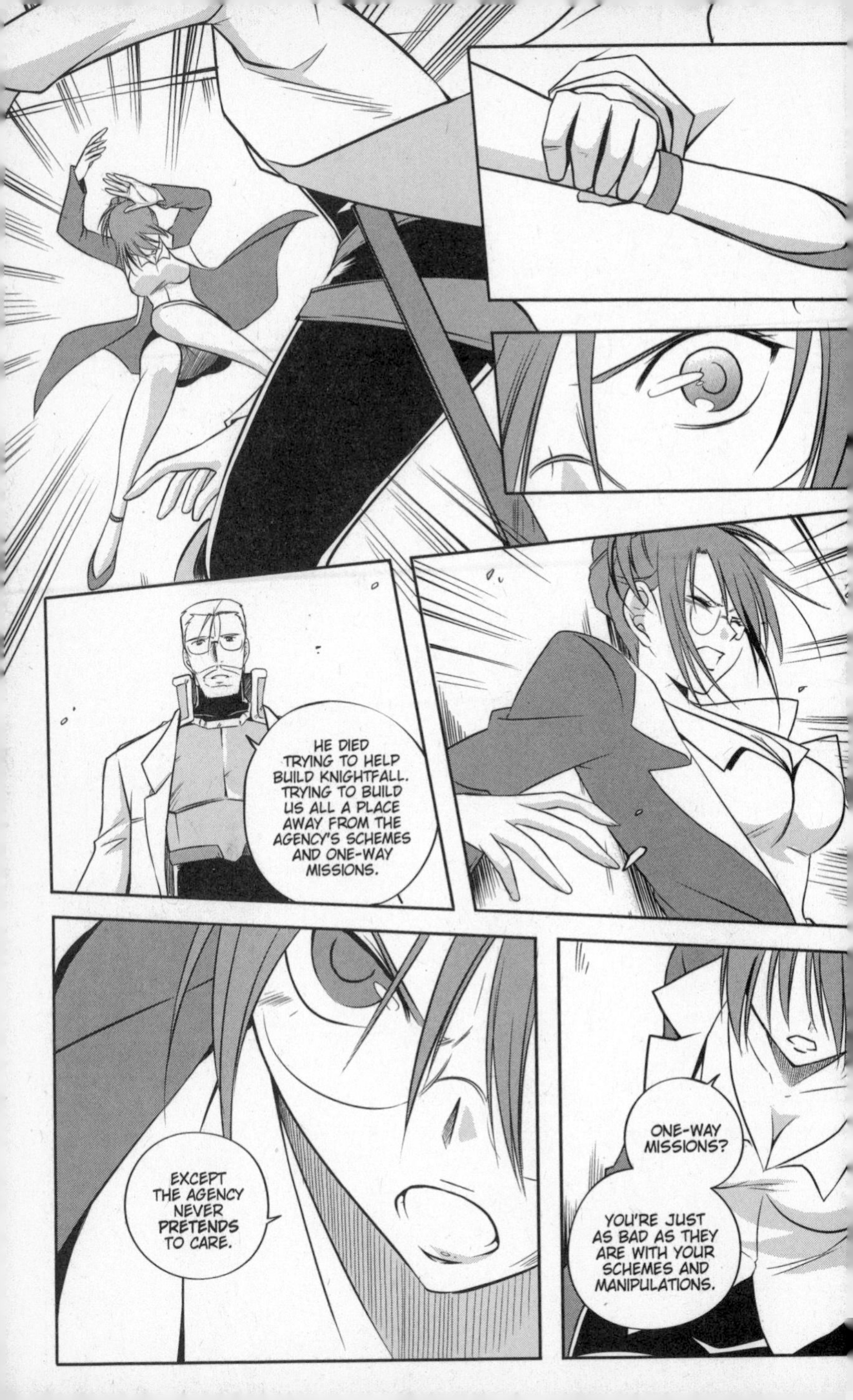
HE DIED TRYING TO HELP BUILD KNIGHTFALL. TRYING TO BUILD US ALL A PLACE AWAY FROM THE AGENCY'S SCHEMES AND ONE-WAY MISSIONS.
ONE-WAY MISSIONS?
YOU'RE JUST AS BAD AS THEY ARE WITH YOUR SCHEMES AND MANIPULATIONS.
EXCEPT THE AGENCY NEVER PRETENDS TO CARE.

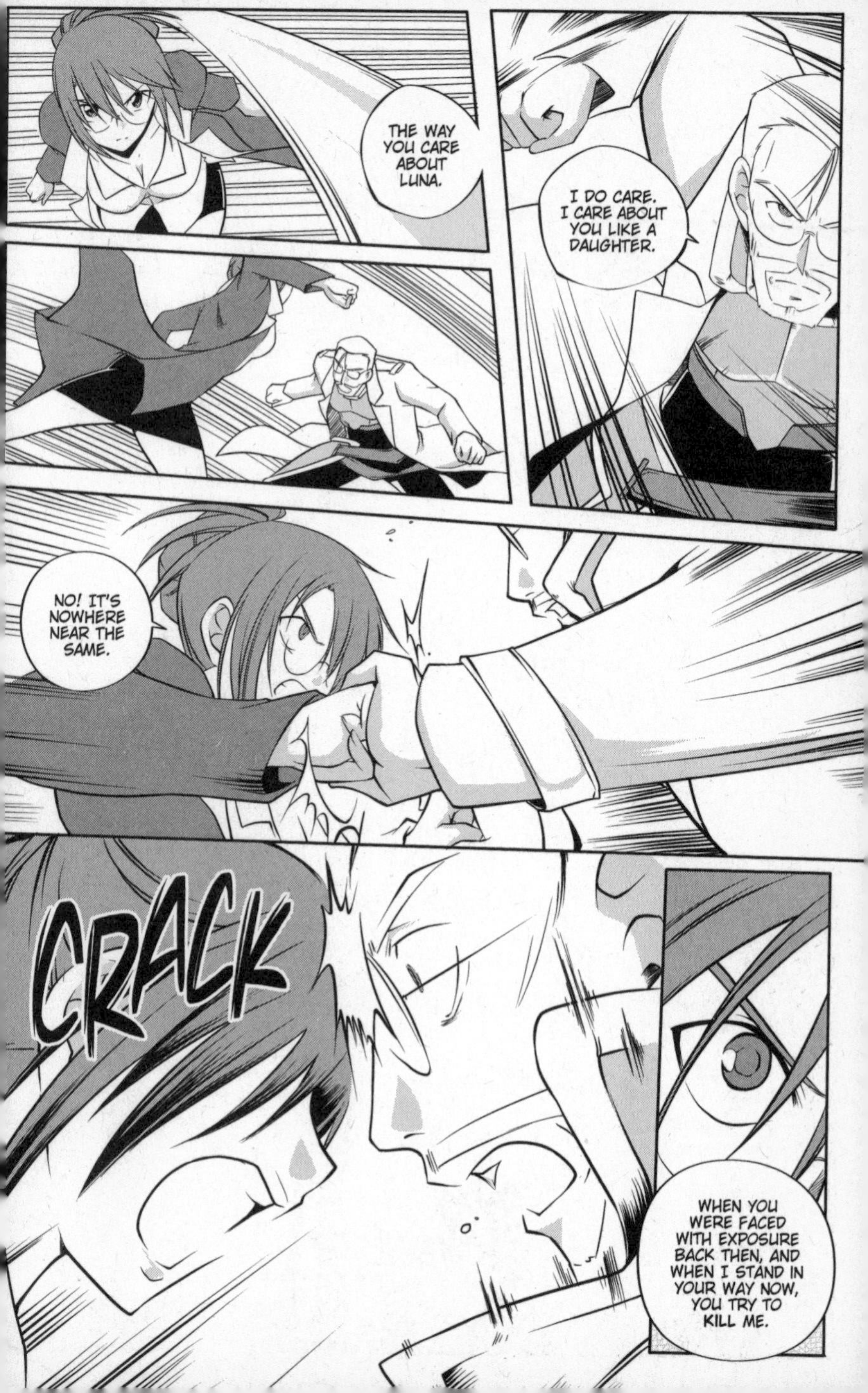
I DO CARE. I CARE ABOUT YOU LIKE A DAUGHTER.
THE WAY YOU CARE ABOUT LUNA.
NO! IT'S NOWHERE NEAR THE SAME.
WHEN YOU WERE FACED WITH EXPOSURE BACK THEN, AND WHEN I STAND IN YOUR WAY NOW, YOU TRY TO KILL ME.
CRACK

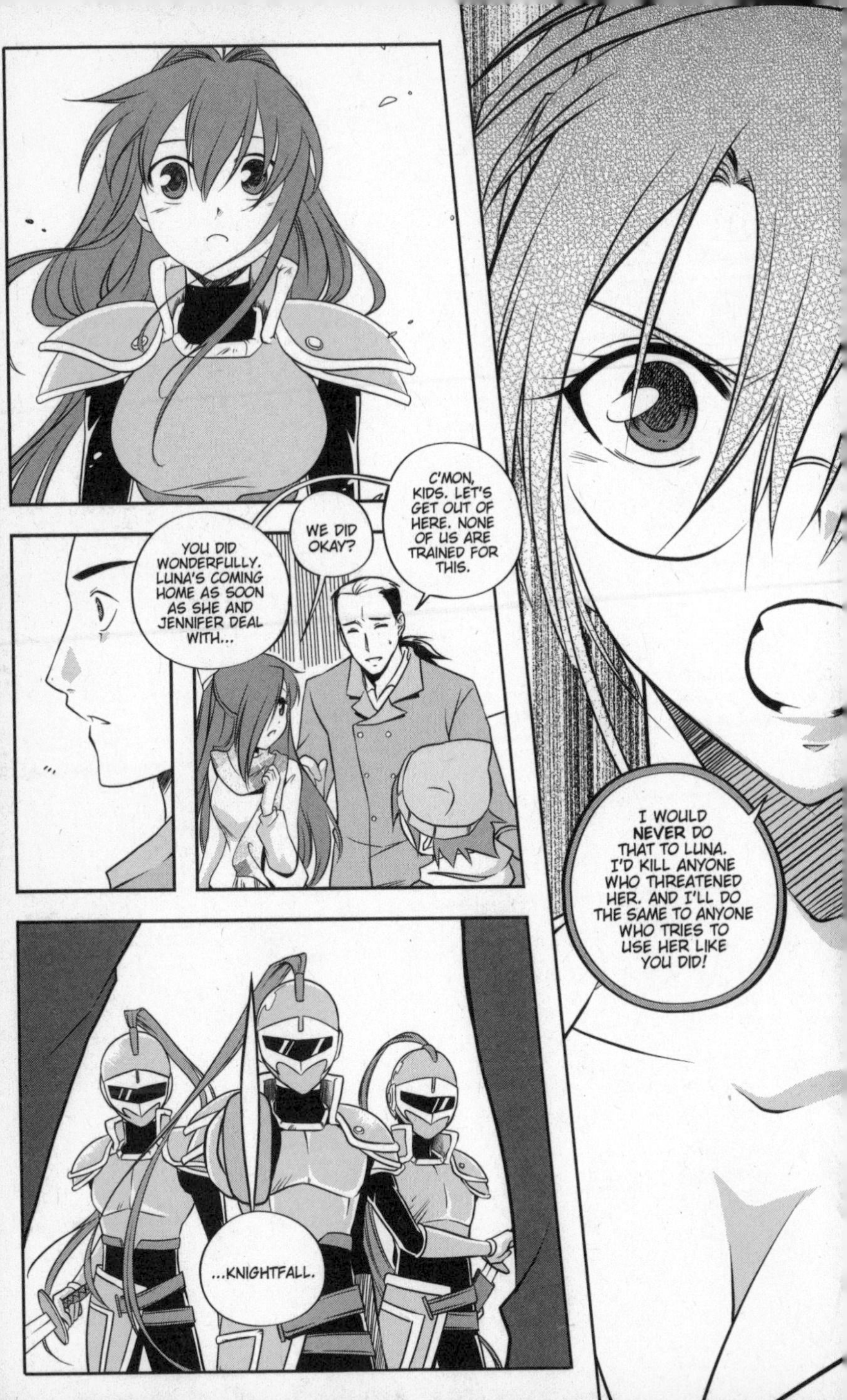
I WOULD NEVER DO THAT TO LUNA. I'D KILL ANYONE WHO THREATENED HER. AND I'LL DO THE SAME TO ANYONE WHO TRIES TO USE HER LIKE YOU DID!
C'MON, KIDS. LET'S GET OUT OF HERE. NONE OF US ARE TRAINED FOR THIS.
WE DID OKAY?
YOU DID WONDERFULLY. LUNA'S COMING HOME AS SOON AS SHE AND JENNIFER DEAL WITH...
...
...KNIGHTFALL.

I'M NOT GONNA LEAVE YOU.

YOU TWO... RUN!

ROLL

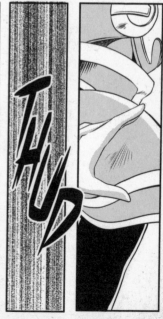

THUD

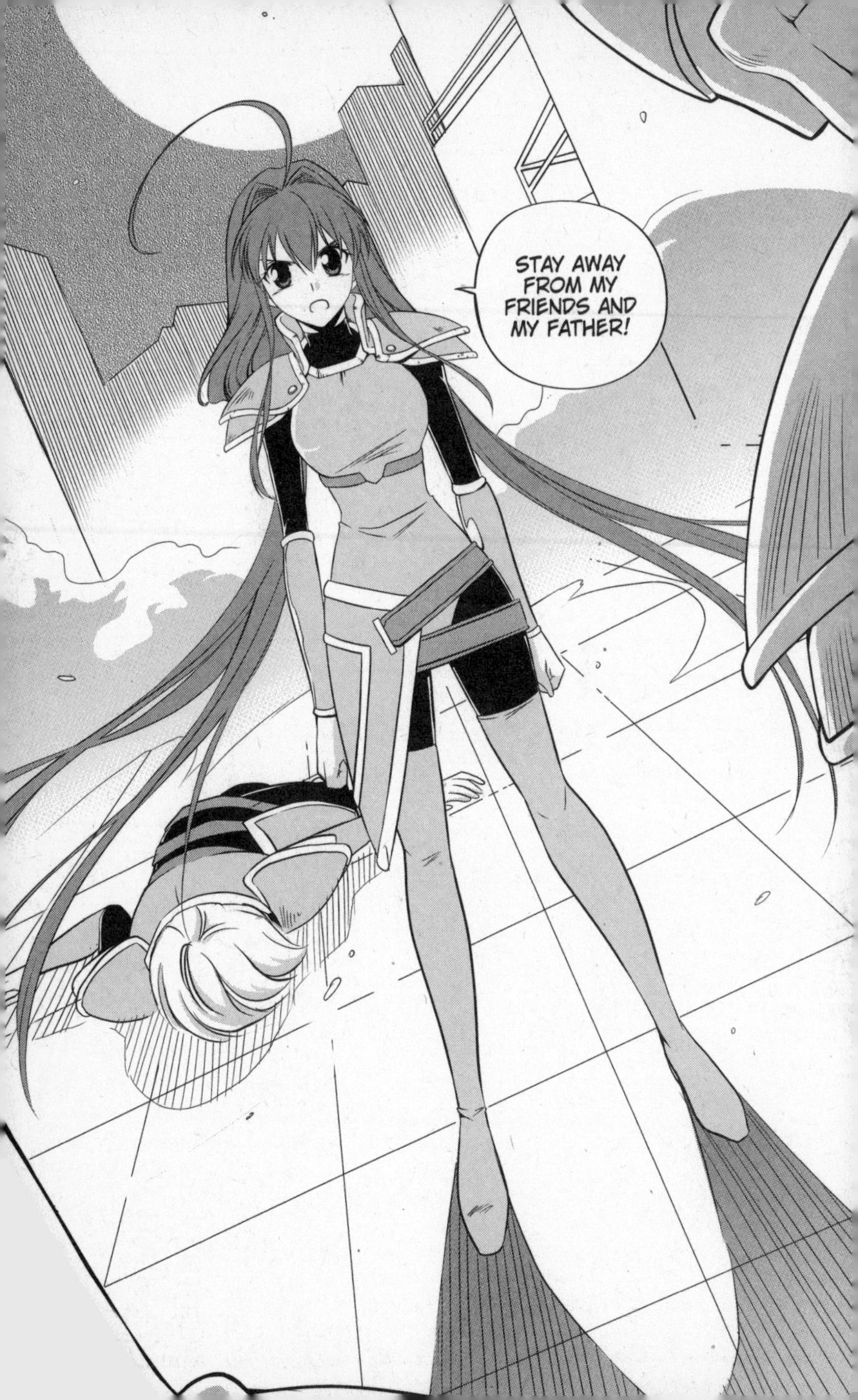
STAY AWAY FROM MY FRIENDS AND MY FATHER!

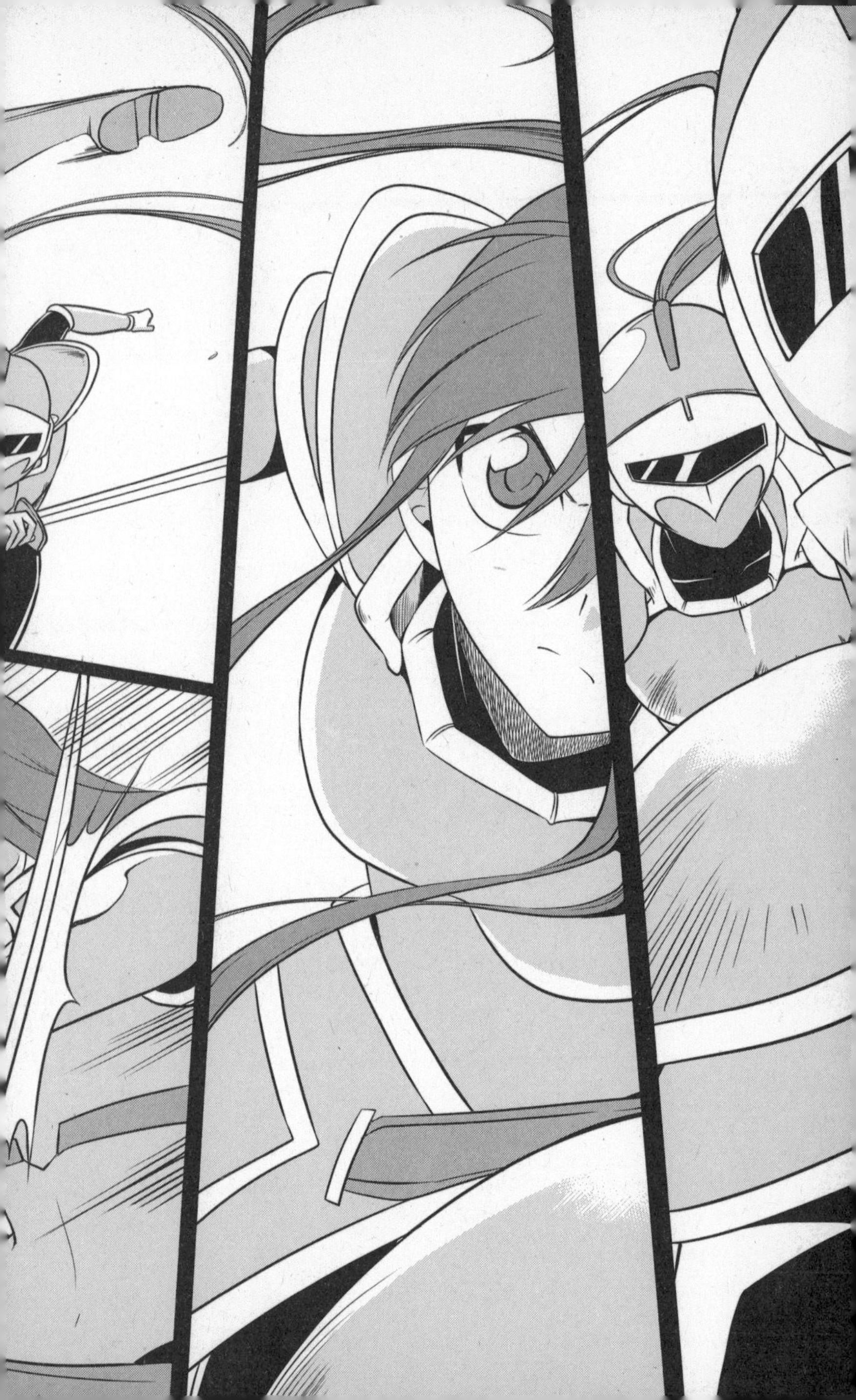

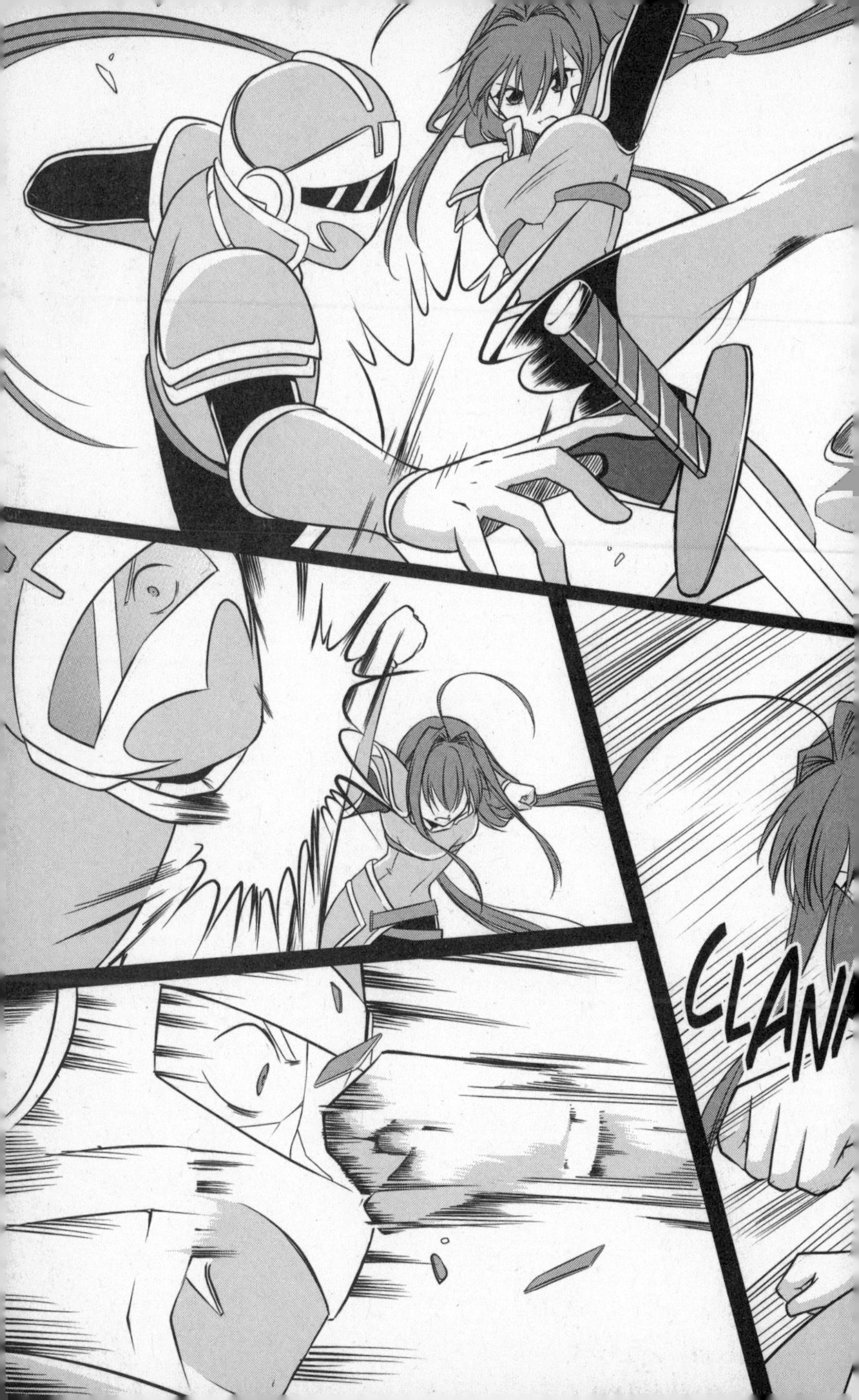
CLANA

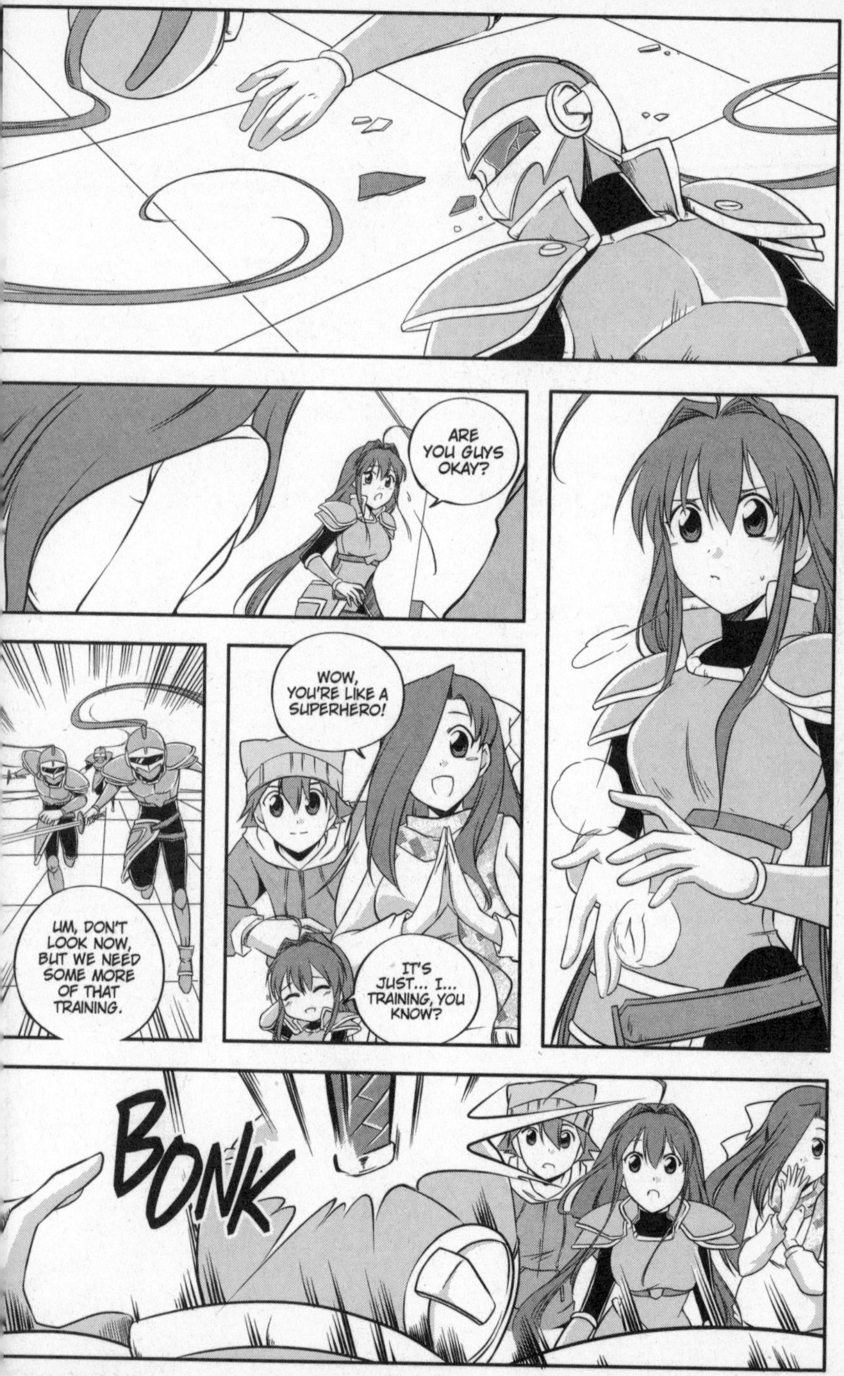
ARE YOU GUYS OKAY?
WOW, YOU'RE LIKE A SUPERHERO!
IT'S JUST... I... TRAINING, YOU KNOW?
UM, DON'T LOOK NOW, BUT WE NEED SOME MORE OF THAT TRAINING.
BONK

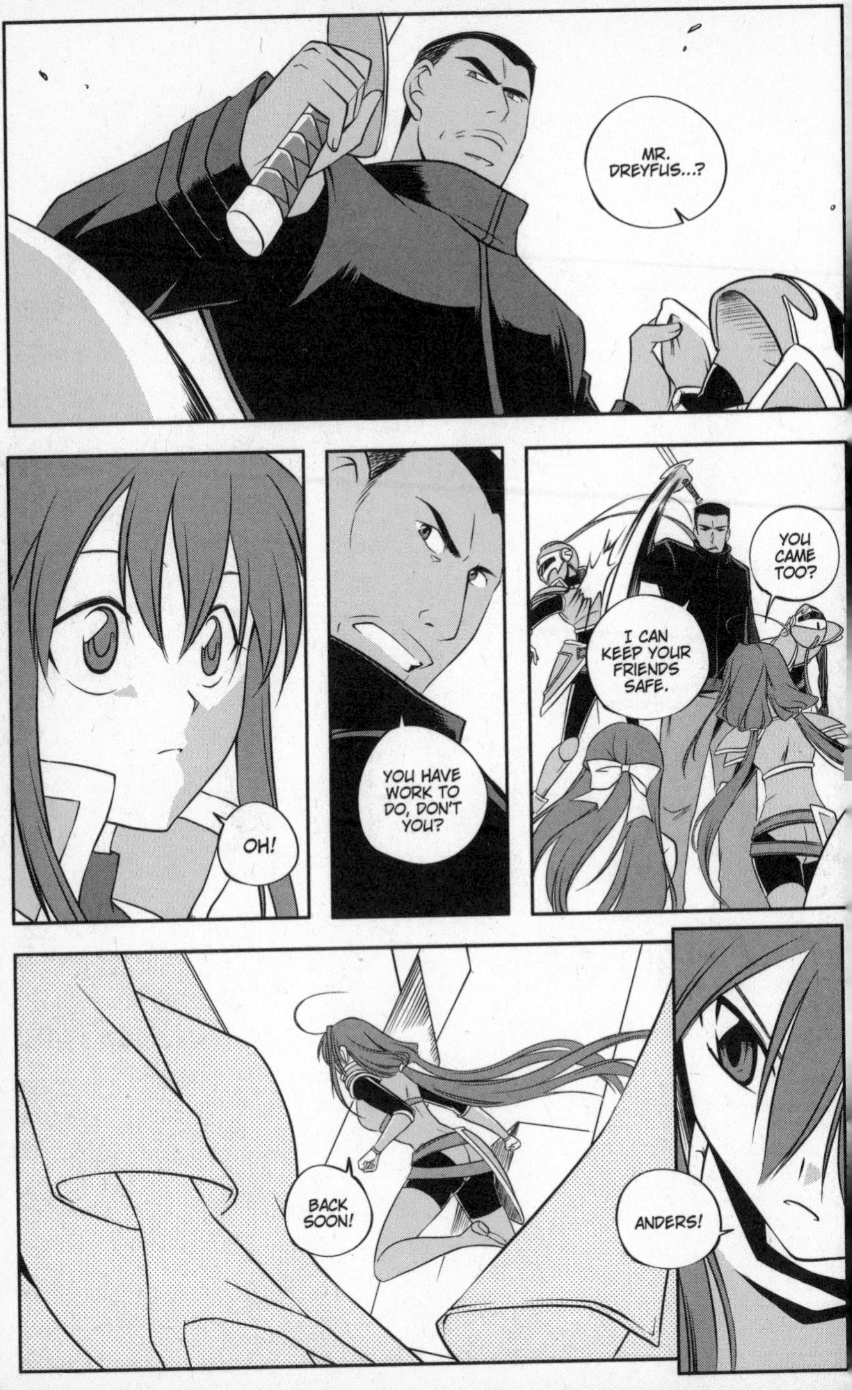
MR. DREYFUS...?
YOU CAME TOO?
I CAN KEEP YOUR FRIENDS SAFE.
YOU HAVE WORK TO DO, DON'T YOU?
OH!
ANDERS!
BACK SOON!

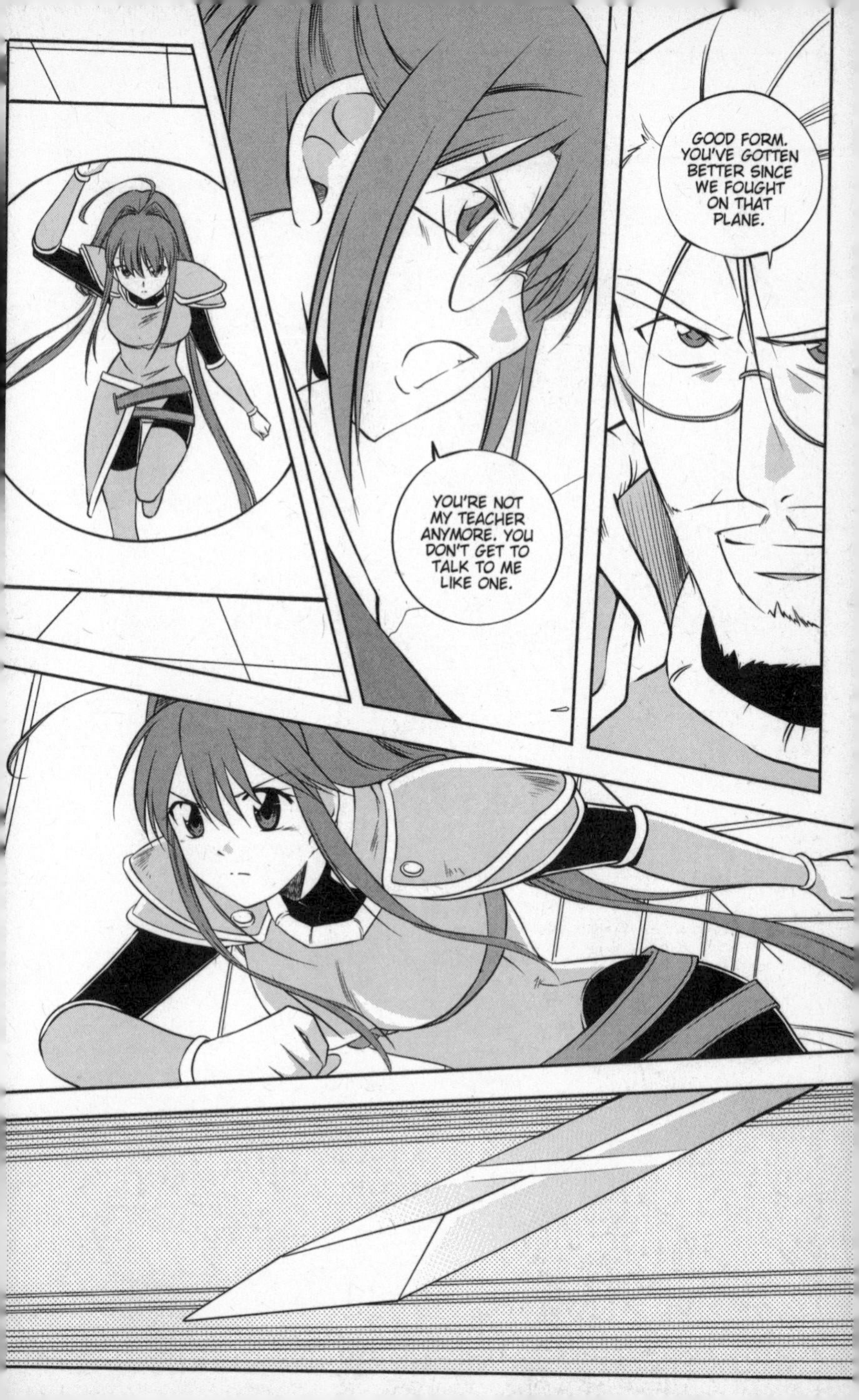
GOOD FORM. YOU'VE GOTTEN BETTER SINCE WE FOUGHT ON THAT PLANE.
YOU'RE NOT MY TEACHER ANYMORE. YOU DON'T GET TO TALK TO ME LIKE ONE.